The Vision for You

How to Discover the Life You Were Made For

ALSO BY DAVID CLAYTON

The Way of Beauty: Liturgy, Education and Inspiration for Family, School and College

The Little Oratory: A Beginner's Guide to Praying in the Home
(co-written with Leila Lawler)

The Vision for You

How to Discover the Life You Were Made For

by DAVID CLAYTON

Foreword by Rev. Marcelo J. Navarro Muñoz, IVE

Copyright © 2018 David Clayton

All rights reserved.

ISBN: 9781980665236

For Alexander and Victoria

CONTENTS

Preface   i-iii

Foreword   v

PART 1

Introduction   Pg. 1

1   Finding God   Pg. 15

2   Leading a Life of Superabundance: The Paradox of Love   Pg. 41

3   Religion, Worship, and Joy   Pg. 57

4   The New Evangelization   Pg. 80

5   Our Personal Vocation   Pg. 100

6   Think and Grow Greedy   Pg. 116

7   Misery is Optional   Pg. 124

8   The Dark Night of the Soul and Christian Joy   Pg. 141

9   Blessed Are the Poor in Spirit, For They Shall See God   Pg. 156

PART 2

10   A Routine of Prayer, Meditation, and Good Works   Pg. 167

11   A Spiritual Exercise: An Examination of Feelings, Thoughts, and Actions   Pg. 179

    Part One – Rooting Out the Cause of Our Unhappiness   Pg. 179

    Part Two – Writing Down Our Resentments, Our Fears, and an Analysis of Our General Conduct   Pg. 193

	Part Three – Confessing Our Self-Centered Impulses to Another	Pg. 222
	Part Four – Making Restitution for All Harm We Have Done to Others	Pg. 228
	Part Five – Common Objections and Questions	Pg. 238
	Part Six – More detail of my personal experiences of this part of the process, and how my life improved as a result	Pg. 253
12	The Deepening of the Mysteries	Pg. 258

PART 3

13	The Vision for You	Pg. 278
	Epilogue	Pg. 309
	Appendix 1 - Eight Principles for Progress	Pg. 321
	Appendix 2 - The Daily Routine	Pg. 323
	Appendix 3 - The 17 component forms of self-centeredness used in this examination of conscience	Pg. 325
	Appendix 4 - A summary of the method of reflection called conspectio divina for easy reference	Pg. 330
	Appendix 5 - A summary of how to discern your personal vocation and to follow the call	Pg. 333
	Appendix 6 - Tips for Sponsors	Pg. 335
	Appendix 7 - Some More Scriptural Quotations that Support the Principles Outlined in This Book	Pg. 338
	ABOUT THE AUTHOR	Pg. 342

Preface

Read this before you start:
What this book is about, who it is for, and how to use it

The *Vision for You* is the name of the process by which we, who have been through it, discovered our true calling in life – what we call our 'personal vocation.' Through this process we discovered the Great Fact – that we have a choice in life. We can *choose* to be happy or to be miserable.]

The goal is to be happy and to become, more and more, the people we were meant to be. We aim to lead a life that is good, true, and beautiful. We call this path the *Way of Beauty*. I believe that anyone who has a sense that their lives ought to more fulfilled can benefit from this book if they are prepared to follow its directions as best they can.

The purpose of this book is to present detailed information about the *Vision for You* process. I first went through the *Vision for You* process nearly thirty years ago and still practice it today. My hope is that you will get all that I have gotten from this and perhaps even more.

At this point, I am going to issue a **Trigger Warning!** This book talks about God and the Catholic Faith. Nevertheless, even if you are not Catholic, please relax.

You don't have to be Catholic or even Christian for this process to work. You just need to be open-minded enough to do what is suggested. The principles this book contains come from the ancient tradition of Western spirituality going right back to the Church Fathers. You don't need to accept the Christian understanding of why it works in order for to work. You just need to take the actions it describes and be willing to believe that there is a God. In other words, act as though he exists regardless of whether you believe it.

I was an atheist when I started this process and had no interest in Christianity, yet still I had spectacularly good results. I did need to be open at least to the possibility of the existence of God, but beyond that nothing else was asked of me.

However, since this time, I have converted to Christianity and became Catholic. I make no secret of my current belief that the greatest benefit will be had by anyone who is a believing Catholic too. The only way for you to find out if what I say is true is to come into the Church too. If you cannot accept this, then I still want to encourage you – you can still benefit greatly from what this book contains without taking that final step.

While I want all who are curious to be able to read this book and understand it, I have in mind especially those people who have already been through the process and are now ready to take others through it. We call this sponsoring people through the process. I see this text as something that sponsor and sponsee can potentially work through together. At times, therefore, I intentionally go into great detail in order to anticipate the sort of questions that sponsees ask sponsors. I have nearly 30 years of experience sponsoring people through this process and have included answers to every question I can remember being asked by my sponsees over the years. Even so, I've probably not anticipated every situation that you will face in life. If you have a question that is not answered directly in this book, please feel free to contact me through TheWayofBeauty.org.

Similarly, if you are looking for a sponsor to help you through this process, then feel free to contact me also. I will try to put you in touch with someone.

It may also be that you have stumbled upon this book and wish to attempt to go through the process on your own and without a sponsor. If so, I wish you well but be ready for what might at times be a dry read.

Finally, I would like to thank all who have taken the trouble to read what was a very rough manuscript and who made suggestions for change: Mariellen Gallagher, Kathleen Robe and Fr. Norbert Wood of St Michael's Abbey, Orange County, CA., and Marcello Navarro, IVE.

Foreword

The *Vision for You* is the name of a process by which we, who have been through it, discovered our true calling in life – what we call our 'personal vocation.' Through this process we discovered the Great Fact – that we have a choice in life. We can *choose* to be happy or to be miserable.

These words of the preface by David Clayton present us with this project or vision full of insight and experience, where the author addresses essential elements to offer contemporary men and women a fulfilling vision according to their vocation in life.

If you are familiar with David Clayton's works you cannot help but make a connection with *The Way of Beauty*. *The Vision for You* is a practical extension of the truth contained in his previous book. His clear conviction on the importance of liturgy and new evangelization in the worship of God, self-examination and prayer are among the main topics the author presents with conviction based on experience and real faith.

I believe this book has an enormous value in helping people discover God's call in this life and so help them attain Eternal Life.

Rev. Marcelo J. Navarro Muñoz, IVE

Rome, 2017

THE VISION FOR YOU

Introduction

Trust in God and do good and you will be granted your heart's desire

'If you trust in the Lord and do good, then you will live in the land and be secure. If you find your delight in the Lord, He will grant your heart's desire.'

Psalm 36(37):3-4

This book is a description of the transformation of life through a set of spiritual exercises called the *Vision for You* – it is a structured 'process,' or 'program,' of prayer, reflection, and good works. I describe how by using this process I discerned my personal vocation and followed that call so that it became a reality. It has been, right to this day, a joyful journey and a beautiful path to a final destination that is, as yet, only partially realized. I have been on this path for nearly 30 years and am still moving forward.

Along the way many wonderful things have happened to me. One example: I was invited to serve on the faculty of a college in the United States as Artist-in-Residence. For this dream job, the U.S. government was prepared to grant a working visa to a UK citizen – despite the fact that I possessed barely any of the formal qualifications ordinarily connected with the work I had been employed to do.

This book is also in large part a description of my unanticipated conversion story, for the 'way of beauty' that led to the fulfillment of my dreams, setting out at first just to be an artist, was the same one that led to my conversion to Catholicism. All of this was freely chosen in order to have a happy life.

This story begins when, in my mid-twenties, I met someone in Chelsea in west London whose name was David Birtwistle.

I had arranged to meet my friend Dennis for coffee when I was living in London nearly 30 years ago. I can't even remember the particular reason that we did so, at this point – we had known each other a few months. I liked his company and I probably just wanted to catch up with him. Early in the conversation, he mentioned to me that immediately afterwards he had arranged to meet a friend of his, David, at the same café and I was welcome to join them if we wanted to. I didn't particularly want to meet David, so I planned my excuses to leave before he arrived.

As it turned out, my conversation with Dennis went on longer than anticipated and David arrived while I was still there. David was a small man, perhaps about 5 ft. 7 in., and my immediate impression before he even opened his mouth was that he was well-to-do and upper class. He wore polished brown brogues (wingtips for the Americans), well-pressed pale-yellow broad-ribbed corduroy trousers, a dark blazer, blue-and-white striped cotton shirt, and pink tie. He had a silk navy blue-and-white spotted handkerchief in the top pocket of his blazer. He had straight grey hair which was combed and parted, thinning a bit, and wore dark horn-rimmed glasses. I guessed he was in his sixties (he was in fact 63 years old).

I had noticed him before Dennis did – a man coming towards us with a slow and erect gait, walking with a stick. I found out later that he walked like this because he suffered from severe angina and became breathless with the effort of taking just a few steps. Because he gave no sign of being uncomfortable, the impression was of bearing and dignity, one who was calmly at ease and in control of the situation.

Finally, Dennis noticed him too and immediately interrupted our conversation to get up and greet him: "David! Good to see you."

"Good to see you too, lad. How are you?"

David had a firm confident voice and used the appellation 'lad' like a Scot might. This was a strange idiosyncrasy of David's – he called anyone younger than him 'lad' or 'laddie.' I found out later that he was from Lancashire in the north of England, and his family was extremely wealthy – they had owned cotton mills in Lancashire. He had gone to an exclusive boarding school and his accent, that of a well-spoken BBC announcer, had been formed by this. However, it is not usual for someone like this to call others laddie, and I don't know where David got it from. When we became friends, he would start calling me 'lad' or 'laddie' too. Initially I didn't like it; later I realized it was a sign of affection.

My friend Dennis was in his mid-twenties, educated middle-class like me with a faint southern English accent (a similar age and background to me, except I have a faint northern English accent). He was not of David's social class. I wondered how they knew each other.

Dennis introduced me and then we sat down and ordered coffee. David asked me how I knew Dennis (through friends in London) and about what I did for a living (recruitment consultant for charities). Then he and Dennis had a short and focused exchange about something that was on Dennis' mind. Dennis was asking advice about some difficulties that he was having at work with his boss. David gave firm and clear advice that was as much about moral conduct as it was about getting on in his career.

I remember being struck first by the fact that Dennis wanted to hear this advice. Dennis had never told me about any difficulties in his life. In fact, he had seemed to me to be someone who was happy and seemed to be able to handle these things quite easily.

After this short exchange, David turned to me again and engaged me in the conversation. As we talked to each other he revealed a few details about his life – he was a bachelor and lived in a flat quite close by; he had retired due to ill health after a serious heart attack. All these details were given without any sense of complaint or embarrassment, just cheerfully and matter-of-factly, but without revealing so much that it embarrassed me.

My impression of David was of a content and happy man. I would describe him as calmly and quietly joyful. He was self-effacing and seemed interested in me, which I liked! I do not remember how long we talked. It wasn't long, certainly no more than 15 minutes before I had to go.

Later I telephoned Dennis and asked him about David. Dennis told me that he had met him, a bit like me, through mutual friends and that he had become a sort of mentor or life coach to him. David was a wise gentleman, Dennis told me, whose advice had transformed his life. Dennis then told me how hopeless and directionless he had felt just a few months earlier, how David had offered to help him, and what a great impact he had had on his life.

I had not known anything about this. Dennis and I weren't long-time or close friends, but I liked him, and we were getting closer. I started to wonder if the things that had helped Dennis could help me too – as he talked about how he had been, I realized that a lot of what he was describing applied to me also. I was unhappy and thought I might be suffering from depression, and I was frustrated with my personal situation and afraid of what the future might bring. I wanted the sense of purpose that both Dennis and especially David seemed to have.

I hesitated and then asked Dennis more about what sort of things David had been telling him. He gave me some information but suggested that I meet up with David and ask him myself. He could arrange it if I wished.

So, I did just that. I met David again, this time on my own. In this second encounter he told me a lot more about his own life journey and how it had changed when he started to do certain things that had been passed on to him by an old friend. It all sounded a bit mysterious, but I wanted to know more because I wanted what he had. Despite his many physical difficulties, I could see that he was happy. Impressed by his story and by the example of how he conducted himself, I was convinced, even after just two meetings, that he had something to offer me. I was impressed also by how things seemed to have worked so well with Dennis, whom I knew better. This led me to believe that I could have a happy life too. So I asked for help.

The *Vision for You* – a process or program that shows us the beautiful path to a life beyond our wildest dreams

David told me that if I followed the suggestions that he was about to give me, the result would be a life 'beyond my wildest dreams.' I was skeptical but trusted him just enough to give it a try – which was perhaps the best decision I have ever made. He called this a process or a program (he used these words interchangeably) – the *Vision for You* – telling me that the spiritual exercises he would give me would allow me to see clearly the beautiful and joyful path that leads to happiness and fulfillment. He used those words a lot – beauty, joy, and happiness.

The Vision for Me! I liked that.

My life at the time was miserable. Miserable enough that I was actually prepared to swallow my pride and listen to him – and that is pretty miserable. Many would have looked at my situation and said it was full of promise – I had friends and a social life, I had many interests beyond work, I had been to one of the best-known universities in the world and my prospects, on the face of it, looked good. However good things looked on the outside, internally – that is emotionally – it was different. I couldn't shake off a sense that my life was drifting away from me and that all of these positive things were pointless. My personal relationships were unhappy and so I felt lonely no matter how entertaining the company, or how intimate the contact. I was drinking too much and couldn't stop, and when I looked at the life ahead of me, it appeared lonely, dull and boring, at best.

David told me that there was a way out of this. He said he had been in a similar state in his mid-forties (about 15 years earlier) and he offered to show me how he had escaped. He described what life had been like for him then and contrasted that with what it was like now, telling me in somewhat general terms what he had done to change his life. Listening to him talk, I realized that he understood how I was feeling because he had experienced something very similar to what I was going through. The fact that David had been through what I was experiencing made me think that perhaps what he had done to get out of his miserable situation might work for me too… Tentatively, I asked him to show me. In response he gave me a program of meditation, prayer, and loving action. Then a couple of weeks later when these had become daily habit, he gave me a series of what he called spiritual exercises, where I analyzed my feelings. This took a few days of intensive work. Next he showed me how to make my dreams come true. Following these suggestions had such a dramatic effect on my life that much of it is still part of my daily routine.

Things are not perfect now, but the loneliness I had been experiencing evaporated within a few weeks of following the course David laid out for me, and it has never returned. I do not feel lonely even when I am alone. I am no longer afraid of what the future will bring, and I earn a living by doing things that at the time I met him I didn't even know people did for work. I am enjoying life. I even stopped drinking abruptly the moment he agreed to help me, and still do not drink today.

David didn't describe it in that way at the time, but I think of the path he set me on as a pilgrimage. I continue on that pilgrimage today, and it has as its final destination union with God in heaven. If he had told me initially that this is what he was offering to me, I probably wouldn't have continued taking direction from him. Such was my prejudice against discussion of God and religion.

I am grateful for the sensitive way he presented the benefits to me (which I will describe later). As a result, my prejudice was not aroused, and David set me on a journey in which the benefits are so many and so great that it is almost impossible to list them all.

In this book I have decided to focus on three benefits in particular because I think that these are things that many people want for their lives:

- A life of joy regardless of personal circumstances.
- A method whereby I can discern my personal vocation and fulfill it.

- A route to transformation that forms me as someone who, despite all my failings, can attract others to the source of these gifts – just as David did all those years ago.

It is the spiritual exercises and the prayer life described in this book that have opened the way to these rewards. It is my firm belief that if you do what I have done, then you can have these rewards too. David died over 15 years ago (suddenly, of a heart attack when he was in his seventies while walking across St. James Park near Buckingham Palace). My motivation in writing this book is to preserve what he told me and to make it available to others who might be interested.

Since my conversion to Catholicism in the early 1990s, about five years after I first met David, I have found that participating in the sacramental life in conjunction with the spiritual exercises of the *Vision for You* program is a most powerful combination. Because the exercises of the *Vision for You* process are essentially traditional prayers and devotions in the Western expression of Christianity, I naturally assumed that Catholics would be doing this or something similar, and so would have the joy that all of this was giving me. As the years progressed, however, I realized that this was not the case. Most Catholics have not had the benefit of such guidance and are not aware of this aspect of their spirituality. All people, Catholic or not, can benefit from what I was shown by David, and so I would encourage people of all faiths to follow the principles he outlined; this was one of the main intentions I had in writing this book. However, I have a particular desire to see Catholics pick this up, for I believe that the greatest joy of the *Vision for You* process is open to those who are living the sacramental life of the Church.

Part one of this book describes in detail what this book offers. In it I draw on my own experiences. I recount how the path to joy is one which leads us to God, and it is a joyful journey. I explain in more detail what a 'personal vocation' is, how it is linked to our capacity to draw others to God, and why both are so important in our search for personal happiness. I also describe why a prayer life centered on the worship of God in the Sacred Liturgy is so important and that it is only when our ultimate goal is the worship of God in the Sacred Liturgy that these fruits are given to us in greatest abundance.

David's great achievement was to lead me into a prayer life that was consistent with this hierarchy of goals in such a way that even a bitter atheist like me was prepared to take the necessary action. I relate many personal anecdotes about David and how he communicated what he had to offer, throughout this book, partly to make it a more entertaining read, but more importantly because I consider the way he passed on the information to be a model lesson in sensitive spiritual direction. I started out as a sour and cynical atheist. Despite that, he directed me onto a path that very eventually led to my reception into the Church. He was sometimes tough, at other times encouraging, while always taking into account my personal situation and temperament. If he had not done this so very skillfully I would probably never have begun 'the process' at all.

The Instruction Manual

Parts **two** and **three** of this book are instructional, designed to tell you how to do the process.

In the ideal you will do this process with a 'sponsor' – someone who has been through the process and can show you personally how to do it. Just like David showed me. Then this book is a great aid to that process. However, with God's grace, it is possible to do from the instructional manual alone, so if you are in that position, pray to God for help and dive in.

Part two describes the series of spiritual exercises referred to herein as 'the process.' The process begins with some reflection, by which we meditate upon the hopelessness of our lives without divine help and acknowledge our need for him (don't worry if you are an atheist, we will lead you through this!). Simultaneously we begin the action – a program of regular prayer, reflection, and good works in which we develop the habits that will sustain us on this path, potentially, for the rest of our lives. Once we have adopted this routine as habit, we undergo a thorough self-examination in which we consider all the causes of our unhappiness and see how we can be happy regardless of what is happening to us. Always, we found, our unhappiness is caused by our self-centered responses to events around us. This causes unhappiness because it separates us from God, who is the source of our joy in life. Once we recognize those causes in us, we are shown how that relationship with God might be repaired so that we are closer to him and more joyful.

Now, we are in a better position to hear God's call and to discern our personal vocation. We are ready for part three.

Part three describes how, once having undergone the necessary spiritual preparation, David showed me how to discern a personal vocation and make it happen. Once I reached this point, the process of discernment was more straightforward than many people imagine prior to doing the process. It works, essentially, by assuming that God wants us to be happy and part of that is doing what we love to do. So we start to ask the question, what would I like to do in life, in my wildest dreams? Then we work towards that goal and provided that what we want isn't inherently evil, then there is no reason to believe that it isn't worth striving for and won't happen.

I have met many people who are seeking to know what God wants them to do by other methods, and they seem to spend years agonizing over discovering what God wants them to do and then are fearful of moving forward in case they are making the wrong decision. This is not how it was for me. The path was clear, and I could see progress immediately.

God's providential care

At this point some people reading will think that this book is like those that promise to give you everything you dream of. If you go to the self-help section of the book shop you can find any number of books that talk of the 'law of attraction' and how to harness it to realize your dreams. I have read many of those books and I would say this process is similar to those but crucially different. This is not a positive thinking program – it is a faith program. It is based in trust in Providence.

Ultimately, because he loves us, he gives us only what we need to be happy. If we are mistaken and what we want won't make us happy, then we won't get it. Sometimes his answer to our prayers is 'no!' But because he loves us, he doesn't leave us dangling either. He gives us what is good for us. In other words, if we don't get what we want it is because God has given us something even better.

This is saying, in effect, your wildest dreams are not the best you can hope for, they are the least. The only reason you won't get them is because you are given something even better and decide to have that instead. I talk about this at length in the chapter called *Think and Grow Greedy*.

And this is why the *Vision for You* process is, in my estimation, so much better than everything else of a similar nature on offer (and why I have continued to practice it ever since).

This works

I have seen how the *Vision for You* process works, for those who work it time after time with spectacular results. It continues to work for me, and I believe that it will work for you too, if that is what you want.

On the next pages I list a summary of the process: the Eight Principles for Progress – three reflective and five active – followed by a description of the daily routine, which is more detail about the first principle of action listed in the Eight Principles. Finally, I give a series of steps as to how to discern your personal vocation and make it happen. This is adding detail to the fourth principle of action of the Eight Principles.

Everything contained in this book is related to these three simple lists. The rest of the book was written to explain why I think they are worth doing, and to help you to do them.

When I describe the general principles of the program I describe what 'we' – all those who have been through this process successfully – have done.

Here are the principles:

Eight Principles for Progress

This is what we did:

I. Reflection – the Three Acknowledgements

1) We acknowledged that we are the cause of our own unhappiness through our self-centered behaviors, thoughts, and feelings (otherwise known as *sins*); the cause is not other people or circumstances, no matter how unfortunate.

2) We acknowledged that we are unable to control our thoughts and actions perfectly and decided to rid ourselves of that unhappiness, which is in the form of resentment and fear.

3) We acknowledged that our sole hope for happiness is in God. We set ourselves this ideal for living: with God's grace we can do his will, be free of resentment and fear and have a good, beautiful and joyful life. Once we have accepted this truth, then we *do* have a choice and we can say that misery is optional.

II. Action – the Five Spiritual Exercises:

4) We adopted a daily routine of prayer, reflection, and good works.

5) When the daily routine had become habitual, we undertook a detailed written self-examination, looking at our past thoughts, feelings and behaviors in order to root out the resentments and fears arising from our self-centeredness. We admitted our shortcomings to God and to another trusted person.

6) We made amends for any harms done (provided that to do so would not cause more harm).

7) We discerned our personal vocation by consideration of what we would like to do *in our wildest dreams*, and then worked towards that goal.

8) We continued to deepen our spiritual lives through the practice of a daily routine of prayer, reflection, and good works.

A Summary of the Daily Routine

We adopted this routine of prayer, reflection, and good works until it became a habit of life:

Prayer:

1. In the morning, on your knees in an action of humility, say something like: – *'Please God, take care of me today so that I can be of service to you and my fellows.'*
2. In the evening before retiring, again on your knees say: – *'Thank you, God for looking after me'* – it's good manners to say thank you!
3. Reactive prayers during the day:

    1. If you are angry or annoyed at someone? Pray for the person repeatedly until you feel better, e.g., *'Please give [the name of the person] everything that I would wish for myself.'*
    2. If you are fearful or anxious? Say the Serenity Prayer repeatedly until you feel better: – *'God grant me the serenity to accept the things I cannot change; the courage to change the things I can; and the wisdom to know the difference.'*
    3. When you have been through the detailed **self-examination** as outlined in our spiritual exercises, apply this process to resentments and fears that crop up during the day as needed to remove them and to have a happy life.

Personal Reflection:

1. Write a gratitude list and thank God for each blessing that you find.
2. Spiritual reading: Read something each day that gives you an ideal to live by. For example, the *Just for Today* card (the text for which appear later in the book).

Good works:

1. We adopt a general attitude of seeking to be of service to others. We ask what we can give to the world, rather than what we can take.

2. We make a regular voluntary sacrifice of time devoted to the service of others in a manner of our choosing (perhaps by establishing or contributing to a meeting created to pass on the *Vision for You* process to those who need it. Or by sponsorship – giving time to meet with others personally in order to take them through the process.).

3. We strove to 'do the right thing,' that is, to lead a good and virtuous life.

1 Finding God

Developing a life of faith as the foundation for a joyful life

'I tell you therefore: everything you ask and pray for, believe that you have it already, and it will be yours.'

Mark 11:24

Some years ago, long after I first encountered David, I met a priest who is an internationally known art historian. I had some ideas about how to create an art school that would train artists to serve the Church and I decided to describe them to him to see if he thought they were sound. I also hoped that he might like the ideas so much that he would help me, or even better, introduce me to wealthy donors who could fund the project.

This priest lived in Florence and because of the associations of the place with traditional Christian art he was in great demand. Every budding artist in the city – and there were a lot of them – wanted to get noticed by him because, like me, they thought he might be able to further their careers. As a result, you needed an introduction in order to have any access at all. Ordinarily, an unknown like me, a student studying portrait painting at a small studio in the city, would have little chance. Through an introduction by Stratford Caldecott, a friend and authority on cultural renewal who was well known in Catholic circles (you will hear more about Stratford later), I met a Spanish bishop while visiting Spain. In the process of making small talk, the bishop asked me if I knew this Florentine priest. I told him no but said I would like to meet him. Try again and mention my name," he answered. I did so and very quickly received a message instructing me to meet him at a particular time and place. Informed that the meeting would last about half an hour, I rehearsed my description of the school and was ready with the standard follow-up question, "Do you know anyone who can help me?"

I went to his residence, which was attached to the Duomo in Florence, and pressed the buzzer. He told me to come on up so I climbed a tight, narrow set of stairs to his apartment. A tall – taller than me, and I am 6 ft. tall – grey-haired man in perhaps his late fifties with glasses perched on the end of his nose greeted me at the top, two floors up. He spoke in a soft voice with a gentle American accent that went perfectly with his previous role of Yale college professor (he had not been a priest long) … and made me even more nervous. We exchanged pleasantries and I launched into my spiel. Listening intently, the priest said nothing for the several minutes that I spoke. When I finished he asked one or two pointed questions. Then he gave me a very encouraging assessment of my proposition, helpfully making several good suggestions for changes. I was heartened by this – it seemed that he liked what he was hearing and was ready to help. I asked my key question, "Do you know anyone who can help me?"

He paused. Then he said, "I am sorry, I can't think of anyone and I don't have time to help you myself."

I felt downcast. I was about to thank him for his time and interest when he added something entirely unexpected: "But I don't think that matters."

I wondered what he meant and he elaborated, telling me that he believed that it was my personal vocation to try to start this art school and that in his opinion I had an obligation to follow this path. He further assured me that while he couldn't promise me any success, provided I was ready to ride through any discouraging periods I would feel fulfilled in the effort. Most importantly, he said that in striving to make this happen "I would attract people to the Faith."

He then explained that this is what a personal vocation is: **it is the means by which we can and will draw others to the Faith most effectively.** When we find our personal vocation, we are living the life that God wants for us, and we flourish as Christians. We shine with the Light of Christ just by doing what we love to do. People are attracted to what we have, and they associate it with our faith. This in turn encourages them to investigate further. This may mean that they immediately start asking us questions, but that will be unusual. It is more likely that even if we have made a positive impression, they will say nothing to us directly. Also, it could take years for them to take action. Perhaps the contact with me will become just one event in whole series of events some of which are yet to happen, and that whole series will finally influence the person to respond to God's call in their lives. We just can't predict. For the most part, therefore, we will be unaware of the effect we have on other people.

This priest articulated very clearly just what a personal vocation is. But he was not the first one to tell me that God was calling me to do what I wanted to do. When I met him, I was in fact already some way into my journey, and several others had reinforced the conviction that I was doing the right thing. The first person to direct me along this path was, of course, David Birtwistle.

When I met David, I had dreams about what I would like to do and be, but very little conviction that it would ever happen. I assumed I had missed my chance by making the wrong choice when I went to college and was therefore pretty much stuck with the decisions I had made about my future when I was 18. I had studied science and engineering at university and had decided that I didn't want to work in that. Unsure as to what else to do I had drifted into a job with a recruitment company in London, where I spent my day interviewing candidates for clients. Even if I had suddenly been empowered to try and follow my dreams, which meant getting enough money from somewhere to pay for it all – perhaps by winning the lottery – I lacked the confidence in myself to believe that I had the necessary ability, nor would I know how to go about making it happen.

All that changed once I met David. As part of the program he gave me, he showed me a way to order my dreams so that I could discern what I really wanted to do, and then make it all happen. The process was essentially one that began with the development of a living faith. Then, with guidance, I began to be able to recognize within me what that inspiration is and how to act in accord with it. David made clear to me that what he was suggesting simply wouldn't work without that foundation of faith. To try the process of discernment without the foundation of faith might result in making absurd decisions.

When I started the process, I had no faith and would have called myself an atheist. Thus, the first set of exercises given here are those that David gave me to enable me to establish a personal relationship with God, and then deepen it. This required quite a lot of work. Only after I had done this first phase did he begin to show me how to discern my personal vocation.

If you are already a believer, then, unlike me, you will not need to establish that first contact with God. However, the exercises will very likely deepen your faith. Even if your faith is deep enough that you are confident you have no need for the first exercises yourself, I encourage you at least to look at them – perhaps you will be better able to help others as a result. Furthermore, I suggest that reading the description in part one of this book of how a living faith was transmitted to a defiant atheist like me might be useful to you in the future, should you wish to pass this process on to others who are not already in possession of a deep faith.

Getting the most of out of what this book contains

With this last point in mind, I strongly suggest that you aim to do *all* the prayers and spiritual exercises this book sets forth even if you think you personally don't need them all. Except in particular instances where the book itself directs you to do so, try to resist the temptation to pick and choose some parts and reject others. Do the whole process in the order in which it is presented. No one will be harmed by doing this since nearly everyone can benefit in some way from the exercises even if they already possess a living faith – just as nearly everyone can benefit from doing any spiritual retreat – and even if your spiritual life is so well developed that it cannot be improved by such work, doing it anyway will enhance your capability of drawing others to the faith.

Pass it on to others

One thing that David impressed upon me from the start is the importance, for anyone undergoing this process, of being prepared to pass on to others what you receive. When you have been through the process that this book describes, ask God daily to show you how to help the next person who needs this process and resolve to be ready to respond to opportunities to help others when they occur.

My motivation for writing the book you are now reading is an attempt to fulfill this particular aspect of the process. I want to pass on to you what was passed on to me by others who were living joyfully and wanted me to be able to live joyfully too. My hope is that you will receive what I was given.

Finally, this book is intended as a companion to another book I co-wrote with Leila Lawler called *The Little Oratory: A Beginner's Guide to Praying in the Home*[1]. So here is my next suggestion: read the two together. Of course, readers will benefit hugely from reading each in isolation and putting into practice what each describes. But the greatest benefit is to marry the two, as each reinforces the other. The connection between them will become clearer and clearer as you read on (especially in Chapter 3), but to put it in simple terms, you could summarize how they relate as follows: *The Little Oratory* describes how the liturgy – the love of God in the ritual worship of the Church – can be harmonized with daily living in the home and the community. The *Vision for You*, by contrast, focuses on personal prayer and spiritual exercises that will help you to order your day-to-day activities so that all is in harmony. This will lead to a life of greater joy. In a sense, the personal spiritual exercises help in the process of making us capable of responding fully to God's love in the context of the liturgy, and in our daily lives.

Between the two books, the hope is to develop a prayer life that affects a harmonious balance between liturgical prayer and personal prayer. When we have this balance, our personal path of joyful living opens up before and within us. We cease to struggle against all that happens around us and start to work with it – or, alternatively, effortlessly pass by all that

---

[1] Pub Sophia Institute Press, 2014

seems to be opposing us. We have a sense that we are moving towards an ideal where all that we do, in some way, contributes to our ultimate end: full and joyful union with God.

A motivating thought – write down your six wildest dreams

Right at the start of this process, it was suggested to me that I write down my six wildest dreams on a piece of paper, then put the piece of paper in an envelope, put the envelope in a drawer and leave it there. Then, I was told, I should take a look at it in a year's time and if I had given my best effort to the process I would find that I had "sold myself short!"

I didn't ask why six, so I can't tell you the answer to that question. But I did do what I was told. I put down a mixture of abstract goals connected to happiness, such as peace and fruitful relationships, and material goals, most of these are too personal to relate. I was encouraged not to feel that each item had to be 'spiritual' or 'holy' necessarily. And because I didn't have to tell anyone what was on the list, I was able to just put down the first things that came into my head.

After a year, five out of six had happened, and the promise of finding that I had "sold myself short" came true in a way I didn't expect. My whole sense of what would make me happy had so developed, that by the end of the year I was looking for different things from life. Many of these new goals were already beginning to happen in my life, too, and the result was a life that was better than I had been able even to imagine at the start of the process – literally, therefore, *beyond* my wildest dreams.

The best way that I can characterize this change is to illustrate with reference to the first couple of lines from an old blues song: *I've been down for so long, that it feels like up to me.* This phrase describes me when I was miserable. I didn't know what the good life was. The only good life I could really imagine was one in which the bad things were absent – such as the ability to stop drinking so heavily. I couldn't imagine what it was to have a life that was good in itself.

Only once I began to experience the process, did I start to get an inkling of what was really on offer here. Gradually my tastes developed and my idea of what was good changed. As a result of this process and as time has gone on I have been given things that I wouldn't have appreciated at the beginning of the process, but which now I value greatly.

This development has continued ever since. The things I want now are very different from those I wanted five years ago, which in turn are different from what I wanted 10 years ago and so on. They are both different and better.

So let's get started. Begin where I began. Write down your six wildest dreams and look at the list in a year and see if they have come true. You can put them in an envelope if you want or create a Word file and bury it deep in the folders on your computer hard disk. If it helps you to crystallize in your mind what it is you want, then put photographs there too.

In case you're wondering, the sixth remaining item on my first list, which has still not materialized many years later, is to have a million pounds in the bank. That still hasn't happened to me. However, I no longer depend on money for my happiness, thanks to 'the process' – although some days, I admit, I have to work harder to be content with less than others. But neither does that stop me working towards a goal of wealth. I know that when having money will help me to do his will, God can give me billions if he wants to!

Back to your list – don't forget to visualize and write down those six wildest dreams.

Here is a summary of the key suggestions so far:
- Try to do all that this book directs you to do; and do it in the order given.
- Be ready to pass on all that you learn so that others will benefit from this too.
- If you can, have in mind the long-term goal of doing what this book contains in conjunction with liturgical prayer – the ritualized worship of God – so that you will have a balanced prayer life centered in a liturgical piety. This can be done if you put the contents

of this book into practice in conjunction with the pattern of prayer contained in the book *The Little Oratory*.
- Write down your six wildest dreams.

Now we go to the source of all that is good, God.

How my own faith began to develop
As I have already mentioned, my own story begins at a place that was pretty low. My life was characterized by a hostility to the idea of God, and generally by bitterness, frustration and dread of the future; and most damagingly as I have already mentioned I had a drinking problem that I could not control. Now, through this process, my life has transformed to one in which, generally, I have joy, inner peace, a sense of personal fulfillment and, generally, a lack of fear about the future. And along the way I converted to Catholicism (over 20 years ago now).

You may not be as low as I was, but I am convinced that you could finish as high as I have and, for all I know, higher. You do not need to become Catholic in order to do the *Vision for You* process. If you can follow these simple directions, then you will, I believe, discover your personal vocation and experience a life of joy, regardless. Nevertheless, as a result of my own conversion, it is my conviction that the greatest joy in life is open to those who are Catholic. That is why I became one myself.

David did not talk about Christianity or the Faith at all when I met him. He talked a bit about his own faith journey though. He had had his own personal crisis 16 years earlier and had undergone his own transformation some years before when he met someone else – whom I never met, called Ronnie – who had showed him the *Vision for You* process. Before he met Ronnie, he had been terrified of God and was certain he was going to hell, he told me. He had been argumentative and even been banned from pubs for fighting.

I could imagine the David who once was argumentative and sarcastic – he had a biting wit and was always outspoken and fearless in standing up for the truth when I knew him; it was easy to imagine this being misdirected. David told me that he had been lonely even when with people. He was a bachelor but he told me that at the age of 47 he had broken down crying in the arms of his last girlfriend. When she asked him what was the matter he had told her he was lonely. This was mystifying and insulting to his girlfriend, but he couldn't explain why, and they had broken up shortly afterwards. He was at his wit's end. Fewer and fewer people would spend any time with him. He had virtually no friends and was contemplating suicide. There seemed to be no future for him, for whatever he tried he alienated everyone and ended in conflict.

He said this all changed when around this time he met Ronnie, the man who had shown him the process. He told me that as a result of this he believed he had found what he referred to as 'the pearl of great price' (I didn't realize he was quoting a line from St. Matthew's gospel, chapter 13). His life had transformed. He said that he had never had a bad day since he had introduced the daily routine into his life. He knew that his natural inclination was towards misery and conflict with others and so he had rigorously followed the process and never let up because he knew it was the only hope he had.

Most importantly he now believed in a loving God whom he was sure wanted him happy, joyous, and free, and all he had to do was cooperate. David said that he was certain that this was open to me too – 'he wants you to be happy, too, lad and you can have a life beyond your wildest dreams. I am certain of it!' No longer was he afraid of God. He knew that God was on his side, was good, loving, merciful, and all-powerful.

The change had been so dramatic and positive that he had decided very quickly that he would devote his life to passing on this 'pearl of great price' so that as many people as possible could benefit from what he had been shown. I have no idea how many people he helped altogether, but when he died nine years after I met him, over 600 people came to his funeral in London; and these must have been just a fraction of the total number he had helped.

He told me just a few details about his personal sponsor. Ronnie was Irish and working class and David initially resented being given direction by such a man, even though he was being helped by him. David would tell this story to illustrate how arrogant and intolerant he had been at this point because he, an upper-class Englishman educated in an exclusive boarding school, found it difficult to accept that a working-class Irishman had anything to tell him about how to live his life. Then David told us that despite the fact that he felt this, he had never openly argued with him, for he wanted to keep receiving the guidance from him.

What David said to me was that in order to change my life, I had to do what he had done. I had to change my whole outlook in life radically. This made sense to me. David reinforced this so well by repeatedly referring to his own experiences and the directions that he was given. Then he would often look me in the eye and say that he was certain that this was available to me too, if I could just do as he had: swallow my pride and take directions.

It required great trust and it didn't come instantly, but as I started to feel it working for me, I began to trust David and the process more and more.

This new life meant examining motives as well as actions. This is difficult for me because I am a proud man. Even now, all these years later, I am still capable of justifying selfish acts as God's will, and still to some degree I am handicapped by the need to be admired and appreciated by others. But I have come a long way (no credit to me, I might add).

I was fortunate in two respects: first to be shown this program of prayer, spiritual exercises and good works; and second, I was ready to listen. In my case, that willingness to listen was given to me through suffering before I met David. My pride had taken a sufficient beating for me finally to be able to admit to myself and some others my utter inability to wrest happiness out of the life I was leading.

My experience is that once I was shown how to do certain things, even though I started by practicing them tentatively, I felt a great change.

The first lesson I had to learn was to cultivate joy. I had to accept that my happiness depended upon my relationship with God and not, as I had previously believed, on external events occurring around me. If this really was the case, then I could be happy no matter how disagreeable or painful those externals might be.

As you read this, you might feel that your need for the process is not so great as mine was. Perhaps things are generally quite good and you are looking for life that might be even better. Perhaps without being bitter about your current situation, you nevertheless lack some direction and feel that things could improve. Nevertheless, it is worth doing the process. All of these are perfectly good reasons to do what this book contains.

You don't have to be desperate like I was… but it helps!

If it worked for us; it'll work for you too

Underlying the writing of this book is the assumption that there's a good chance that something that worked for me and others who have done this process, will work for you too; although, of course, I can't prove it. It's only in trying it out that you'll find out for sure.

I don't see myself as particularly gifted in my ability to understand or apply these principles, but I do think that a very important part of this was my willingness to do what was being presented to me.

I was willing for two reasons: first, as I have said, I was desperate. Nothing else I had tried had worked for me. I had nowhere else to go and no one else to turn to. Second, the people I saw who were following the process told me that things were changing dramatically for them too. Although I was skeptical, there was enough in what they told me and the way they told me, to convince me to give it a try. It wasn't so much the material changes in their lives, although sometimes spectacular things did happen, but rather, the way they were. There was something about the way they conducted themselves and interacted with others that spoke of an inner happiness and ease with themselves that attracted me to their way of life.

I want to take you back to that first conversation with David, so that you can see how he gave me hope even in that first meeting. When we first spoke in that café in London, he asked me the usual conversational opening questions about myself, and I remember that as usual I managed to direct this into a series of complaints about my life. He listened patiently and would chip in with one or two comments that indicated he was listening.

Soon I was describing how badly I had been treated by my former girlfriend. She was someone whom I could not get out of my mind even though I had not even seen her for nearly a year. I remember telling David that the strange thing was that I didn't think that I had ever even known her well enough to be able to say I loved her, and, saying something that was truer than I realized, I told him that I thought it was mostly my pride that was hurting. I was upset, I said, because I couldn't bear the idea that this person should have such a hold over my emotions and yet did not care about me and so casually discard me.

I can remember clearly what he said to me in response to that, "It may be just your pride, but even so it's still very painful isn't it?" This stopped me in my tracks. I stopped talking for a few seconds and thought about his response; it struck me that he really did understood how I felt.

Later I asked my friend, Dennis, about him. He told me that David was a wise man whose advice had been helpful to him. Almost jokingly I said, "Do you think he could help me?" Without hesitation my friend said emphatically "Yes."

Spurred on by encouragement from Dennis, I called David. In our next meeting he gave me the daily routine of prayer and meditation and asked me to commit to help others whenever the opportunity arose. Then in a process that took several weeks (because I had to fit them around my work schedule and his), he took me through the spiritual exercises described in this book. These were designed to help me establish a deep personal relationship with God. When I had completed these, and he was satisfied that I was doing my best to lead a life according to spiritual principles, he told me how to discern my personal vocation.

After those first months that it took me to go through this process, he urged me to continue to deepen my relationship with God by continuing this daily routine and by spiritual reading. He would suggest book titles to me. I had no idea until very late in this process that David was Catholic. He never proposed at any stage that I start going to church. Only once he knew, years later, that I was going to church, did he make any suggestions that directed me towards Catholicism, and even then, he did so gently.

David was an elderly man when I met him, and he has since died – over 15 years ago now. Part of my desire to write this book is to capture as much as I can remember of the wisdom he passed on to me; and to try to capture his method of doing so.

I hope that by reading this book, you will not only get a sense of what to do, but also of why it is worth doing. To this end, I will make many references to my own story and to the stories of others (sometimes anonymously, for reasons that will be apparent).

How David piqued my interest in those initial conversations

In my first few meetings with David, I can see now, he was gradually steering me towards the acceptance of some basic premises, which once accepted, would open the way to a life of joy.

First of all, I had to accept that my misery was of my own making because it resulted from my defective and self-centered response to circumstances around me.

Second, that I was powerless to change my response by my own will or intellect alone to remedy this.

Third, that only by cooperation with the help of a loving Higher Power could I overcome this misery. He told me that to the degree that I cooperate with him, I will have great joy because that Power is all-loving, all-powerful, and wants me to be happy.

David brought me to the point of accepting these things during our first conversations by asking me to tell him about my life and to describe my experiences. He gently pointed out how my best efforts had resulted in misery so far. He then related his own experiences, describing what he used to be like and how his life had changed as a result of doing the things he was passing on to me.

The following reflections arose out of those conversations and give an account of how I reconciled my experiences with what I now believe to be fundamental truths.

We are the cause of our own unhappiness

One of the biggest obstacles to happiness and to personal change is the idea that other people or the circumstances in which we find ourselves are the cause of our unhappiness. That is not to say that bad things don't happen sometimes, or that there are not malicious people out there who really do treat us unjustly. Rather, it is saying that even taking that into account, what is causing us to feel low is the way that we react to these things. These reactions can be purely internal – what we think and feel – or can be manifested in action as well: I might angrily take things out on others… or the gatepost!

Before things could change, I had to be willing to accept this principle that my problems were caused by me and not by this other person or that situation. Rather, it was how I reacted to these things.

Second, even if I accepted the idea that my reactions to events were the main factor in my unhappiness, there was the question of how I could change my reactions. In the past I had responded by trying to change the way I felt through trying to change people and external circumstances. When this failed it lead to the constant pursuit of superficial pleasures so as to distract myself from my inner turmoil. This, of course, was just a temporary sop because I wasn't dealing with the underlying problems. It wasn't until I had done one of the spiritual exercises described in this book, a focused examination of conscience, that I could understand how to deal with my unhappiness constructively.

It was through this process of guided self-examination that I accepted that my unhappiness was derived from my previously false view of living. Up until that point, my picture of reality had been distorted because I looked at the world through the prism of my own selfishness: I believed that if only the world would change itself to suit me, things would be fine.

To discover the error of looking at things this way was great news because it meant that now there was an answer to my problems. I could see that in order to have a happy life, I only had to change myself, which is possible; rather than change my surroundings and other people to my perfect satisfaction, which is impossible.

Life is good. A permanent truth that applies to all of us.

At the root of this new outlook there are more assumptions: for example, life is good and I have a loving God looking after me. If this is true, then it follows that all that happens to me is good and in accordance with God's will; or is permitted by a loving God so that a greater good can come out of it. No matter how bad the situation may seem, goes the assumption, God always gives us the grace to deal with it.

I cannot prove such an axiom, but I can describe the life I get by adopting it. I have found that when I lead a life on this basis, then things work out for me. Circumstances teach me to be patient and grateful for what I have when times are tough, and then when times are good I can enjoy the good things that come my way. It is a win-win situation. It works, I believe, because the assumption is true – there really is a God who is looking after me. I don't think that it could have worked so successfully and for so long if I had been deluding myself about this and I had been living a life based upon false assumptions all these years.

My experience is simply this: that a life lived according to these starting assumptions is a happy life, and life gets better the longer I live this way. Of course, bad things still happen to me. Nearly every day there will be things that happen that I don't like. But most things change in time and most bad things go away in the end. Even when they don't, I find that during the bad periods, I receive a solace that transcends the suffering. By that I mean that even though the suffering is not eliminated, the joy of trusting in God is greater than the suffering I am experiencing, and this allows me to bear it patiently, even joyfully. Perhaps tomorrow there may be something to which this does not apply, but so far in nearly 30 years it has worked every day that I have tried it.

The greatest examples of lives that demonstrate the truth of this to me are those of the saints and especially the martyrs of the Church. I have read accounts of people praising God as they experience horrific torture; I have read letters from saints in concentration camps in the Ukraine urging their relatives not to petition for their release because their greatest joy was serving their jailers and the other prisoners. I read a letter from St. Thomas More to his daughter describing how joyful he was while imprisoned in the Tower of London.

I hope and pray that I never have to go through what any of these people bore, but I have to believe that it is true for all of us that where there is evil or suffering, then grace abounds all the more. God will give me what is necessary to go through life's trials joyfully too.

All this is fine and dandy, you may be thinking, but surely there was more to it than simply and mechanically adopting these assumptions? Wasn't it necessary to have a faith – a real conviction – for all of this to work? Surely, wanting God to exist doesn't give me the faith that he does… does it?

If you are thinking these things, then you are just like me. These were exactly the questions that I had at the start. I felt as though I was in an impossible situation. I couldn't just choose to switch on faith like flicking on a light switch. How, I wanted to know, could I create a faith that would open the door to the happiness promised?

Being willing to believe – introducing the idea of God

In order to have faith in God, I was told that all that was necessary initially was to be *willing* to believe. Willingness meant, in the way that David used the word, being ready to take *action*. It didn't matter from his point of view if I was full of doubt and skepticism. Provided I had enough faith in a basic idea of God to do actions in accord with his existence, then the results would come, he assured me. And this is exactly what happened. In time, as a result of the repeated experience of things working out day after day, my faith grew and doubt was dispelled.

The first action to take if I was willing to admit to the existence of a loving God was *prayer*. I began to pray for the first time, even though it felt forced. I felt silly and wondered if my thoughts were just floating up ineffectually into nothingness, but I did it anyway.

As well as praying to God, I started to lead a better life, a morally good life. When I met David I was without a developed sense of morality, so I allowed myself to be guided by him. Only later did I realize that he was passing on the morality of the Catholic Church to me. I didn't suspect anything because when he presented a particular course of action to me, if I questioned his reasons he justified them using arguments from natural law.

David told me initially to choose my own idea of God. While my idea of God could be unique to me, I was told I couldn't pick any idea of God. The God that I was willing to believe in had to have certain essential characteristics, which I will describe in the next paragraph. He told me this, I now realize, for my own good, not in order to assert a dogma for its own sake. What he was presenting was the barest minimum necessary for me to accept in order for the process to work and for me to have a happier life.

An idea of God – this is personal!

God is not an inanimate force I was told – my relationship with him is personal, loving, and powerful. I wasn't ready for the idea of the Trinity yet and David didn't mention it at all. In fact, he said at this stage, we didn't really need to get into deep discussion about the nature of God (remember he is dealing with someone who, barely 10 days before, would have described himself as an atheist). What he did tell me was that I did have to see God as *someone*, not something.

David constantly asserted the idea that God loves me and is interested in me personally; he wants me to be happy and wants to help me. Also, God is all-powerful and so has the power to help me; and because he loves me, he won't force himself on me. However, the moment I seek him and ask for help, he could and would act on my behalf.

I was willing to accept the basic idea of a God that David gave me. And so now I had to start praying. Prayer is the means by which we seek him.

We can have an incomplete picture of God, but we don't want a false idea of him

It is important not to have false ideas of God. We might have a limited idea of him, in the sense that we cannot know all there is to know about him, but we don't want false ideas. If we build the foundation of this new life on false premises, then error will build on error and life will be unhappy. This is because if everything I did was consistent with a false start, it would lead to wrong behavior that would lead me further and further away from God and so to greater and greater unhappiness.

A life that is not rooted in truth will eventually collapse in misery. A life that is rooted in truth, I have found, will reveal yet more of the truth as we go forward, provided we can keep an open mind. At the time of writing this, it is 29 years since I first met David. I believe that if my life was not rooted in truth right at the start, the cracks would have been beginning to show by now and I would have had to find another lifestyle. While my beliefs and ideas are not restricted to those simple starting facts of all those years ago, nothing I have learned since has contradicted them. In fact, quite the reverse. My life experience has confirmed their truth.

If I place my trust in something that is untrue, then at some point in the future I will either have to swallow my pride again and abandon those false premises as the misery grows, or else go on suffering the consequences with life getting worse and worse. In extreme cases it could lead to unhappiness so great that it results in depression and mental illness.

Here are some of the false ideas of God that I heard from others and had to reject:

God is not an inanimate force

In contrast with the idea of a personal God is the idea of God as an inanimate force. This cannot work. This program is not a process of learning a new law of cause and effect, like a scientific law, that I can then manipulate for my own good. Rather, God is a person who is all-powerful and all-loving and who wants us to be happy. This God has a will and is choosing to help me because he loves me; but because he respects my free will he won't force me to do what is good for me. David was going to show me how to accept God's love and return it. I cannot demand such love or take it for granted. It is there as a gift and when I realize this I can be grateful for it. This is a program of transformation through love, and we cannot love an inanimate force.

God is not me

I had to be clear that God is not me and possesses more than human power alone. It may sound strange that we even have to say this, but although very few would claim to be God, many do live their lives as though that was the case. Fully accepting this means that the process is about conforming my will to the will of a loving God so that he can help me. It is not about making God do what I want.

I am *not* tapping into my 'higher self' or any such thing. It *is* true to say that by allowing God into my life, I might become a better person than I ever dreamed possible, but I must be clear that the source of the power that makes this happen is not me, it is God.

Certainly, I want to be the best person I can be and in this sense be transformed into my highest self. But I cannot do this through my own power. To suggest such a thing is to say that I am God. This is patently absurd. If I was God, how had I managed to get into this predicament in the first place? I knew that I had to look beyond myself for answers. Drawing from the waters of self-affirmation had been my approach for the whole of my life up to this point and that well had run dry long ago.

God is not the universe – He is greater than that

This is another tempting idea, especially to anyone who loves the beauty of Creation; but again it is a false, diminished idea of God that ultimately will limit my happiness if I accept it. He is not even the Spirit of the Universe or the Soul of the Universe to the degree that these phrases identify him with the universe itself. God is separate from the universe, greater than it, and it is subject to Him. This is how he can arrange all things for our benefit because he has power over them. Making God the universe or the soul or spirit of the universe – in a way that is analogous to how the soul of man is connected to his body – raises other questions about man's place within the universe. If man is part of the universe too, as a material being, and the universe is God, then man is God, that is, I am God… and I have already rejected that idea, so this idea must be wrong too.

All is one… not!

Saying that 'all is one' is very similar to saying that God is the universe. It allows for the possibility of the existence of things beyond the universe, but it still identifies the universe with God. This is because if all is one and God exists, then all is God. The objection to this is the same therefore as in the previous case – if all is one and all is God, then I am God… and we can't have that!

God wants us to be happy. We obtain happiness by doing God's will for us – the Power of Positive Action!

Nothing could be further from the truth, in my experience, than the idea that God wants us to be unhappy. One of the great things that inspired me to believe that God wants me to be happy was seeing how David dealt with his personal misfortune. Although only in his early sixties, because of acute angina he had to walk slowly and with a stick and to pause for breath every 10 yards. Despite this he always had a dignity and self-possession that was impressive. He spoke continually of how good life was, rather than how difficult it was, and he did not indulge in self-pity at all. His interest was in others' rather than his own difficulties.

So when he told me that God wanted me to have joy and freedom with absolute conviction, it was believable because despite the difficulties he was experiencing, his life was joyous and free. It was the example he showed me that transmitted the first flicker of a hope that this might be available to me too.

Here is the simple truth: God wants us to be happy, so if we do his will, we *will* be happy. To do his will is to do what is right – that is, to lead a morally good life (as well as a beautiful life). In my case this meant big changes.

Adopting a whole new principle of life is frightening and to be faced with this choice feels like having to take a leap in the dark. As I made my first changes, I needed regular reassurance to believe that it would work. It was easy to believe that even if this worked for others, that I would be the exception and give in to sloth and self-pity and do nothing at all. I was inclined to think that my situation and the workings of my mind were unique and beyond hope. David would counter this by continually affirming that this had worked for him, and that he had had doubts too. Furthermore, he told me, he had seen it work for many other people who had been willing to follow the directions he was giving me; and finally, he would tell me how certain he was that this would work for me too. He told me often that he was sure that God wanted me to be happy and that in order to be happy all I had to do was God's will. In order to receive these blessings, he reiterated the point that all that was necessary was a faith sufficient for me to take the actions he would present to me. This was not so much about the power of positive thinking as the power of positive *action*.

I realized pretty quickly after meeting David that I needed a new way of deciding what is good. After all, my way had resulted in unhappiness to the point of despair. Clearly, I had to look beyond my own feelings and inclinations about what was good and look to some external standard to which I could conform. I started to ask advice from people I trusted, and for the most part at the early stage this was David. In time, David would say to me that I should start looking beyond him for guidance because he was fallible and that I needed to find a moral authority that came more directly from God. This began the process by which, after considering different religions and then denominations, I found the Catholic Church.

At the beginning I would speak to David regularly and ask questions about what I was thinking of doing and David would suggest a course of action. Then gradually he started to explain the principles by which he was judging what to do so that I could start to apply them myself.

Some of this instruction was about deciding what not to do. He taught me that I had to drop the idea that superficial pleasure – what feels good in the short term – as the principle by which I choose what to do. This is the trap into which we fall when we seek to escape unhappiness by seeking out distraction. In its extreme we see it, for example, in a drug addict who avoids dealing with his problems altogether through his habit. I had to learn also that sometimes doing the right thing is not always going to make me popular or feel good immediately. It might involve work or discomfort. But in the end, I learned, I will feel good as a result. This way offers a more stable, deeper happiness that exists in my core, rather than a superficial temporary pleasure or a distraction that does not change anything permanently.

I was taught that the best approach was to apply the right principles so that reason was directing my actions. Rather than using feelings and emotions alone to decide what is right action, I use reason to decide, and then the good feelings and emotions *follow* right action; and this is what I am seeking.

… and God wants for us what we want for ourselves – happiness!

The greatest happiness is when we want what God wants for us and we realize that, deep down, it's just what we always wanted anyway.

I have come across people who wish to do God's will and then agonize over what that is. When I talked to them I usually found one of three fallacies was the cause of this anxiety: first is the false idea that God wants me to be unhappy and so I am afraid to find out what his will is because it might lead to misery; the second fallacy is that God makes it difficult for me to know what his will is; and the third is that even when I know what his will is for me, he makes it difficult for me to do it and so even to try will be frustrating.

In my belief these ideas are wrong. If God wants us to be happy, and he loves us, then he will do all He can to make that happiness attainable.

True, we will all at different times suffer physical hardships, pain and ultimately death (and if the experiences of the martyrs are anything to go by, potentially even a painful death). We will be subject to injustice, temptations, economic setbacks and uncertainties, derision and contempt from our fellows, and rejection by those we love. But (and here is the great news), *these need not be a cause for unhappiness.* Once we accept that bad things happen for a good reason and we are open to God's grace, we can experience and demonstrate a Christian joy which transcends our suffering; even extreme suffering. One special purpose of this in God's plan, I believe, is that others will see in the way we react to adversity that Christ is working through us and they will be attracted to him and to the Church.

I used to be so upset when some little thing didn't go my way, that I allowed it to color my impression of the whole day. When, with David's help, I started to look at my life honestly, I could see that, in fact, most of the time, good things were happening. The blessings of my life far outweighed the burdens. One of the daily spiritual exercises suggested in this book, writing the gratitude list, demonstrated to me unequivocally just how many and how great the blessings were in my life. When I started to reflect further on this I realized that even in the moments of my greatest misery, prior to going through the *Vision for You* process, so many good things had been given to me. I had been blinded, by self-centeredness, and had not appreciated them. Only once I went through the process did I realize just how ungrateful I had been all my life up to this point.

David looked me in the eye and told me that he was certain that God wanted me to be happy and that a joyful life was on offer regardless of any setbacks and circumstances. Furthermore, he said, if I just did my best to do God's will, then there would be many blessings and good things in my life too. He told me that I could become the person that deep down, I felt that I wanted to be and ought to be; and that God's plan for me was in accord with what I wanted at my core. God made us, he said, and so our deepest desires are in accord with what is truly good for us. First is the desire for God. After that, all that we want should be in accord with this. Everything we do, right down to simple and mundane choices that we make almost unthinkingly in our daily lives will be either in accord with or undermining the highest desire that arises from our human nature, and that is for God.

This being so, the question then becomes one of working out exactly what it is that we want to do, deep down. It may surprise some people that this is relatively quick and simple once you know how to do it, provided you are able to distinguish between the attractions and temptations of temporary pleasures and those things that are genuinely good for us. The prayers and spiritual exercises described in this book are directed toward developing that faculty in us. So that when we come to look at what we want to do, we can put aside those things that are bad for us and will distract us from the path of true happiness. Much of this is developing the habit of *doing* what is good until we start to *like* what is good for us too. The more we move along that road, the more we travel on that path to sanctity. Sanctity is worth having, by the way, because it gives us a happy life. We can say that for a saint, the statement 'I like it,' is the same as 'it is good.' For the rest of us, this is not always true. Our goal is to move toward that goal and develop in sanctity so that for us *I like it* and *it is good* are the same thing.

Many agonize over the choices they have to make in life, unsure of what to do because they believe that God makes his will for us a mystery. This reduces the personality of God into one of those irritating acquaintances who seem to delight in knowing more than you do. In order to make sure that you know this they continually drop hints and give out enough little bits of information to arouse your curiosity, and then when you ask them about it they say that they're not allowed tell you. The image of God of those who struggle to know God's will is similar: he commands that we do his will and then won't tell us what his will for us is. The method that David showed me (and which I pass on to you in a subsequent chapter on the discernment of our personal vocation) is very simple and assumes that God is showing us constantly and clearly what he wants us to do. Once we accept that then, although we might need some help in learning to recognize the signs initially, it is relatively simple to read them and to follow the path God has set aside for us.

In order to move forward on my path of a happy life, I had first to acknowledge three basic ideas that summarize the discussion so far. With David's help I was able to do so.

The Three Acknowledgements

1) I acknowledged that I am the cause of my own unhappiness through my self-centered behaviors, thoughts and feelings (otherwise known as *sins*); the cause is not other people or circumstances, no matter how unfortunate.

2) I acknowledged that I am unable to control my thoughts and actions perfectly and to rid myself of that unhappiness, which is rooted in resentment and fear.

3) I acknowledged that my sole hope for happiness is in God. I believe that with God's grace I can do his will, be free of resentment and fear, and have a good, beautiful, and joyful life. Once I have accepted this truth, then I *do* have a choice and we can say that misery is optional.

A program of prayer

Now that I understood that God is personal and someone I can communicate with, I needed to know how to start making contact with Him. This was the beginning of my prayer life.

Under David's direction I began with a simple program of prayer, which is described in the chapter on the daily routine. This routine established contact with *this God I was willing to believe in*. Prayer establishes a personal connection with God. Although this program is consistent with reason, it is not simply an intellectual process by which I puzzle my way out of my problems. It does not rely on modern social science, psychology or philosophy to explain human behavior. All of these things can be in harmony with the process but any that rely on these disciplines alone cannot solve my problems. This offers something that is higher than all of them. It is a spiritual process – one of *supernatural* transformation through the grace of God.

I began by getting down on my knees each morning and asking God to look after me that day so I could be of service to him and others. Then at night I thanked him for doing so. I was told it was only good manners to say thank you. It is these simple daily actions by which I made my first response to his love in which I acknowledged him. This is the beginning of a happier life. The first part of the second section of this book, when we actually get down to following the process, describes this in more detail.

Now to love. Love is not an easy subject for an Englishman who doesn't like discussing his feelings, but I'm going to try...

But before I do that I am going to ask something of you. First, pray:

Bend my heart to your will, Oh God.
I ask this in the name of my Lord Jesus Christ.

2 Leading a Life of Superabundance: The Paradox of Love

A life devoted to love of God and constant thought for others will give us all we ever wanted for ourselves.

'You shall love the Lord your God with all your heart, and with your soul, and with all your mind. This is the great and first commandment. And the second is like it. You shall love your neighbor as yourself.'

Mt. 22:37-39

'If you love me. You will keep my commandments.'

Jn. 14:15

To do God's will is to lead a life of love

If we were to examine the personal vocations of any number of human beings, they would all be different. Each person is unique, and so the detail of how God intends for us to work his plan in our pilgrimage of life is different. However, if there is one thing that all those personal vocations will have in common it will be that we are to lead a life of love. In the broadest terms this is what God's will is for us: to lead a life devoted to love. We are made to love, and it is through love that we have the joy that is promised to us. To the degree that we fulfill this ideal we will be happy: we will want all that we have, and nothing more; and we will have all that we want. A life that is devoted to love – one of constant thought of others – is the one that will, paradoxically, give us what we want for ourselves.

This life of love is consummated in one love. That is the love of God. We are bound to love all others too; this is characterized in scripture as 'love thy neighbor.' The two are inseparable: it is in loving God that we are made lovers capable of loving our fellow man, and it is in loving our fellow man that we are transformed so that we are better able to return God's love for us.

God loves us first. He has already loved us, all of us, and patiently and lovingly awaits our response. In loving us first, he gives us the power to respond if we choose to do so. When we respond by accepting his love for us, it is the beginning of our life of joy, and if we continue to accept his love, our joy intensifies.

I've got that bad lovin' feelin' – it's not all about feelings

David told me that love is not so much about passion as it is about action. I thought the measure of how much love was in my life, whether giving it or receiving it, was how I felt. The greater the lover I was, according to this logic, the more passionate I would *feel* about the object of my love, and this passion would in turn attract love from others.

By that measure, I knew I wasn't much of a lover. While I craved love so much that it made me miserable, I didn't seem able to give it. I rarely felt great passion for others and I was pretty useless at getting people to love me. This, I thought, was the root of my unhappiness. I looked at the romantic and popular rhetoric and feelings of love in songs, poems, and films, and I felt inadequate. My feelings didn't match these.

At one point I tried to *become* emotional and express the passion that I felt I ought to feel. This was a short-lived experiment. This might work for some, but my experience was that each manufactured and clumsily expressed emotional gesture drove people away from me faster than if I was deliberately insulting them. I must have looked like as much of a fraud as I felt. At the point where I had met David I was beginning to wonder if true love was something I would never have.

THE VISION FOR YOU

I remember once, shortly after I had met David, hearing a mother describe how her son was suffering, bursting into tears as she did so. I was so self-centered at this point that I did not think much about her love for her son; rather, I began to ask myself if I loved anyone enough to cry if they were suffering. I couldn't remember ever crying because someone I loved was suffering. I was falling short, I thought, in the post-macho popular psychology of how modern man was supposed to be – emotional. I thought that I should start to cultivate my ability to cry. It was part of my general sense of myself that I was somehow handicapped – that I couldn't 'express my emotions,' or that I was 'emotionally inarticulate.' I had heard that women admired these qualities in men, so it mattered that I should become capable of displaying them.

I asked David about this and mentioned to him that I wondered if I should be one of those late-20th-century men who cries more often. David asked me how I knew that I didn't feel things as strongly as this crying mother. Of course, I couldn't know for certain. I had assumed that, because she was crying, she felt emotion more strongly than I did, but perhaps, David said, "she just cries easily. You don't know." He told me that I should not manufacture emotion according to some modern stereotype of what I ought to feel. We feel what we feel, he said, and we can't control it because our emotional responses are involuntary. This is true for all of us, 'reconstructed' or not. The goal, he said, was to be in control of our emotions, when responding to events, so that we could be of the greatest service to God and those around us, directed by reason. This is the only right route to the emotion that we all seek, and it leads ultimately to the one emotion that is really worth feeling intensely: joy.

It was a relief to hear from David that while it was a good thing to 'feel' loving toward someone, it was not a necessary condition to be able to love them. In order to love someone, I must *do* the loving thing. The important thing is loving action. Loving action is that which is directed towards the good of the person I love. Regardless of how I feel, when I do what is good for someone and with that intention in mind, I am loving that person.

I found out also that being a loving person doesn't always mean that what I do for other people will make them like me. What is good for a person may be the last thing he wants, and he may well resent me for it, but that shouldn't necessarily stop me from doing it.

To do the loving thing requires us to use good judgment. Therefore, in order to love well, all that I do must be informed by reason. Sometimes loving requires self-sacrifice and courage. On other occasions, we need restraint in order to stop ourselves from doing what our passions tell us to do.

Virtue

The personal qualities that enable us to do what is right are called virtues. The word virtue is derived from the Latin word *virtus,* which means strength of character, which in turn is derived from the word *vir* meaning man. These qualities of wisdom, courage, temperance and justice were recognized as those shown by people of strong character and identified in ancient Rome as inherently masculine attributes. Now we would not identify strength of character with men only, but the point still holds: we need to have strength of character and self-control so that we can be prepared to override our emotions at times in order to do what is right.

I'm guessing that some people will worry about this. It sounds, perhaps, like a robotic approach to life in which cold reason is king. In fact, I am not suggesting at all that emotions are unimportant or that they should be suppressed. On the contrary, the whole point of this book is to open the way to a happy life, and happiness is about how we feel as much as anything else (there is a whole section of this book devoted to describing the emotional aspect of happiness). Good feelings are the goal of the way of life I am describing. So, I am profoundly interested in emotion. The point here, though, is that if we make a decision based *solely* upon how we feel prior to the event, then we cannot rely on that choice being a good decision. There is every chance that it will end in unhappiness.

We ought to select our preferences from among those choices that reason tells us are right and good. The initial judgment might on occasion be made after careful deliberation – this would be wise for major life decisions – or it might be done instantaneously after only a little reflection, as is the case with most of the decisions made in the course of daily living. For these quick decisions we tend to rely on plain common sense and draw on personal experience. Nevertheless, if they are good decisions, they will be consistent with reason. The way to have the greatest happiness, I believe, is to choose what we want to do most, but only from a selection of those options that we know are consistent with reason.

Every lover needs a beloved

In his encyclicals, Pope Benedict XVI has described the dynamic interchange of love in detail. Love requires two interacting persons because nobody can love without having someone to love. In this loving interaction, each person, in relationship with the other, is acting for the good of the other. In this sense they are offering themselves as a gift to the other person. In his encyclical, *Deus Caritas Est,* Benedict uses an ancient Greek word for love, *agape*, for this act of self-giving. Then he makes the point that this gift of love is not consummated until it is accepted by the other. Therefore, there are two potential desires in a loving interaction. One is agape, by which we wish to make the gift of love to the other; and the other, which he called *eros*, is the desire to receive the love of the other. In a loving personal relationship each person is drawn to the other and is simultaneously giving and accepting graciously the gift that is offered. According to Benedict, *eros* can be distorted into a desire to possess and control the other, but it can also be purified and transformed into a gracious desire of acceptance of the gift of the other. Ultimately, he explains, this desire is a desire for God, and the personal relationship that governs all others is with Christ. All our love for others is derived from and points to the relationship we have with Christ, who offers himself to us first.

Man, he says, "cannot always give, he must also receive. Anyone who wishes to give love must also receive love as a gift. Certainly, as the Lord tells us, one can become a source from which rivers of living water flow (cf. Jn 7:37-38). Yet to become such a source, one must constantly drink anew from the original source, which is Jesus Christ, from whose pierced heart flows the love of God (cf. Jn 19:34)."[1]

---

[2]Deus Caritas Est, 7

With mention of the word *eros* we immediately think of erotic love (no surprise, the word erotic is derived from *eros*). What Benedict describes certainly includes, but is not limited to, a properly ordered romantic love and that includes the desire for sex within marriage. If this aspect of *eros* were properly ordered it would be directed only to the one person that God has called to be our spouse. Clearly this is an ideal that no one in this life is capable of! This is why it is so important, as in all matters but in this area especially, to consider rationally what is objectively right in governing our conduct, and not just be bound by what we desire.

Every human interaction no matter how mundane or ordinary can reflect this *agape-eros* dynamic of mutual self-gift and acceptance of the other. In each particular relationship its form ought to be properly ordered to the nature of that relationship. Ordinary friendships participate in this dynamic of love. Even superficial exchanges between acquaintances or business relationships can participate in this loving dynamic. Only the persons of the Trinity and the saints and angels in heaven are engaged in a perfectly realized harmony of *agape-eros*, but by degrees and by God's grace we can move towards that ideal in the here-and-now and in all our personal relationships.

When this dynamic is not properly ordered, one aspect takes over at the expense of the other, or one party dominates the other unfairly, or both. We can easily observe this disorder in our own interactions and those of others, especially in relationships between men and women. When *eros* dominates at the expense of *agape*, then even if each person is entering the relationship willingly, you have a relationship which is not the exchange of love. Rather it is two people using each other for the mutual fulfillment of selfish desire. Each is consenting to allow themselves to be used. Each desires first to possess the other, rather than to give to the other. This is immoral because it is a reduction and distortion of love, and so ultimately will lead to unhappiness for both parties. Much of the modern pop culture glorifies this distorted, unpurified *eros* and thus promotes unhappiness.

The irony is that much of what the spokesmen for the culture say about love is true. The Beatles were right for example in singing, 'All you need is love.' This statement becomes a problem, however, if we have the wrong idea of what love is. If we examine the form of love that most pop singers are singing about, the actions and motives that they describe are consistent with selfish pleasure-seeking rather than true love – the *agape-eros* dynamic.

The logical extension of the philosophy that promotes only a distorted *eros* and neglects *agape* altogether is profound evil. In its extreme, one party seeks to dominate the other regardless of what the other wants. This perversion is a dangerous path that can lead to all forms of abuse, of sexual abuse, and rape.

God is always present where there is love

When, however, we live a life that participates in the divine *agape-eros* dynamic of love, God is present in a special way. We can think of the action of love as having three components: the lover, the beloved, and the love itself. In a truly loving encounter, one which has this *agape-eros* dynamic, each person is simultaneously lover and beloved, both a giver of himself and the object of the love of the other who graciously accepts the gift of that love. Then we can think of the relationship as an entity in itself which connects the other two. This is the love. And because God *is* love, that means that God is there too.

God is love. He is more than one who loves, He is love itself. He is the inspiration behind all our love. Therefore, we cannot give love unless we have first accepted Him. Even those who do not acknowledge God are able to show love to others only because at some level within themselves they have accepted the love of God, albeit unacknowledged and anonymous. And this acceptance of love is the source of any joy in our lives. There is a chain of events here: God loves us, we respond to that love with love of God and man, and we are joyful. This is scriptural. For example, in John's gospel we read:

> "All this I have told you so that my joy may be yours and the measure of your joy may be filled up. This is my commandment, that you should love one another as I have loved you… It was not you that chose me, it was I that chose you. The task I have appointed you is

to go out and bear fruit, fruit that will endure; so that every request that you make of the Father in my name may be granted you."

John 15:11-12, 16 (Knox translation)

It takes three to tango: Lover, beloved, and the love

This means that where there is love there are *three* entities present: the lover, the beloved, and the love. It is impossible to love without those three essential components being present. And when we love we can be sure that, in fact, they are all there. God, who is love, is there in person in a special way, with us and connecting us.

The astounding mystery of love – it is *super* abundant. This is the pearl of great price… and it is free

For me this is the most amazing thing about love and the life of love. I cannot see how anyone who really understood this would not want what is given to us in the life of love and do all that they can to accept that gift. The life lived by the principle of love is one that benefits all who come into contact with it. The measure of such a life is superabundance.

Many popular motivational and self-help books entice you to buy them by promising a life of 'abundance,' but what they offer is a reduced form of what the Church herself offers in its fullness. *Superabundance* is the actual word used by Pope Benedict XVI in his writings and sermons for something offered to us that is beyond measure. He is reflecting an idea that is right at the center of traditional Christian thinking. We are offered a life that is plentiful to a degree that we cannot even imagine. The source of the superabundance is the love of God that gives beyond measure and even has the power to create something out of nothing. By living the life of superabundance, prosperity, wealth, and the measure of all that is good in the world increases.

This is so because love is always fruitful. In its most striking form this superabundant love created the universe itself and maintains it in existence. It can create human lives, as it does in a marriage. Or it can create wealth as it does when two people freely exchange money for goods. Through loving action, we can participate in the continuing process of creation and the molding of what already exists into what is good for us and for the world. Provided that we seek to conform to God's will, this superabundance has no limit. The only limitation is our own capacity for love, and the main barrier to that is pride.

Here is what I was promised: if I can live a life which is devoted to trying to do the loving thing then I will have a life beyond measure. By writing this book I am passing on the very simple directions that I was given which have enabled me to do so, giving me rewards that I couldn't have imagined… and it keeps getting better.

The superabundant life of love is the happy life. All the great benefits and rewards of such a life arise from making our primary aim the reception and return of God's love for us. If we seek first the kingdom of God, then all else will come to us.[2]

But exactly how do we love God?

If, when I was beginning this process, David had suggested to me that I start to love God, my reaction would have been to want to escape as fast as possible. I would have assumed that I was being asked to generate artificial feelings for a God whom I barely knew at this point. I just couldn't have done it and would have been embarrassed to try.

This assumption came from my jaundiced view of Christians and the nature of Christianity. As far as I could see, Christians were just a group of frightened people who were unable to face the day without seizing up with anxiety. The only way they could cope was by clinging to each other for comfort. The practice of Christianity, I thought, was one of being nice to each other, avoiding conflict and doing your best to avoid hurting the feelings of others at all costs. All this was done to avoid the ultimate horror of life, which is… not being liked by others.

In my picture of them, Christians were so mild and meek in their pursuit of niceness that they ended up being respected by no one. They all bore the mark of whoever stamped on them last. What little personal dignity

---

[2] Cf. Matthew 6:33

they retained was smothered by the feverish pursuit of warm and fuzzy feelings. This involved always wearing a forced smile and frequently gathering for communal activities such as clapping and singing banal and syrupy folksy songs.

The songs they sang seemed to be modeled on bad nursery rhymes, and no one past the age of five, it seemed to me, could retain their dignity while singing them. Yet here they were – grown men and women apparently oblivious to this fact and singing at the top of their voices, smiling away, swaying and waving their arms without a trace of self-consciousness. It was the fact that they seemed to think they were cool that made whole thing even more excruciatingly embarrassing, indicating to me how clueless they were. I know this sounds harsh and uncharitable, but it is how I felt at the time and it influenced my response to David and what he was offering.

Because I had such a bad impression of Christianity, right from the first moment I started to work with David I was also extremely suspicious that I was being lured into this repugnant sort of religion. As David started gently leading me along the path to an encounter with God, I was sharply on the lookout for anything that smacked of this stereotype of tambourine-waving, Kumbaya Christianity. Had I picked up the slightest indication that this was where we were headed I would have bailed out quickly. Fortunately, David realized this.

Give until it hurts

David's approach to introducing me to the way of love was to begin by encouraging me to help others. He didn't tell me that it would lead me to love God, he just told me that I would start to feel better if I developed the habit of considering others instead of focusing on myself. He said that I should put aside time every week in which I would make a commitment to volunteer to help others. This became part of my new routine of prayer and spiritual exercises from very early on. I volunteered for a group that helped homeless people in London. I was told that making the habit of doing something loving, even if at times unpleasant and unappreciated, would make me feel better about myself.

Through this habitual practice of the action of love, by degrees and despite myself, he said, I would become a better lover, and this would affect all my other relationships. I might not be conscious of what I was doing differently, but I would be different. The ideal I was pursuing was that I should do enough service that it constituted some sort of meaningful sacrifice. "Give until it hurts!" was the way that David put it. This meant always doing just enough to pull me out of my comfort zone. This might sound like a tall order, but in fact it was easier than it sounded. At this point in my life I was so selfish that I barely had to give anything before I was out of my comfort zone. I am the sort of person who by nature is so self-centered that it hurts me just to give somebody the time of day.

Love of God through love of neighbor

What David was doing was helping me to love God by helping my neighbor. David was passing on to me the advice of St. Augustine who about 1,500 years ago wrote:

> Always and everywhere, bear in mind that you must love God and your neighbor, *love God with all your heart, and with all your soul, and with all your mind; and love your neighbor as you would love yourself.* You are told "Love God." If you say to me "Show me whom I should love," what can I say except what John says? *No man has ever seen God.* But you must not think yourself wholly unsuited to seeing God: *God is love,* says John, *and whoever dwells in love dwells in God.* So, love whoever is nearest to you and look inside you to see where that love is coming from: thus, as far as you are capable, you will see God. So, start to love your neighbor. *Share your bread with the hungry, bring the homeless pauper into your house. Clothe the naked, and do not despise the servants of your kin.*
>
> What will you get from doing all this? *Your light will break forth like the dawn.* Your light is your God, your dawn, because he will come to you to end the night of this world – he who, himself, neither rises nor sets but is eternal.[3]

---

[3] St. Augustine: *Tracts on St. John;* quoted in the Office of Readings, Jan. 3rd

David also reiterated to me that this is not driven by feelings, we are less interested in generating a passionate feeling for God or for neighbor than we are about doing the loving action. Nor are we to be driven by other people's feelings. Although it is easier and, in some ways, preferable that when we do good others appreciate it, we cannot make that appreciation of what we do the primary motive for doing it. The life of love is not about always being nice, or always being liked for what you do. It is about doing what is right – what is good. Sometimes the hardest decisions are for those whom we love the most. Parents who deal with difficult teenagers will know that if they do what is good for them it will not always be appreciated. Sometimes in very difficult situations, such as when a son or daughter is addicted to drugs, doing what is right for them can cause estrangement for years. We may not all face such extreme examples, but all of us will have to deal with similar dilemmas at some point in our lives.

To aim for a virtuous life is to aim for an ideal that requires so much wisdom and courage that without God's help, it is a task beyond our capabilities. This indicates why we must pray if we are to be good lovers – we need to ask for that help in leading a virtuous life. The lives of the martyrs speak to this point: they led holy lives yet were so disliked that they were killed. Christ led a perfect life yet it provoked anger in others that was so intense that he was brutally tortured and murdered.

The experience of my ordinary and imperfect life so far is that trying at least, to do what is right, regardless of how I feel about it beforehand and regardless of what others feel about it, is worth the effort. Deep down, at the very least *I* know that what I am doing is right, and so this is how I build up a healthy self-esteem, based upon truth. Also, generally speaking, good actions appeal to what is good in others, and those who recognize this will respect you for it. While sometimes the minority is more vocal in putting you down, many others will recognize the good in what you do and respond well.

Love changes the world; it even changed me

As I followed David's directions and loving action became more of a habit, I noticed changes. People around me started to behave differently toward me. Some relationships that had been constantly antagonistic become steadily less so to the extent that sometimes I welcomed the company of those who previously had been causes of irritation. As I was the only common denominator in these interactions, I could only conclude that the change came about because the others were reacting differently to me. It seemed that what David had predicted was happening. By constantly doing loving things, I was being transformed into a better lover, despite myself. Sometimes I was deliberately treating others differently, but it seemed that this was something beyond that – my natural, instinctive mode of behavior was improving. Some people did not like what I was doing, but that mattered less too because I became less dependent on the opinion of others for my sense of well-being.

Mirroring this was a change in my attitude toward others. As I mentioned, I volunteered to help the homeless. David told me of the importance of doing good for others regardless of whether or not I felt compassion beforehand. This was just as well for me! My problem at this point was that I really wasn't interested in the well-being of others; I was absorbed in my own difficulties and didn't really know how to be interested in things that didn't naturally grab my interest. I was so clueless that David even had to coach me into asking people open questions about themselves, starting with "how are you?". When I did this, people would start to talk about themselves. This was different from the one-way street of my old conversational technique – my telling others about my life.

So now, coached by David into doing something different, here I was helping people. My motivation was far from saintly, however. I was interested in doing good for others because of what I would get out of it and any appearance of interest in others was feigned. I realize now that I was still objectifying people – making them objects of 'love' for my benefit.

However, even approaching the idea of doing good things in such a tainted, self-centered way forced me to think to some degree about the other in order to make a judgment as to whether or not what I was doing was good for them. Although impoverished in many ways, it was still a big step forward.

And despite myself, I was gradually transformed. I remember one day asking someone the standard question, "how has your day gone so far?" As usual, the person started to tell me. Then something happened that I noticed for the first time. I realized that *I was actually listening to the answer*. Normally while the person I was in conversation with was talking I would be trying to think of the next open question so as to keep the conversation going when he stopped. But here I was *genuinely interested* in knowing about this person's day and how he felt about it. When he complained about things I tried to offer solace not only because that was the right thing to do, but because part of me *actually wanted him to be consoled*.

I described this to David later and although pleased and encouraging, he didn't seem surprised. He told me that this is why he had encouraged me to volunteer to help strangers because it would affect me more profoundly. While I am bound, of course, he said, to give love to all, there is always the thought that it will impact me directly for the better if I like them already or am related to them. They are still *my* friends and *my* family. When I help others without any thought of direct return, as I did in this group simply because they are unable to make any return, then that is in some ways a purer love that will have a more profound effect on me.

The idea, articulated so well by St. Augustine, is that by loving my neighbor whom I can see, I am transformed in love, so it intensifies my capacity to love God, whom I cannot see. But I was only able to love others at all because God loved me first and I had accepted his love. By grace I had become capable of loving others. So, without being aware that this is what was going on, in order to love others, I had first to draw closer to God. The result of drawing closer to God is greater joy. This is why our joy in life is increased by helping others.

To the degree that I cooperate with grace, each time I do this I am transformed and my capacity to work within this dynamic of personal relationships is incrementally increased. It is a positive feedback cycle. This is also why it is so important that prayer and faith in God (or the gradual development of these things) are there alongside the practice of good works. We need to develop that connection to the source of love if we are to become better lovers.

Love in community

The dynamic of love has been described as though love is always a self-contained binary system. There are two lovers, two beloved, and each is loving the other. However, a loving society is not simply the vector sum of the love between pairs of lovers. In fact, it allows for an even higher expression of this *agape-eros* dynamic within itself, which binds us together in harmony. When God loves us, we might accept that gift of love so that it is consummated. But it is likely that we will return the gift and give ourselves to him as completely as he makes the gift of himself to us. In fact, we may not even acknowledge this love. But if we are able to love anyone else, and we all can to some degree, we have passed on that love of God to others. God knows that most of us will do this, but He gives nevertheless. This after all, is the nature of a gift – it is unconditional. This is the ideal that we aim for – giving without thought of return so that others are helped and are in return able to help others, even if it is others, and not us, who are loved in return. By this, a community is created founded on love and rooted in that first love of God. And here's the paradox: When we love others without the expectation of love in return, we love God more. We are engaged in an *agape-eros* dynamic of love with God, but one which has drawn the love of others into its expression. How wonderful that is! And there is no limit to how many can be part of this loving society.

This last point does lead us into an answer to a question that some might have: good as it is, is this indirect form of loving God as close as we can get? Is there a way of encountering God personally? The answer, of course, is yes. That is what the next chapter will describe.

As I write these words on love, it occurs to me that many who know me may look askance and wonder what sort of example of love I think I am. There is a saying, *"Can't do? Teach! Can't teach? Become a critic!"* Just as the art critic can't paint and the theater critic can't act, my writing about love does not presuppose that I am a great lover. Rather it is a recognition that I am not one. As I look to the ideal of love that I describe, I am painfully aware that it makes my deficiencies even more obvious. The best I can hope for is that those who knew me 30 years ago and know me now would say that at least there is an improvement. Certainly, I am happier than I was, and my own perception is that my relationships with others, though far from perfect, are better. Nevertheless, I recognize the need in my life for constant work and improvement and ever-renewed transformation in Christ. I know that if I am to be a better lover, then I must first accept God's love for me and that this will be the source of my love for others.

The next chapter is about love of God in worship… but first, pray:

Bend my heart to your will, Oh God.
I ask this in the name of my Lord Jesus Christ

3 Religion, Worship, and Joy

The spirit of man longs to worship God as much as the body craves air, food and water.

The liturgy is the summit toward which the activity of the Church is directed; at the same time, it is the font from which all her power flows.

Sacrosanctum Concilium, 10.

If love is not primarily about generating feelings but rather about taking loving actions and developing, through the aid of reason, the right motives for doing so, then what actions constitute a love of God?

The answer is prayer. Prayer is most direct, most effective, and most powerful when it takes the form of worship in the Sacred Liturgy of the Church, which is the phrase used by Christians to describe public worship of the Church, i.e., what we do when we go to church.

When I first met David, I was not ready to accept any suggestion that I worship God and he wisely didn't even raise the matter. He was sensitive enough to my prejudices that he didn't even let on for a long time that he was a practicing Catholic.

This reluctance to talk about religion and the worship of God did not arise from a lack of profound respect for either. It was because he was aware of my prejudices. When, years later, I started to attend Mass with him regularly, I found out that this was something he took very seriously. To illustrate, I had been fairly relaxed about the way I dressed for Mass. Then one day, I went to Mass in jeans and a baggy blue sweater. I thought I was pretty cool, but he pulled me aside as we were leaving church.

"I hope you don't mind me bringing this up, lad," he said. "But I think you should dress more appropriately for Mass. Wear a jacket and collared shirt at least." As usual he was immaculately dressed, with suit and tie, or jacket and tie, polished shoes, and that spotted handkerchief in the top pocket. "Don't you realize," he said, "that when you go to Mass it is Almighty God who is present?" Then he paused and said more slowly, softly and deliberately (which had the effect of emphasizing how important he thought this was), "Almighty God. Almighty God! Out of respect you should be acknowledging this in the way you dress. What do you think, lad? Does the way you are dressed seem right for meeting the person who created you, gave you life and maintains it, and who has given you all that you have ever had that is good?" Then he used an argument I heard him use often to persuade people to dress respectfully. "If you were going for a job interview and there was something in it for you, you would want to show respect and dress smartly. So why not now?"

Although he did not talk about the Sacred Liturgy during the first years that we knew each other, what he did do was give me a pattern of personal prayer and meditation that was derived from and so pointed to the essential elements of the worship of the God in the Sacred Liturgy. By doing this he was, in a sense, priming me for the worship of God. This habitual pattern of prayer was stimulating my spirit in such a way that I became ready to worship.

The spirit is the name given to that part of my soul that is closest to God and which, in the proper order of things, governs all other activities of my soul, and hence my body (because the soul governs the body). This is why we do spiritual exercises if we want to improve our relationship with God.

The *Vision for You* spiritual formation was effective. When sometime later I encountered Solemn Mass at the London Oratory it had such a profound effect on me that I still cite it as perhaps the single most influential factor in my becoming Catholic.

Religion and worship

Before my conversion, the worship of God seemed to me to be the least justifiable aspect of religion. I viewed any ritual as man-made practices that reinforced, it seemed to me, not the existence of a personal loving God, but the idea of the existence of a vain God who needed adulation.

It would be a strange and rather emotionally stunted divine person, I thought, that craves attention so much that he actually creates underlings within whom he bestows a driving purpose in life to give him that attention. This would put 'God' at the maturity level of a tin-pot dictator who gains emotional succor from terrorizing people into praising him for his benevolence.

My view of the nature of God changed, however, as I began to pray daily. I had adopted an idea of God that I could accept, as I have described before, and started to pray to Him daily. Through this my sense of God began to develop. As I felt the improvement in my life it made me desire a deeper understanding and a deeper relationship. I started to read books about God.

While I was in the early part of the process, David never tried to stop me from such reading, but I could tell he was wary about my doing it. He said that I should be careful that my reading didn't lead me to doing things that might distract me from the spiritual exercises that he was showing me. Otherwise I might end up like a headless chicken moving from one spiritual flight of fancy to another and getting less and less out of it.

He changed this attitude later, however. Once I had completed 'the process,' David began to encourage me to do my own spiritual reading and research. He knew that the process he had given me was a great foundation for such a quest. I now had a firm faith in God along with a set of principles and experiences that provided some measure of truth to guide me on my journey forward. The effect of the process on me had been so profound that I was convinced it was rooted in truth, and so it became the yardstick by which I measured truth in spiritual matters, working on the principle that I would reject anything that contradicted directly what I had learned up to that point but be open-minded to everything else.

David directed me to a particular book shop in the Covent Garden area of London that specialized in spiritual books, telling me to browse the shop and look at the titles. If one caught my eye I should pull it off the shelf and leaf through it, and as I did so I should pick passages to read at random and see how I got on with the text. If I didn't like it when I was dipping into the text I should reject it, he said, but if I did enjoy my sampling, then I should buy it. He also told me that even once I had started to read it, I should not feel any sense of obligation to finish. If it was helpful and enjoyable, carry on, but if I got a firm sense partway through that this was wrong, I should stop.

From time to time he would ask me what I had been reading and what interested me and then suggest other titles. He first suggested a book called *The Road Less Traveled*, which was a psychiatrist's account of the necessity of faith for mental health. Gradually, depending on where I was in my journey, he would suggest others that were more overtly religious and Christian, such as G.K. Chesterton's *Orthodoxy*, and even more obviously Catholic works of medieval English mystics such as the *Cloud of Unknowing*, the *Scale of Perfection* and *Revelations of Divine Love*, Thomas Merton's *Seven Storey Mountain*, and Eugene Boylan's *This Tremendous Lover*.

Another writer that I found helpful at this stage was Malcolm Muggeridge. Muggeridge began writing as a left-leaning atheist in the 1930s and, as such, was typical of the educated class of his day… and mine. However, he rejected communism early on in his career (he was one of the first journalists in Britain, for example, to describe what was really going on in Stalin's Russia) and later in life was attracted to Christianity. For many years Muggeridge drew back from full conversion and lived a large part of his life on the brink of becoming Catholic. He was eventually received into the Church when he was 79 years old in 1982. He was great reading for someone like me who came from a similar philosophical starting point and was now considering Christianity in general and Catholicism in particular. Plus, his writing style is pure joy to read. Simple and direct in some parts, poetic and allegorical in others, the words flow off the page like honey. In reading his books I encountered more than 40 years of his life within the period of perhaps a couple of months of mine.

Had I read them too early on in 'the process' I would have not have enjoyed these books. But because I read them after I had completed that foundation, I understood enough, at least, for them to be stimulating and helpful.

If I can't be in a 'religion of one,' which one can I be in?

As a result of all this reading I gradually lost what had been initially a deeply ingrained prejudice against 'organized' religion. At some point it occurred to me that if there was one God and if we all share one human nature then one would expect there to be common elements in all spiritual activity that truly allow us to relate to God.

Thus, if I refused to join a religion I would be in effect creating a religion with a membership of one, a religion in which I was the authority deciding everything. What are the chances, I thought, of my being the only person in the whole of human history who has got this right? If there are common activities, then one would expect to see many people doing them. If I do those things in common with someone else, then immediately I am participating in an organized religion. Furthermore, assuming that human nature has not changed (since the Fall, at least), one would expect to see many people over a long period of time doing the same things in order to achieve the same goals. And that would be a religion. The essence of a religion, I concluded, is a group of people who share common practices of loving God. This being so, I concluded, I should be open-minded enough to start investigating the different religions, and then pick the one that seemed to reflect what is true.

Another question that seemed important to me was: who decides what is the best way for humankind to relate to God? The answer, surely, is God himself… Therefore, I decided to choose a religion that I believed spoke with divine authority.

Not all of my motivation for wanting to join a religion came through rational thinking, of course. Part of it was emotional. I wanted to be with people who thought as I did and with whom I could travel a common path. I felt the need to be part of a community of people with whom I could make a shared journey. I now believe that the social character of 'religion' is essential to it, too.

A religion is more than simply a collection of individuals who are connected to God – the individuals are also connected to each other, both indirectly (but nevertheless profoundly) through God, and directly through personal relationships. I believe that man by nature desires this social aspect of religion. He wants to feel that he is worshiping God as others do. I also believe that if man misdirects or attempts to erase or ignore this desire, he will be psychologically impaired, and his happiness will not be as great as it could be. Even an isolated hermit celebrating Mass alone is aware that he is worshiping in harmony with the whole of God's Church.

Although I considered nearly all the religions I was aware of, most of the time my search was focused on Buddhism, Islam, Hinduism and Christianity. I can't remember why, but I didn't look at Judaism very much – perhaps because I knew that it wasn't particularly evangelical and so wouldn't make it easy for me to join.

One thing I discovered very quickly is that it is a modern myth that all religions are essentially the same. It didn't take much serious reading to see that they said different things about the essentials of their faith, about moral conduct, and practices of worship. It simply wasn't possible to agree with them all, because they didn't agree with each other.

I rejected Buddhism and Hinduism first because of their descriptions of the nature of God. They seemed to be saying that all is one and all is God (if he exists). Both religions appeared to me to be pantheist or perhaps even atheist (in the case of some Buddhist texts I read). Neither of these was consistent with the concept of God that I had acquired at this point, so I rejected them.

This reduced the choice to Islam or Christianity. I rejected Islam when I read its moral code. The books about Islam that I read, written by adherents to Islam who wanted to convert me, encouraged forgiveness of others for harms they had done to me but, critically it seemed to me, allowed also for special exceptions when the harm was so great that it was 'unforgivable.' I knew enough of my own nature to see that this was a loophole that I would take advantage of in order to justify bearing grudges against just about everybody! This had been made very apparent to me after going through the 'moral examination' in which I examined all my negative thoughts and feelings as part of the process (you will understand why when you have done this). I knew after doing this process, that I couldn't have peace unless I strove to forgive all those who had harmed me, no exceptions. The Christian ideal was one of perfect forgiveness for all harms done to me. It seemed to me that while there were plenty of Christians who were justifying vengeance in response to harms done, but when they did so then they were acting in a way that was contrary to the teachings of their faith.

Why Christianity?

It is reported that G.K. Chesterton was once asked if there were any arguments against Christianity. "Just one," he replied, "Christians."

His answer reflects the fact that the conduct of Christians themselves, right up to and including some popes, does not always match up to the morality that Christianity espouses. I have often heard this used by others as a reason for rejecting Christianity, but for me this has never really been a problem. It has always seemed to me that wherever there are people, human failings will be present too. Therefore, it was no surprise to me that Christians have done many bad things; or that they would try to claim that good was on their side as they did what looked like bad things. As the American motivational writer and protestant Christian 'Zig' Ziglar would say with a chuckle whenever anyone objected to going to church on the grounds that the church was full of hypocrites, "Come on down and join us, there's always room for one more!"

I found myself much more inclined to focus on the ideals that the faithful adherents of a particular religion were striving to live up to. The higher the ideals, the more obvious it would be when people fell short, I thought, fully expecting that as a natural consequence of this, the religion with the highest ideals would have greatest numbers of 'sinners.' At the same time, because the religion with the highest ideals would also have more people with a higher standard of behavior (since those ideals would be continually drawing people to something greater) the actual behavior overall of adherents of the religion with the highest ideals should in fact be better than the actual overall behavior of non-adhering people.

Under this sort of examination, it was Christianity that came out highest for me. In the lives of the saints, who best matched up to these ideals, we had the greatest models of behavior. This encouraged me to believe that not only were the standards of Christianity high, but that also it was possible for someone as imperfect as me to make at least some progress towards perfection, even if I didn't actually attain it.

Why the Catholic Church?

It was one thing, of course, to decide that Christianity was not contrary to my fundamental principles, but another to say that it was good enough for me to commit to it. This meant I had to start looking in even more detail at what being a Christian means in terms of belief and daily living, and then decide whether or not I could commit to doing it. This is where I began to differentiate between the different Christian denominations in order to decide which one to join. It was not possible for me to be a generic non-denominational Christian without starting my own 'religion of one.' I had to pick one and be ready to commit, and this meant committing not only to a set of beliefs – a 'credo,' so to speak – but also a set of actions including a mode of worship.

So now, in addition to my reading, I started to attend church services of various denominations and to talk to individual Christians about what they believed. Wherever possible I would speak to ministers and priests.

I don't remember being treated badly by any, but I was impressed by the responses of the Catholic priests that I spoke to. For one, they were noticeably more curious about my journey. They asked lots of questions about David and the process he had taken me through. What struck me particularly was that when I described the details of the process, they seemed to understand it and encouraged me to keep going with it.

In contrast, people from the non-Catholic churches seemed less interested and often would discourage me from continuing. What they seemed to be saying was that it was good that the process had got me to the point it had, but I should drop it now and let them take over.

I was struck also by the fact that the Catholic priests were simultaneously willing both to believe that prayer could produce miraculous results and to use reason to examine their validity. Not until I met David, I think, had I seen anyone else who was like this. This indicated to me that if I became a Catholic I was not going to be asked to suspend the faculty of intelligence. In fact, as I was to discover once I became a Catholic, the reverse was true. Engaging with the Faith would be intellectually stimulating and would take me right to the limits of my intellectual capacity. There was always more to know and to understand.

As I talked to Catholics – lay people as well as priests – I began to recall certain people, perhaps two or three, who had made an impression on me at different points in my life and had been Catholics. Not all the Catholics I was speaking to now, not even all the priests, struck me in quite the way that these lay people from the past had. But now, in a deeper way, I was beginning to make a connection between the way these good people in my past behaved and the Church they were part of. I could see that if I too strove after the ideals encapsulated in good Catholic living, I might become like them and experience the joy that they possessed.

Another important point for me was the way that daily examination of conscience and confession is emphasized by Catholicism. Along with the Orthodox and high Anglicans, among those I investigated, the Catholic Church institutionalized the confession of sins to the priest. It stipulates that Catholics must go to confession regularly and even encourages a daily examination of conscience. My experience of personal transformation as a result of the *Vision for You* process had convinced me of the value of these practices. In fact, I found it difficult to imagine how anyone could be happy without them.

Having come to believe that self-centeredness, and therefore sin, was bound up in my fallen nature, I couldn't imagine that even a single day would pass without my indulging in some selfish behavior or some thought that would take me away from God. This led me to believe that just about everybody sins daily, even saints, and thus that daily examination of conscience is vital to spiritual progress. In pointing this out the Church, far from making me feel guilty, was offering a chance for me to be freed from the guilt and discomfort that I already felt. The sacramental nature of the Church's process of confession gave it even greater weight.

However, this did raise one question: If the process had worked so dramatically before I had become a Christian and without direct participation in the religious rites and sacraments of the Church, why should anyone actually become a Christian? Wasn't it possible to establish a fruitful relationship with God outside the Church? This point of consideration arose in another way when I asked if the rest of my family, who were not Catholics at this point, would be consigned to hell?

When I asked this question of priests, I was told no, being formally received into the Church before death isn't absolutely necessary for salvation. God gives everyone sufficient grace to go to heaven and there may be a full cooperation just before death even by those who are living outside the formal structures of the religion through ignorance, for example. If, however, I am fully aware of the truth and reject it, that might cause me problems.

Fear of hell is a good thing once I accept that it exists. It is rational to do what is necessary to avoid going there. But that is not the full story of why I converted. In my consideration there was a much more important reason that was a positive motivation for converting as soon as possible. I was also told that it is the presence of the Church on earth that makes it possible for anyone to go to heaven, Catholic or not. Therefore, those people who are part of the Church are participating in the means by which all others may be saved. This, therefore, is for Catholics a great act of love for their fellow man, and so a source of greater joy for all.

Pope Benedict addressed this general point of why anyone should become a Christian, saying that "the basic movement of Christianity is the love through which we share in the creative love of God himself."[1] When we become part of the Church we participate more directly in the dynamic of love of God and through this we are transformed; and so now we participate more deeply in the mission of the Church, becoming "instruments of his mercy and loving kindness,"[2] for all mankind. This reinforces the point made earlier, it seems to me: to the degree that this principle of love governs what we do, we live the life of superabundance and we find greater joy. And there is a greater joy on offer to those who are part of the Church, because, through grace, the potential for love of God and man is greater.

Another attraction of the Catholic Church arose from the fact that the priests I spoke to did not criticize other denominations. One thing that seemed to unite the non-Catholic denominations that I spoke to was that they were very conscious of not being Catholic and seemed to find it difficult to resist the desire to differentiate themselves from the Catholic Church at some point in the conversation. I never initiated such a discussion or invited them to comment on Catholic teaching, but often they would. I got the impression that the Protestant and Orthodox churches seemed to understand themselves as much by what they were not – Catholic – as by what they were. This served only to attract me to the Church even more strongly. I considered the objections against Catholicism that I had heard and did some research to see if they were true. In each case, as a result of my additional research I concluded either that the Church's doctrine was being misrepresented by its detractors; even when accurately represented, when I listened to the Church's rationale for such teachings, the Church was right. All of this reinforced

---

[1] Benedict XVI: *What it Means to Be a Christian*, p. 58 (originally a sermon entitled *God Becomes Man and Man Becomes Christlike*); pub Ignatius Press, 2006
[2] Ibid, p62

still further the picture I had of Church teachings of a Faith that was fully integrated with and consistent with reason.

I discovered also that among all the churches and religions, the Catholic Church had the highest ideals that were consistent with a life of love. As such, it shone a light on all others and this was why it forced all others to position themselves relative to it. Through this process of examination, I discovered that the Church had never (despite what I had been told) reversed or changed any dogma since its inception. This made sense to me. I did not believe that man had changed as a species since ancient times and so what was good for man in times past would be good for man now.

Although I didn't understand why until much later, something else marked out the Catholic Church from the Protestant churches (though, in this case, not from Eastern Orthodox and High Anglican churches). This was the importance they attached to worship, or to use the word they used for their worship, *liturgy*.

Initially, while I had accepted that going to church with others was important, I saw it more in terms of fulfilling my own personal desire for human solidarity and fellowship than anything else. As I continued to delve into this phenomenon I began to see that it was about much more than this.

While some of the liturgies I attended were beautiful and reverent and ultimately profoundly influential in drawing me into unity with the Church, it was in the liturgy also that many of my negative stereotypes of Christians and Christianity were confirmed. This was true in even within the Catholic Church. In fact, I would go further than that and say that the Catholic Church seemed to have both the best and worst liturgical experiences that I encountered.

It was the music used in the liturgies that especially affected me. Music has always been important to me. As a teenager I had seen music as much more than personal entertainment. For me it was an identifying label. I chose my friends based upon the music they listened to. In my case in the

1970s it was esoteric forms of progressive rock and jazz fusion – I used to like to be overheard talking about the music of bands such as King Crimson, Camel, Be- Bop Deluxe, PFM and Return to Forever.

When I was a cynical high school student, I can remember my impressions at the time: the most uncool crowd when I was at school was The Christian Unions – the group that tried to be cool by listening to Christian rock bands, but didn't have a clue. The music and the words at the vast majority of church services I attended all these many years later were absolutely not cool. The more fervent the hand-waving and swaying of bodies from the congregation, the more it looked to me like a very unconvincing attempt by a lot of socially inadequate and lonely people to seek distraction from their unhappiness and social inadequacy by whipping up emotion. They were trying to be groovy long after the word 'groovy' had ceased to be groovy. 'Sad' was the word that came to my mind when I saw this. From my perspective this sort of 'liturgy' had all the attractiveness and cultural sophistication of a pre-kindergarten Peter, Paul and Mary.

When I met David, I was in my late twenties and my musical taste had changed. I listened to classical and jazz music, and a broader range of pop. I no longer thought of musical taste as the most important way of labeling someone. Furthermore, I was more open-minded about Christianity. I recognized that my youthful response of the past had been gut reactions that were in part derived from prejudice, and I tried to put them aside. I really did my best to look for the good in what was offered. Even still, nothing – absolutely nothing – could convince me that I would ever grow to enjoy this sort of experience. It was so syrupy that it still made me sick. I really mean that – the reaction was powerful, visceral, and negative.

I thought back to my youth and pondered over my memories of The Christian Unions crowd from when I was at high school. I had definitely not been one of the cool guys at school whom everyone admired; but I wanted to be. I could see who was succeeding at it, and I wanted to be admired and liked by them. The Christian Unions crowd always struck me as wanting to be those things too, but failing in such an obvious way that you had to feel sorry for them. They were trying valiantly to be accepted but could not overcome the biggest handicap of all. They were Christians. Their problem, and I knew this even as a teenager, was that they were trying to compete with the non-Christian world on terms that were intrinsically non-Christian. It didn't matter how hard they tried, they couldn't seem to understand that the Christian faith is not about being cool.

Evoked by the songs and music, all this prejudice came up again as I attended these services. I am certain that there were many good people in those congregations who did not correspond to my stereotype, people who were living out their Faith in a genuine and substantial way. However, when they worshipped God in their peculiar style of liturgy it did not speak of a deep and genuine Faith to my ear, but of something far less substantial.

I tried to be open-minded. I wanted to get past my sense of embarrassment at so many of these liturgies, but I was finding it difficult. Then one day, David offhandedly suggested that I go to a church called the Brompton Oratory in South Kensington in London. He didn't tell me what denomination it was and I didn't think to ask.[3] This opened the way to a whole new world. It was attending the Solemn Mass in Latin at the Brompton Oratory that opened my eyes to a different view of the place of the worship of God in the Christian life.

The music was traditional plainchant and High Renaissance polyphony. Finally, here was a use of music for worship that didn't even try to be cool. It spoke of something else altogether. There was no pale imitation of either youth culture or aging hippie culture or any other sort of secular culture. Crucially, and paradoxically, this sort of music spoke to people from all cultures because it spoke of another world altogether. This was a true multiculturalism in that it participated in every culture. It seemed to come from a place that was higher than this world, somewhere mysterious and better, but for all people. This is what I was looking for.

---

[3] I give a more detailed description of the impact of this first exposure to beautiful sacred liturgy in the chapter on Sacred Liturgy in my book Art, Beauty, Liturgy, Culture.

The paintings and the architecture and the overall unity of these things with the music, art, and the activity of worship indicated a refinement and depth. But it did not smack of an exclusive elitism of any sort. There was neither the affected elitism of the 'cool' of youth culture (which adopts a persona that says, 'I am happy with myself and I don't care whether you like me or not'); nor of that of grown-ups' cultural elitism (which adopts a persona that says, 'I am cultured and have eclectic tastes, I am more refined and am more intellectual than you are').

This liturgy at the Oratory pointed me to something noble and perfect, and crucially something loving and inclusive. I am sure those who attended were not all perfect people, but regardless of the personal qualities of the people involved, their liturgy spoke of a new and beautiful world beyond them which beckoned to me. It refused to even try to compete with a secular culture on its own terms. It set its own standard and was inviting me into something wonderful and different.

Although I knew that the liturgy at the Brompton Oratory was not what I would see at most Catholic churches, my attendance then and subsequently many times before I converted gave me a sense of what the liturgy could be at its height. From then on, I identified the Faith with the beauty that I saw there, rather than with the banal forms that I saw elsewhere. Despite this, I did not convert immediately. There were still aspects of Church teaching on morality that I struggled with and I had to work through these. But thereafter, knowledge of the beautiful ideal drew me in and made me want to understand. By the time I converted to Catholicism, in May 1994, I understood that every licit Mass is good regardless of my appreciation of the external forms, for there is always something beautiful at its heart. I understand now that not all churches have the resources of the Brompton Oratory, but still I do look forward to the day *every* church offers a liturgy that points to the heavenly ideal, however simply, rather than distracting us from heaven by speaking of lesser things.

What is worship?

I discovered that worship is about more than the fulfillment of a need for human fellowship. During my quest I was struck by the fact that worship seemed to be a feature of nearly all the faiths and churches that I investigated. Even Buddhism had its temples, despite not seeming to acknowledge a God. It was more of a philosophy than a religion. I saw people in Buddhist temples in Thailand reverently lighting candles in front of giant statues of the Buddha. I reflected on my own experiences and what I knew of religions and concluded that it was intrinsic to man to want to worship and that he will be happier if he does so. Certainly, this is true for me.[4]

And for all my adolescent cynicism, I could even remember this tendency in me coming through in strange little ways long before I became a Christian. At the high school I attended in Birkenhead in the north of England, all of us had to attend morning prayer. The choir sang the psalms every day in the chapel and the rest of us were supposed to join in. It amused my crowd of friends to insert the names of rock stars when the Trinity was invoked so that we would sing: 'Glory be to Peter Gabriel, Robert Plant and Jimmy Page…' I don't think any of us would have gone so far as to propose that these seventies rock stars were actually divine, but it was disconcertingly close to it. We did use the word 'gods' to describe them – I might actually have said at some point 'Peter Gabriel is a god' – and we did try to dress as they did and model our lives on theirs (as far as we could get away with it under the careful eyes of our parents and teachers). Also, the very fact that we connected the religious service with our admiration for these people indicates something, I think. What was on our minds would probably not be described as full-blown worship, but we were paying homage to them as an expression of our admiration and we were doing it in a religious way.

The closest I came to actual contact with any of the stars I admired was each time I made the pilgrimage to the Liverpool Empire – a local theater – to see them in concert. I would make sure that I was fully adorned in the appropriate length hair, wearing clothes embroidered with the design from the latest record cover. These were the signs that marked me out as a devotee, a true 'believer.'

---

[4] It seems from an article that I read recently that scientists seem to think that it is generally true http://relationshipsinamerica.com/religion/are-religious-people-happier-people, study by the Austin Institute, 2014

The rock musicians whom we admired responded in different ways to this adulation – some seemed to enjoy it and I can see now that others were embarrassed by it and wanted people to like their music instead. I still listen to this music today occasionally[5]. However, I long ago stopped being so star-struck and now think that the idea that someone is worthy of that level of admiration simply because they are good at singing or playing instruments is absurd.

The recollection (not without some embarrassment) of this aspect of my immature, teenage past gave me a sense of what right worship is. It is the natural response of homage which is given freely to one that we admire. God is greater than all creatures and so it is appropriate that the homage given to him is greater than that given to flawed rock stars or even genuinely saintly people. My problem in the morning prayer at Birkenhead School was not my desire to worship, it was the object of my worship. Worship is the highest form of homage – an expression of love which is appropriate only for the highest being. There is nothing wrong with paying homage to others, but it must be to the degree that is appropriate to the person. So, I can send an appreciative letter to a musician if I feel inclined, thanking him for his music; I can venerate saints as great people and ask them to pray to God for me; but worship is due to God alone. Each of the appropriate but lesser acts of admiration are good in that they are analogous to the worship of God and point us to it.

The Sacred Liturgy

What form of worship is appropriate to God? We could not know except that God himself, through his Church, answers this question for us.

Given that we all worship the same God, and given that we are all human, it doesn't seem surprising that we should have common worship. *Sacred liturgy* is the name the Church gives to its public worship, the word 'public' indicating that it is for all people. Certain people might have specialized and differing roles to perform within the sacred liturgy – priests, deacons and lay people all have differing and special roles within the liturgy – but

---

[5] Although not in the liturgy!

they work in harmony as part of something that is directed to the good of all people, including those who are not present and not Catholic. The liturgy is a pattern of prayer which forms us and by which we become able to accept God's love for us and return it in a way that is appropriate to a relationship between God and man. Like all that the Church does, the sacred liturgy is for the glory of God and for our joy. The services we most commonly identify with the term 'sacred liturgy' are the Holy Sacrifice of the Mass and the Liturgy of the Hours (sometimes also called the Divine Office). The Mass is the more essential of these to the spiritual health and vitality of the Body of Christ on Earth, but both are important, and together they represent the most 'powerful and effective' form of prayer there is.[6] Worship of God is what man is made for. To the degree that any prayer or other religious worship is powerful or effective, it is so because it participates in the ideal which is the sacred liturgy of the Church.

Participation in the sacred liturgy of the Church is the optimal means by which we may be transformed supernaturally into the person that God intends us to be and by which we can be happiest. All that the Church teaches and all human activity when properly ordered, is directed to this end. It is the activity by which we accept God's love for us and return it in that *agape-eros* dynamic described earlier.

It is natural for man to communicate through symbols. For example, if we want to communicate our love for someone we could simply say "I love you," but when we give a beautiful bunch of roses or throw a surprise party for the person the message is communicated more strongly. Symbols are not just arbitrary signs that have come into the culture, they speak to us through their connections – offering food and drink is the basic sustenance of life; and flowers, the most beautiful aspect of the plant, are attractive and delicate, each bloom lasting just a few days. This makes them precious and this, plus their beauty, expresses our love of the person to whom we give them.

Furthermore, it is not just what we say, or what we do that communicate the truth powerfully, it is *how* we say and do these things. Gestures and

---

[6] Cf. *Sacrosanctum Concilium*, 7

facial expressions are telling, and we all read them quite naturally when we interact with others. We are hardwired to communicate in this way.

This symbolic interaction with others has primed us for its ultimate expression: the loving interaction, which is the worship of God in the Church's liturgy. Through the mediation of the priest, who acts in the person of Christ himself, God communicates in a symbolic language of action and words that speaks to us naturally of his love. If we allow the Church to guide us in our responses, then our actions and words will speak the language of divine love too. The clothes that each wears, the dignified way in which those that participate hold themselves, even the solemnity of their facial expressions speak symbolically both of the grandeur of the Divine and of the depth of God's love for us, giving us a natural language of response so that we might be transformed into a reflection of that Divine Love.

Ritual is the symbolic part of the way God speaks to us of his love, and the way we speak to God and to those around us of our love for Him. It is formalized because there really is an optimum form for the expression of love. In part cultural, in that ritual emanates from human interactions with each other, it is also in part, and most importantly, emanating from the divine interaction and so comes out of an objective standard that is for all people.

Our greatest joy is made possible by the fullest participation in a loving encounter with God, which is the same as to say that our greatest joy is made possible by active participation in the liturgical life of the Church. All else that the Church teaches and all that we do in our daily lives ought, in the right order of things, to be informed by our love for God as expressed in the liturgy, and so direct others toward it. And in turn, when we do what is right and good in our everyday lives, then that forms us as lovers who can worship God well and so have joy to the fullest. The transformation is not completed in this life, but every participation in the sacred liturgy transforms us by degrees so that when we go out into the world we are better able than before to love our neighbor as ourselves, as Jesus teaches. And to the degree that we do love more perfectly while in the world, we complete the cycle by returning to the sacred liturgy to love God more perfectly as well.

When we participate in the sacred liturgy it enables us to accept the invitation to participate supernaturally in the dynamic of the love between the persons of the Trinity, and thus, to use the phrase of Pope Benedict XVI quoted earlier, "participate in the creative love of God."[7]

There is a cycle of exit and return, by which we encounter God in the liturgy and are transformed supernaturally so that we go out to love our fellows and to love God through love of our fellows. In this way, our work outside the sacred liturgy is directed to the love of God and to the completion of his creative work in us and in the world so that we might draw others into the love of God as he intends. Thus, we are further transformed into better lovers ever more ready to return once again to those acts of worship.

This cycle of exit and return is a positive feedback cycle in which each turn builds on the last and follows a spiral staircase to heaven. When each aspect of this cycle is in perfect harmony all that we do is ordered to its true end, then the distinction between worship and good works becomes blurred, each an extension of and reinforcement of the other.

The Church tells us in the documents of Vatican II that our worship of God is both the end to which all our activity is directed, and also the source of grace and strength by which our love of God and man is possible.

> The liturgy is the summit toward which the activity of the Church is directed; at the same time, it is the font from which all her power flows. For the aim and object of apostolic works is that all who are made sons of God by faith and baptism should come together to praise God in the midst of His Church, to take part in the sacrifice, and eat the Lord's supper.[8]

When I converted to Catholicism I had begun to recognize that sacred liturgy is more than an irrelevant artificial construct, but it was not until

---

[7] Benedict XVI: *What it Means to Be a Christian*, p58 (originally a sermon entitled *God Becomes Man and Man Becomes Christlike*); pub Ignatius Press, 2006

[8] *Sacrosanctum Concilium* 10

quite some time later that I came to perceive it as the highest form of human activity. Indeed, it is the Church's worship that characterizes it more than anything else.

Personal prayer ordered to the pattern of the liturgy

There are four characteristic aspects to the prayer that takes place in the worship of God: *confession*, by which we acknowledge our true place in relation to God and our utter need for him; *supplication* (or intercession) by which we ask for what we need from him so that we might be fit to worship him and able to love our fellow man as ourselves; *thanksgiving*, by which we return gratitude for what he has given us; and *adoration*, which is our expression of love.

When I walked into the Brompton Oratory two things made it possible for me to be so affected by the liturgy: (1) the beauty of the way that liturgy was celebrated, and (2) my readiness to respond. My reading and research had opened my mind intellectually to the idea of worship, and my heart was ready to assent to it because I had been through the process described in this book and had been practicing for some time the daily routine of prayer and meditation David had suggested to me. I can see now that the personal prayers and reflections I had been practicing daily were structured to varying degrees on the four aspects of confession, supplication, thanksgiving, and adoration.[9] I had no idea this is what was going on, but as it turned out, I had been primed to receive God's love and to return it in the liturgical context before I had ever been to Mass.

There is another reason why that Brompton Oratory liturgy spoke to me so powerfully. The actions of the priests, the servers, and the lay people were all symbolic. They communicated through visible means a great invisible truth in a way that was natural for me to understand. I understood at an instinctive level much of what was going on, although I couldn't have articulated in precise detail why people knelt, bowed, stood and sat, or crossed themselves at certain points as the priest held aloft a piece of bread. The incense – which I could smell and see in the shafts of colored sunlight coming through the windows – the architecture,

---

[9] See later chapter, Now for Action for more detail.

the art, and the music were all in harmony with the ritual of worship and amplified the symbolism. All senses were engaged and what was being communicated to me symbolically was the love of God in a way that was natural for me to apprehend. By natural means I perceived the supernatural.

And it wasn't just the prayers of 'the process' that had prepared me for the worship of God. The entire life that the *Vision for You* process had given me was one of greater love and joy and this also was preparation for this moment of liturgical encounter. My new life had been the training, so to speak, that had formed me in love so that I might better be able to accept the love of God and in turn love him and others.

This steadily developing change is one that doesn't stop. The life that is most in harmony with our highest purpose of loving God is that which gives us the greatest joy and it is a life of superabundance. All of this intensifies as we continue on our path. This path is the life we have when we follow the personal vocation God has for us. It is also the life by which we will be most effective as evangelists in drawing others to God.

If we want to be able to respond to God's call and understand it with sufficient clarity, then we must devote ourselves to developing the capability of listening and responding to it. However, we cannot do this without supernatural help. Our very natures must be raised up to something new. That is, we must be transformed and raised up to the state of being capable of relating to God personally. It is the liturgy more than any prayer that enables this to happen. It is the greatest source of grace that opens us up to inspiration, that develops in us the faculty to recognize and cooperate with inspiration when it comes, to follow through and take the path towards our destination. This is the life, described by Pope Benedict and referred to already, in which we participate in the creative love of God himself.

That is why I have described this book, and the *Vision for You* process, as really a companion to the liturgical life. As I have already said, this is not excluding you from great rewards if you do not go to church. I have made it clear that what is presented here will work to a degree even if you are not Catholic and it is still most definitely worth doing (after all, I wasn't Catholic when I went through the process). However, the greatest fruits are available to those whose life is one of liturgically centered piety as part of the Church.

Furthermore, this is not excluding anyone who wants it – this life *is* available to all, because the Church is open to all.[10]

Now pray:

Bend my heart to your will, Oh God.
I ask this in the name of my Lord Jesus Christ.

---

[10] To lead this life, those who are not Catholic would first have to become Catholic. For those Catholics who feel that liturgical piety is something that they could develop further, I would again recommend purchasing *The Little Oratory* (Sophia Press, 2014), a book written with precisely that goal in mind.

4 The New Evangelization

How a life centered on the worship of God transforms us supernaturally so that we lead a joyful life of love that draws others to the faith.

My brothers, I implore you by God's mercy to offer your very selves to him: a living sacrifice, dedicated and fit for his acceptance, the worship offered by mind and heart. Adapt yourselves no longer to the pattern of this present world, but let your minds be remade and your whole nature thus transformed. Then you will be able to discern the will of God, and to know what is good, acceptable, and perfect.

Rom. 12: 1-2

One becomes all that God is, except for an identity in being, when one is deified by grace.

St. Maximus the Confessor, 7th century AD

Evangelization, old and new

The priest in Florence, whom I described earlier in this book, was the first to make the connection for me between living out our personal vocation and being an effective evangelist. What he was describing to me was a mechanism of what many today would call the 'new evangelization.' The phrase was first used, I am told, by St. Pope John Paul II and he was encapsulating themes that had been discussed since the Second Vatican Council. The idea resonates, I think, because many in the Church have a strong sense that we need a new form of mission. If we consider the traditional mission as one in which we bring the gospel to those who haven't heard the Word before, then we need a new evangelization by which we can reach people of a Western, post-Christian culture – people who have no faith, but think they already know enough about Christianity to be hostile to it. As John Paul II put it in *Redemptoris Missio*, 30: "Today the Church must face other challenges and push forward to new frontiers, both in the initial mission *ad gentes* and in the new evangelization of those peoples who have already heard Christ proclaimed."

Although many Catholics have heard the phrase, I suspect that most are unsure as to how to go about it. When I asked my students once, some years ago, what they thought the *New Evangelization* might be, they suggested that perhaps it meant trying to convert people using new technology such as Twitter, Facebook and so on. After all, they told me, even Pope Ben himself tweets regularly! In fact, the clearest articulation of the New Evangelization that I have found was written by Pope Benedict. He did not tweet, post or blog it, but rather published it as an essay.

Benedict XVI on the *New Evangelization*

In this paper, written in 2000[1], Benedict doesn't rule out making use of new methods of communication, but his discussion focuses instead upon recovery of the original means of demonstrating the Faith which were so successful in the early days of the Church. In other words, there are traditional principles for evangelization which are unchanging but which, if necessary, modern means of communication can serve.

If people are to convert, Benedict says, we have to aim to answer the fundamental question of life: "How can I be happy?" This is the question that drives all that we do – and the one that had driven me to my conversion.

---

[1] Joseph Cardinal Ratzinger: *Address to Catechists and Religion Teachers: the New Evangelization, Building the Civilization of Love*; 2000

If people believe we have a better answer to that question than anyone else, then they will want to acquire that knowledge from us. And they will think we have the answer to this question if they see joy in our lives! So we answer their question not so much with our words but with the Word: Christ. We aim to show people Christ. We want people to see Him in our way of life. As Benedict puts it in his paper:

> Human life cannot be realized by itself. Our life is an open question, an incomplete project, still to be brought to fruition and realized. Each man's fundamental question is: How will this be realized – becoming man? How does one learn the art of living? Which is the path toward happiness?
>
> To evangelize means: to show this path – to teach the art of living. At the beginning of his public life Jesus says: I have come to evangelize the poor (Luke 4:18); this means: I have the response to your fundamental question; I will show you the path of life, the path toward happiness – rather: I am that path.[2]

There is an important distinction being made here. Evangelization is not so much telling people about Christ or the Faith, as it is *showing* them Christ, a person. Christ is both the person to whom the path of happiness leads, and the path itself.

Showing people Christ *in us*

This is a little puzzling, for how we can show non-believers a person who ascended into heaven long ago?

Fortunately, Benedict goes on to describe how we do this.

We present Christ by showing him alive *within us*. By dedication to fulfilling the will of God our Father moment by moment we tread Christ's path ourselves, and are transformed supernaturally by grace as we do so. We tread the path that both leads to Christ and is Christ. Through a personal

---

[2]Joseph Cardinal Ratzinger: *The New Evangelization*, 2001, available here: http://www.ewtn.com/new_evangelization/Ratzinger.htm

encounter with Christ we become, by degrees and by God's grace, the person that he intended us to be. We present Christ to others by our conduct, our joy, our way of life. People see him through us for we become sons of God too, partaking of the divine nature.

This is consistent with the words of the Catechism of the Catholic Church:

> For this is why the Word became man, and the Son of God became the Son of man: so that man, by entering into communion with the Word and thus receiving divine sonship, might become a son of God.[3]

We become walking icons of Christ

By means of our personal relationship with the divine person Christ, as man, we partake of his divinity because Christ is both God and man. Then we too shine with the Light of Christ as seen by the apostles at the Transfiguration. We become walking icons of Christ, and the "light" that others see in us is the love of Christ as manifested in our own personal relationships. What attracts people is the joy we possess, and we transmit this joy to others through our personal interactions. This is how the Light of Love is manifested in our as yet imperfect, but nevertheless significant and real, participation in the humanity and divinity of the transfigured Christ.

Hope overcoming suffering

There are two aspects of the Christian message that resonate today (as indeed, they resonated when presented to pagans two thousand years ago) and Benedict advised us to focus particularly on showing these to people.

The first is that we can overcome suffering by uniting our sufferings with the suffering of Christ. To overcome suffering does not mean that as Christians we will have lives in which there is no physical pain, hardship,

---

[3]Catechism of the Catholic Church, 460, quoting St. Irenaeus

disappointment, or anguish. These are inevitable consequences of living life to the fullest. Perhaps we could escape them somewhat by disengaging from full interaction with others and leading a life of less love, but this would be also a life of less joy. The Christian answer is not escapism.[4] Rather, our response when we face adversity is to cheerfully make use of it in order to demonstrate how being united with Christ allows us to rise above it and meet it with dignity. Again, this is only possible through cooperation with that grace by which we are receiving "divine sonship," to use the phrase quoted above from the Catechism.

Typically, when trouble occurs, there are two things I can do. One is to work hard to remove the trouble myself as best as I can, and the other is to pray that God help me by removing the trouble Himself. Sometimes my efforts get results, sometimes the prayer is answered, sometimes both and the job offer arrives or the illness is cured.

Sometimes, however, I cannot get rid of the problem by my efforts and it appears that my prayers are not being answered either, because the difficulty remains. The Christian life is one in which the consolation of grace *transcends* – takes us beyond – the suffering that we experience. This demonstration of the cheerful acceptance of suffering which results is a powerful force in drawing people to the source of our strength: The Church. It counters the hopelessness felt by many people today who have made the mistake of relying on modern science and modern institutions to deliver to them a utopian life free of suffering. It may be perfectly reasonable to look to these things to alleviate human suffering, but there will always be a limit to what they can do. They cannot touch us spiritually and only a spiritual solution can really allow us to overcome suffering. In other words, we will always need God as well.

If we are overly reliant on things that cannot help us completely, then in times of severe difficulty the result will be despair. And at the point of despair one might react in a number of different ways. One might

---

[4] Even the most cloistered monk does not disengage from the ups and downs of ordinary living.

be to reach for the only true solution, God. Another might be to seek escape through false religion and superstition. A third might be to seek forgetfulness of the problems with powerful distractions and superficial pleasures such as are offered by alcohol or drugs.

Benedict expresses the importance of uniting ourselves to the person of Christ so that we can overcome our own sufferings in the following way:

> The cross belongs to the divine mystery – it is the expression of his love to the end (John 13:1). The Sequela [chain of events that always results] of Christ is participation in the cross, uniting oneself to his love, to the transformation of our life, which becomes the birth of the new man, created according to God (see Ephesians 4:24). Whoever omits the cross, omits the essence of Christianity (see 1 Corinthians 2:2).[5]

Life after death

The second aspect of Christian life that we should hope to communicate to others, Benedict says, is the fact of life after death and a just and merciful judgment by the Christ.

When we hope for a future that reaches beyond death we are given purpose in this life. We have a sense of something good that follows this life and toward which this life is directed. This hope in salvation is something that secular materialism cannot offer; nevertheless, it is something that all men yearn for. When we joyously await final judgment from a loving and merciful judge, then that fear for the future, which so many today experience, is removed more powerfully than it could be by even the most generous pension scheme. Hope for the future gives this present life real meaning:

> This can be seen: It isn't true that faith in eternal life makes earthly life insignificant. To the contrary: only if the measure of our life is eternity, then also this life of ours on earth is great and its value

---

[5] Joseph Cardinal Ratzinger: *Address to Catechists and Religion Teachers: The New Evangelization, Building the Civilization of Love*; 2000

immense. God is not the competitor in our life, but the guarantor of our greatness. This way we return to the starting point: God.[6]

It is so very often assumed by non-Christians that the Faith *creates* a fear of death and judgment. Many who hold this view, I have found, are amongst those who have fallen away from the Church because in part they were instilled with a fear of final judgment as a tool for getting them to behave when they were very young. Many of these people are still haunted by a fear of future judgment. Leaving the Faith does not remove the fear, but it does at least liberate them, as they would see it, from the shackles of morality so that they can indulge in an excess of superficial pleasure as a way of distracting their attention, if only temporarily, from the fear that is still with them.

Christ is a judge who always judges justly and does not condemn because he is always merciful to the contrite. A fear of facing Christ is misplaced. On the contrary, divine mercy is something to be embraced, provided we can acknowledge truly before him our faults. Condemnation, on the other hand, *is* something to be feared, but condemnation does not come from God, it comes from ourselves when we reject God and, through pride, refuse to face Christ – acknowledging his just judgment with confidence in his infinite mercy.

Many people are aware of this self-condemnation and talk of "forgiving themselves" and "not being so hard on themselves" because of the need they feel to escape it. However, escaping condemnation is something that we cannot do by ourselves. When examining our pasts and our sins we do not have the authority to forgive ourselves, and no matter how hard we try to "give ourselves a break," the refusal to face God is itself a continual act of self-condemnation. This is real. It is something we instinctively feel in this life. Only when we place our sins before God, acknowledge our faults, humbly ask for forgiveness and accept it, can we be freed from the weight of condemnation in our consciences.[7]

---

[6] Ibid

[7] I was told that to refuse to accept God's forgiveness is arrogance, for we are placing ourselves above God who does have the authority to forgive.

If we wish to communicate the mercy of Christ to others we must show them that Christ is a merciful judge and we do this first by showing this aspect of Christ in us and demonstrating justice and mercy in our everyday dealings with others. What others see in us as a result will be attributed to the one we pay homage to, its ultimate source: Christ.

In both of these instances, along with so much else of the Christian message, these are truths better humbly demonstrated than spoken of. If we tell others, for example, how well we are dealing with adversity, it is difficult not to sound self-satisfied as though we are giving ourselves the credit. It can also be interpreted as a lack of sympathy for others who are suffering and are struggling with their difficulties, even if we offer our experience in order to try and help them.

I recognize aspects of what Benedict is describing in my own conversion story. Many things contributed to my conversion, of course, but an important part of it was meeting those few key people along the way who impressed me simply by the way they were. They had something in their lives worth having. I would have had difficulty saying what it was that they had, precisely, but whatever it was, I knew it was good. They treated others well, they had dignity and humility and I respected them. I felt that being with them and interacting with them somehow led me to want to be a better person. Usually, they did not talk much of their faith, but somehow let me know just enough so that I knew that they were Catholic. What was so powerful was precisely this fact: for the most part they *showed* me their faith in their conduct more than they talked of it. If they had spoken of it any more than they did, I would almost certainly have been put off, so hostile was I to the idea of Christianity.

Apart from David, who ended up taking me through the process that this book contains, they were all people who did not play a large part in my life; and by the time I converted I was not in regular contact with any of them. I had never raised the issue of the Faith with them or even asked any questions about their personal philosophy of life. But the impression they made stayed with me. Later, when I had become desperate enough to begin searching for new answers to that question "How can I be happy?" I remembered the example of these people whom I had come across earlier on.

What Benedict seemed to be saying is that if I wanted now to participate in the conversion of others, I should aim to become like these people who had influenced me.

We draw people to the Faith by demonstrating happiness in our lives

It was a tall order! This was much more than just accepting the tenets of the Faith and then telling others about them, however eloquently. I had to become a different person. Benedict XVI commented on this too in 2007:

> Generally, the term *conversion* is used in reference to bringing pagans into the Church. However, conversion (*metanoia*), in its precisely Christian meaning, signifies a change in thinking and in acting, as the expression of the new life *in Christ* proclaimed by faith: a continuous reform of thought and deeds directed at an ever more intense identification with Christ (cf. *Gal* 2:20), to which the baptized are called before all else.[8]

Here is the simple fact: if I wish to lead others to the Faith, I must have a happy life that is rooted in Christ so that I am continuously being transformed supernaturally. Such a person is not shaken by adversity because he possesses a clear purpose in life and a lack of fear of death which contribute to the peace of the moment. To the degree that I have this, my life speaks to the many who lack these things. The deepest poverty is the inability of joy, the tediousness of a life considered absurd and contradictory. This poverty is widespread today, in very different forms in the materially rich as well as the poor countries. The inability of joy presupposes and produces the inability to love, produces jealousy, avarice – all defects that devastate the life of individuals and of the world. This is why we are in need of a new evangelization – if the art of living remains an unknown, nothing else works.

But this art is not the object of a science – this art can only be

---

[8] Pope Benedict XVI, *Doctrinal Note on Some Aspects of Evangelization*, 2006, para 9.

communicated by [one] who has life – he who is the Gospel personified.[9]

This almost seems to be telling us that it is our duty to be happy for the good of others. Is happiness really something I can control like that, I wondered? If I feel obliged to be happy, isn't the worry about knowing I have to be happy going to destroy my happiness?

The only way I can get out of this self-defeating way of thinking is to resolve to do my best, regardless, to follow the directions for prayer and living. Through the process, David showed me how to cultivate joy, regardless of my present mood or situation and this book is written in order to show you all the things that I was shown.

The good news is that, in my experience, if I give it my best shot then my life improves and while it is never perfect I would say that, generally, I am happy and each year life gets steadily better. One hopes that this is because the desired transformation is happening and so in some way, my life is having an impact on others.

It is very likely that I will be unaware of how I am affecting others, so I shouldn't depend on seeing conversions as a sign that I am evangelizing others. This point was made to me by the priest in Florence and is made also by Benedict in his paper. To evangelize means to show someone Christ. Once we have done this, then we have done all we can do. Whether or not people respond is something we cannot control. All we can do is sow seeds. These will quite possibly bear fruit in the end, but we do not know when or how, and it is likely that we will never see those particular seeds bear fruit.

Benedict describes this delayed effect as follows:

> Yet another temptation lies hidden beneath this – the temptation of impatience, the temptation of immediately finding the great

---

[9]Joseph Cardinal Ratzinger: *Address to Catechists and Religion Teachers: The New Evangelization, Building the Civilization of Love*, 2000

success, in finding large numbers. But this is not God's way. For the Kingdom of God as well as for evangelization, the instrument and vehicle of the Kingdom of God, the parable of the grain of mustard seed is always valid (see Mark 4:31-32).

The Kingdom of God always starts anew under this sign. New evangelization cannot mean: immediately attracting the large masses that have distanced themselves from the Church by using new and more refined methods. No – this is not what new evangelization promises.

New evangelization means: never being satisfied with the fact that from the grain of mustard seed, the great tree of the Universal Church grew; never thinking that the fact that different birds may find place among its branches can suffice – rather, it means to dare, once again and with the humility of the small grain, to leave up to God the when and how it will grow (Mark 4:26-29).

The Church always evangelizes and has never interrupted the path of evangelization. She celebrates the Eucharistic mystery every day, administers the sacraments, proclaims the word of life – the Word of God, and commits herself to the causes of justice and charity. And this evangelization bears fruit: it gives light and joy, it gives the path of life to many people; many others live, often unknowingly, in the light and the warmth that radiate from this permanent evangelization.[10]

The foundation of such a transformation, says Benedict, is *prayer*. We cannot transform ourselves, but through an encounter with Christ each of us can be dramatically transformed despite ourselves. This encounter with Christ begins and ends with prayer. It is through prayer that we can go beyond simply knowing about God, or knowing that He exists, to actually knowing him, as one person knows another. Through prayer we develop a personal relationship.

---

[10] Joseph Cardinal Ratzinger: *Address to Catechists and Religion Teachers: The New Evangelization, Building the Civilization of Love*; 2000

The route to happiness – Liturgical prayer, para-liturgical prayer, personal prayer... and love

The prayer life that provides such an encounter, says Benedict, is centered on the liturgy. He says that there are three aspects to this. The first and most essential is *liturgical* prayer – participation in the sacred liturgy itself with the Eucharist at its heart. Then there are what he calls *para-liturgical* prayers, prayers which people say in common, very often structured by repetitions (for example, the Stations of the Cross, the Divine Mercy chaplet and the rosary) that in some ways resemble the pattern of the sacred liturgy. Finally, there is *personal* prayer which is said in private as a uniquely personal response to God. This may be structured on a liturgical pattern, but it will also include conversational prayer.

A well-balanced prayer life contains all three of these aspects with each ordered in such a way that, taking into account our situation in life, they optimize our participation in the sacred liturgy. Seen in this way, personal prayer and para-liturgical prayer will focus on preparing us for that essential encounter with God in the Eucharist. Similarly, sacraments other than the Eucharist itself are also directed to this primary purpose in human life of worshipping God fully through the sacred liturgy and being united with him through a worthy reception of the Eucharist. In the same paper on the New Evangelization quoted before, Benedict explains this as follows:

> There is a complementarity between personal prayer ('in one's room,' alone in front of God's eyes), 'para-liturgical' prayer in common ('popular religiosity') and liturgical prayer. Yes, the liturgy is first of all prayer; its specificity consists in the fact that its primary project is not ourselves (as in private prayer and in popular religiosity), but God himself – the liturgy is *actio divina*, God acts and we respond to this divine action. Speaking about God and speaking with God must always go together. The proclamation of God is the guide to communion with God in fraternal communion, founded and vivified by Christ. This is why the liturgy (the sacraments) are not a secondary theme next to the preaching of the living God, but the realization of our relationship with God.[11]

---

[11] Joseph Cardinal Ratzinger: *The New Evangelization*, 2001, available here: www.ewtn.

All prayer done well is powerful and is transformative of the person who prays, whether liturgical, para-liturgical or personal. Miracles can happen as a result of any of these different types of prayer. But each derives its power from the encounter with God in the Eucharist, and in turn is effective because it reinforces the power of that encounter. So, the non-liturgical forms of prayer derive power from the Sacred Liturgy and the sacramental life; in turn, our participation in the sacramental life is enhanced by the power of non-liturgical prayer. God is not limited by his sacraments, so the prayers of those who do not participate in the Sacred Liturgy might still have power (for example someone who is not a Catholic); but for anyone the greatest transformative power is when all forms of prayer are present. It all begins and ends with God. It is part of a cycle of love enacted and love returned.

Most of us do not know without instruction how to pray well. Even the apostles who had Christ himself before them as an example to follow asked him to teach them how to pray. Benedict tells us that it is important that instruction on prayer is made available to all:

> God cannot be made known with words alone. One does not really know a person if one knows about this person second-handedly. To proclaim God is to introduce to the relation with God: to teach how to pray. Prayer is faith in action. And only by experiencing life with God does the evidence of his existence appear. This is why schools of prayer, communities of prayer are so important.[12]

I was lucky enough to have some instruction on prayer. After my reception into the Church and for many years while I was still living in London, I used to go and see one of the Fathers of the London Oratory for spiritual guidance. The first thing that he asked me to do was to describe my spiritual life. I told him of everything that David had passed on to me. This was a program of personal prayer and good works. He encouraged me very strongly to keep that going because it had brought me to the Church.

---

com/new_evangelization/Ratzinger.htm

[12] Joseph Cardinal Ratzinger: *Address to Catechists and Religion Teachers: The New Evangelization, Building the Civilization of Love*; 2000

Then, once he was satisfied that I was going to Mass appropriately, he introduced me to the Divine Office. He also encouraged me to go and spend a few days at a monastery so that I could experience the regular chant of the office done well.

In the balanced prayer life of liturgical and personal prayer that Benedict describes in his essay (and which is contained with the *Vision for You* process), there is one aspect of liturgical prayer which is often ignored by Catholics, although it is very important: The Divine Office (also called the Liturgy of the Hours), is a form of structured prayer based upon marking times of the day with the psalms. It, in its effect, is an overflowing of the Mass into the entire day in such a way that it acts as a bridge between the Mass and other forms of prayer, and between the sacred liturgy and our ordinary daily activities.

Beyond certain essential elements that all Catholics are obliged to do, the ideal pattern of prayer is different for different people. It has to take into account each person's situation in life. The aim is to have a prayer life that makes the ordinary activities of the day easier, rather than one that adds to the burden by creating a huge workload of prayer that makes us feel guilty when we fail to do it all. When prayer and daily living are in harmony, then each works together so that we are of greater service to our fellow man. In the end this dynamic of prayer and work is all directed to a deeper conformity with my ultimate purpose, the worship of God in the sacred liturgy.

The closer we get to a harmony of living in which each aspect holds its right relation with every other and with the whole, and has God as its object, then despite ourselves we will become the person God intends us to be. We will discern our personal vocation, we will evangelize and we will have joy. When all that we do is ordered to the sacred liturgy, we flourish optimally, for it is the primary source of grace by which we can do so.

Opening a conference on the Sacred Liturgy in Rome in 2013, Bishop Dominique Rey of Fréjus-Toulon put it this way:

The Sacred liturgy is not a hobby for specialists. It is central to all our endeavors as disciples of Jesus Christ. This profound reality cannot be over-emphasized. We must recognize the primacy of grace in our Christian life and work, and we must respect the reality that in this life *the* optimal encounter with Christ is the sacred liturgy.

Domestic Church – the first 'school of prayer' and vital to the New Evangelization

The ideal place to learn to pray is in the home. This is the place where the example of the parents shows the children how to pray so that it seeps into the fabric of their souls. Ideally this will be in such a way that there is a focus for prayer in the home, an image or icon corner, and a practice of properly balanced prayer that supports and is in harmony with family life, transforming the house into home.

A home which is prayed in and which has a visual focus of prayer is a concrete example of the "domestic church". If the family prays at least some part of the Liturgy of the Hours, the dynamic exchange of love that takes place in the Eucharist will by that means be brought directly into the home, so that its grace may permeate the day. Indeed, the *General Instruction* of the Divine Office tells us that its purpose is to "sanctify the day."

This is the first school both of prayer and of love. If the prayer is authentic, you cannot separate love from it, and if the love is full it must be expressed in prayer also. When this happens, God is seen through that home in the family and in the community. Benedict XVI has referred to this directly, telling us that not only is the domestic church helpful to the new evangelization, the new evangelization actually *depends* on it:

> The new evangelization depends largely on the Domestic Church. The Christian Family to the extent it succeeds in living love as communion and service as a reciprocal gift open to all, as a journey of permanent conversion supported by the grace of God, reflects the splendor of Christ in the world and the beauty of the divine Trinity. St. Augustine has a famous phrase: *"immo vero vides Trinitatem,*

si caritatem vides" — "Well, if you see charity, yes indeed you see the Trinity" (*De Trinitate*, VIII, 8).[13]

The Little Oratory, previously mentioned, was written with this fact in mind. Leila's and my hope as co-authors was that the book might inspire the reestablishment of many "domestic churches" and result in an invigoration of the home life for families and singles alike that would in turn further invigorate parish and community life. While the instruction I am giving you now through this book will have a profound effect even if practiced by a few individuals in isolation, the greatest, most glorious – and most joyful – effect possible will happen if it is integrated with a sacramental life centered on the Church and the Eucharist as described in *The Little Oratory*. We cannot separate any of our more immediate hopes in life – the desire for a spouse, for a family, the hopes for the family we have, for a fulfilling job – from the overall purpose in our lives, which is to do God's will. *The Little Oratory* will facilitate that integration by its description of how to harmonize prayer life and daily living in the context of the domestic church.

You don't need a family to create the domestic church

It is important when thinking of the domestic church not to get into the frame of mind that the idea of the domestic church is only for those who are part of the perfect Catholic family. I know many people who are in difficult family situations beyond their control, perhaps who are married, but whose spouses are not Catholic or are even hostile to the faith, or in other cases for one reason or another are single parents. Also, there are many single people who do not feel called to either a consecrated lay life or to religious life but haven't met the right person yet. For all of these people, a residence can become a home if it is a domestic church; and through this prayer each becomes connected to the community of the Church in such a way that they need never feel lonely or isolated.

It is important not to fall into the trap of thinking that people haven't sorted out God's plan for them until the family situations right themselves

---

[13]Benedict XVI: *Address to Plenary Assembly of the Pontifical Council for the Family*; Rome, 1 December 2011

or they commit permanently to marriage or to some sort of religiously defined life. I know for myself that when I think in this way I start to feel as if I am stuck permanently in the waiting room at the train station, waiting for an announcement about a long-delayed departure. It doesn't help, incidentally, to inform single people that the single life engenders selfishness – a remark that always seems to imply that anyone can easily meet someone and get married if they want to. Most people who are single are not in positions to choose to "fall in love" nor do they have the power to induce someone else to "fall in love" with them through an act of will.

Be reassured. Single or not, regardless of our current situation, we can begin walking the path that God intends for us right now and have the same joy. In regard to the domestic church: everyone who has a place to sleep can create the domestic church around them. If you live alone, then you can set up the icon corner and pray. If you share an apartment or house, then you can set up a discrete icon corner, in your room if not in common areas, and pray there quietly. If your situation is such that you cannot even put up images to make an icon corner, then you can have your personal pocket oratory. This is like a small wallet that is opened out to show the three essential core images contained within it. If you do this the benefits are not limited to your home. Prayer will have a profound effect on any communities or networks that you belong to, simply by virtue of your improved interaction with all people.

Why the traditional images in an icon corner are particularly relevant for evangelization today

In *The Little Oratory*, there is guidance on how to arrange images for an icon corner in the home. For those who can't afford to buy expensive pictures (or can't paint their own!) it provides a number of high quality reproductions that can be detached and framed. They are standard sizes so they can be framed easily and cheaply and so you can create your own icon corner as a focal point for prayer.

As the book explains the traditional layout for the icon corner has three essential images at its core. In the center should be the suffering Christ, that is Christ on the cross. To the left should be an image of Our Lady.

To the right should be an image of the glorified Christ. This is most commonly a Christ in Majesty or one of the versions of the face of Christ – a Veronica cloth or similar Eastern image called the Mandylion.

As already mentioned, Benedict XVI spoke of two important messages that people today need to be aware of. First is that we can transcend suffering by being united to the suffering of Christ. Christ on the cross, he tells us, is the most poignant symbol of this. By praying with this image we become a walking icon of Christ who shows others, through the way we deal with our own suffering, how Christ can help them to deal with theirs. We remember this aspect of Christ in sacred time particularly during the penitential seasons of Advent and Lent as an anticipation of the glory of Christmas and Easter.

The second message Benedict emphasized is that we should communicate the sure and certain hope of life after death – and that God is a good and merciful judge through whose judgment we can be released from the earthly suffering caused by sin. All images of Christ glorified, shining with the uncreated light of heaven, communicate to us the glory of heaven and what is in store for us through deification. Furthermore, iconographic images of the face of Christ, and the Mandylion particularly, are painted so as to give us a sense of a good judge. Many who look at traditional icons are struck by the enigmatic expression on the faces. The expression is sometimes referred to as 'bright sadness.' This is the contentment of perfect heavenly peace tinged with melancholy because all saints are aware of our suffering and want more than anything that we should be free from it with them in heaven. This is why we ask them to pray for us, and why they want to do so. Images of the face of Christ have an additional aspect to them – a certain sternness of expression. I was told in my icon painting class that this sternness is deliberate for it is meant to communicate the fact the Christ is a judge and we will face him at the end. It does not, or rather should not, dominate, but it should be noticeable along with these other aspects of peace and compassion, for together all these tell us that Christ is a just and merciful judge.

The special role of Mary in the new evangelization

The third core image in the traditional icon corner is of Mary, the Mother of God. The role of Mary is crucial in the new evangelization, I believe. First, she is the new evangelist par excellence. To evangelize, Benedict tells us, is to *show* people Christ. All that the Mother of God does is show us her son. By fixing our sights on "heavenly things," as St. Paul tells us, we move towards the model we contemplate in prayer. Therefore, we want to have the highest model to move towards, and that is Our Lady. Many images of Our Lady are painted so that her eyes engage us and then in her gesture she is showing us her son.

Mary describes herself in the Magnificat as one whose "soul glorifies the Lord" – that is, increases our perception of his glory. And when we praise God in the words of her canticle at Vespers, contemplating the image of her showing us the Lord, her song of praise becomes our song of praise and we share in her mission. Our souls glorify the Lord along with her, and our spirits rejoice.

The images that we pray with have a profound effect on us. The Catechism tells us that the beauty of visual art can communicate aspects of the truth that words alone cannot. The beauty of music can do the same, incidentally, and this is one reason why singing our prayers while using visual images ought to be the norm as far as possible, and why it is always suggested especially for the liturgy.

The core imagery of the icon corner communicates so many aspects of the Faith all at once, that I cannot possibly relate them all here. However, in regard to the new evangelization, each one has something important to say to us, that makes our daily prayers with them so powerful.

The methods of the new evangelization are timeless

When thought of in this way, the new evangelization is not just new in that it belongs to the present day, but it is also new in a greater sense in that it belongs to the new covenant, ushered in by Christ.

The very first Christian martyr historically, and the first saint celebrated in sacred time after the birth of Christ (on December 26th), is St. Stephen. In the biblical account of his death he is described as shining with that Light of Christ and having the face of an angel that even his oppressors could see. Those onlookers included Saul – the man to become St. Paul,

THE VISION FOR YOU

one of the greatest evangelists himself. In the Liturgy of the Hours for St. Stephen's feast day there is a commentary written by St. Fulgentius of Ruspe, who lived in the 5th and 6th centuries AD. In this he says:

> Our king…brought his soldiers a great gift that not only enriched them but also made them unconquerable in battle for it was the gift of love, which was to bring men to share in his divinity. … Shown first in the king, it later shone forth in his soldier. Love was Stephen's weapon by which he gained every battle, and so won the crown signified by his name. His love of God kept him from yielding to the ferocious mob; his love for his neighbor made him pray for those who were stoning him. Love inspired him to reprove those who erred, to make them amend; love led him to pray for those who stoned him, to save them from punishment. Strengthened by the power of his love he overcame the raging cruelty of Saul and won his persecutor on earth as his companion in heaven.

This passage is a reminder that to be an example of the gospel does not always endear us to those around us. We need God's grace to have the virtue and courage needed to bear the sword of love.

As we pray the liturgy with the Church, using images such as these as focal points, we hope to move interiorly towards embracing the ideas that they portray. We are all aware that we do not match up to the standards these saints embody. Parents are likely to find the fact that they serve as the primary model for virtue for their children a daunting responsibility. Our hope in praying visibly, in the icon corner, and, for example, bowing when invoking the Trinity and looking towards the image of Christ, is that our children will understand that there is a standard higher even than their mother and father, and that is what they should look to as they grow up.

Now pray:

Bend my heart to your will, Oh God.
I ask this in the name of my Lord Jesus Christ.

5 Our Personal Vocation

Each of us has a unique calling – when we follow it we are given our heart's desires and we become the most effective evangelists we can be.

'It was not you that chose me, I chose you. The task I have appointed you is to go out and bear fruit, fruit which will endure; so that every request you make of the Father in my name may be granted you. These are the directions that I give that you should go out and love one another.'

John 15:16-19 *(Knox translation)*

The second time I met David, in his apartment in Chelsea in West London, he asked me about my job and if I enjoyed it. I had joined a company that recruited staff for charities, thinking that working with charities was a good thing to do and thus the job would be fulfilling. In fact, the thrill of getting this job wore off quickly and I was not enjoying it. This is not surprising since I was unhappy with just about everything in my life, and given this state of mind would likely have been frustrated with even a perfect job.

David let me complain a bit about my job without making much comment, and then asked me what I really wanted to do. This was several months before we had the long conversation about the discernment of my personal vocation (more about this in later chapters). However, even at this point I replied that I wanted to paint.

"What do you want to paint?" he asked me.

"Something like these," I said, pointing to some oil paintings on the wall of his apartment – brightly colored idealized cloudscapes and landscapes.

"If you go through this process, you will very likely become a painter, if you want to be," he responded. And then we moved on to a new subject.

What David didn't tell me then was that he had painted all those paintings on his walls! He loved William Turner – and once I knew this I could see the influence particularly of late Turner paintings in which water and sky each blend into the other. David's work sold regularly and at good prices. He told me about it months later, in order to encourage me to follow my own dream to be an artist, explaining how he had even landed an exhibition in Cork Street, where all the top commercial art galleries in London are situated, simply because when he showed his paintings to a friend who was a collector, the friend's immediate response was to ask where he exhibited. Up until this point David hadn't even imagined that his work was good enough to exhibit. But buoyed by the friend's comment he just walked into the Cork Street gallery with a couple of paintings under his arm, and they offered him an exhibition. He wanted me to believe that this could happen for me too, if it was what God wanted for me.

David also told me, as an aside, that when he read the reviews of his work he realized what charlatans most art critics are. He had had generally positive reviews of his show, he said, and he wasn't complaining about that. But what made him so disdainful of them was the way they claimed to understand what he had been trying to do even though none of them had bothered to ask him.

"I'll tell you why I paint, lad," he said. "For the same reason that Bach said he composed music. To bring glory to God and joy to mankind. That's the standard I want to be measured by."

Years later when he died I asked his family if I could have one of his paintings, and they found an abstracted Turneresque oil seascape in which a peaceful sea merges on the horizon into low clouds that touched the water in the distance and then balloons upwards in blended blues, silver grays, turquoises and greens. It was one of the few paintings that I brought with me to the U.S. when I moved here. As a measure of how good it was: burglars once broke into my house in New Hampshire. When surprised, they ran off and left pretty much everything intact – but they did find time to remove David's painting from the wall and run off with that. He wasn't famous enough that his painting could be converted into cash, so I assume the burglars just loved the painting. I hope that eventually it drew them to God.

When I started to pursue a painting career myself, I always remembered David's description of why he painted: to bring glory to God and joy to mankind.

What is 'vocation'?

Depending on who you talk to, you will hear the word 'vocation' used in a variety of associated but different meanings. It means literally *call* or *calling* and so in its broadest sense refers to what God calls us to be. Each of us, therefore has a common vocation of union with God in heaven. The only way to this goal is *the* Way, Christ. It is only by Christ and his mystical body the Church that we can approach Him. Because God loves each of us he always gives us enough information and insight that we are fully free to choose to follow that path. He does not compel us to follow him – each of us is free to reject or ignore the call he makes.

If we are truly free, then a number of conditions must be present. First, we must have the capacity to choose what is best, which means we must possess both the knowledge of what is good and the power to choose it. Second, the choices we make must be made by an act of will, so that we are neither compelled to choose what is good, nor restrained from choosing what is bad. Therefore, if we really are free to choose what God wants for us, he must make available all the knowledge that is necessary to make the right choices, and also give us the power to choose, whether well or badly.

Although each of us has a common vocation, this does not mean each of us imitates Christ in an identical way. The particulars of how we follow the call are different. For example, each of us has a calling to a particular state in life: priest, religious (such as a monk or nun), or as a layperson, the single or married life. This is perhaps the most common use of the word vocation in the Church. When there are prayers for vocations, what they are usually thinking about is the need for more priests for the Church and so they are requesting that men respond to the priestly vocation.

Beyond these broad classifications there are the considerations of the exact details of our path. In this respect every vocation is unique. Every person is unique and each one has a unique path set out for them by God. To distinguish it from the other broader classifications of vocation, this unique individual path is sometimes referred to as a *personal* vocation.

This final use of the word vocation is the one we are discussing in this book: personal vocation.

To consider what our personal vocation is we can consider, potentially, every aspect of our lives: where are we to live, what will we do for a living, what do we want to do for fun, whom are we called to serve in the community? This does include the big decisions about our lives already mentioned, but it is not limited to them. When we are transformed in Christ and are doing what God wants for us, then we will be happiest, and we will be fulfilled. Then we will flourish as people. As part of the Church, each of us has a unique role to play in society so that the Church as a whole fulfills the function that is intended for it. Furthermore, God gives us a unique set of gifts and abilities that are perfectly suited to enable us to fulfill our personal vocation. No one can lead my life better than me just as I can't lead anybody else's better than they can. Each of us is the unique and perfectly crafted peg made for its uniquely shaped hole. When we use the gifts that God has given us to follow the path he intends for us, miracles can happen. We participate in the creative love of God, and all that God can do can happen through us and for us all.

How do we discern our personal vocation and live it?

In order for this to happen we need three things:

- First, we must be transformed in Christ. The prayers and spiritual exercises detailed in this book are designed to help with this and the effect will be most profound when they are seen as supporting the sacramental life of the Church, with the Eucharist at its heart.

Second, we must know what our personal vocation is. In some ways that is very easy. We know that the ultimate goal in life is union with God in heaven. But what are the goals I should be aiming for now, in this life? What constitutes the path that is going to lead me to heaven? To answer this question, we each need a sense of what our perfect life is. This is the one by which we will be close to perfectly happy and which is, at the same time, consistent with the ultimate goal of full union with God in heaven. After detailing prayers and spiritual exercises that open the way to personal transformation, this book then takes us through a process of discernment so that we can know what those lifetime goals should be.

Third, we need to know how to get there. In this view of personal vocation, we live it out starting right here, right now. The path itself – by which we reach our ultimate destination and our various lifetime goals – is our personal vocation. If we are to travel on the path, we need to know what to do today, right here and right now, in order make any progress. Every day when I wake up in the morning I must look at the day and know that what I plan to do today is in accord with both my lifetime goals and my ultimate goal. Again, this book describes how we can know this.

We take it that our personal vocation is the life by which we will be most joyful and flourish fully; and that we are given special gifts to enable us to have that life. This being so, it opens up two approaches for discerning what that personal vocation is.

- The first is to examine our lives up until now and look for the activities that we enjoy doing the most.

The second is to examine our lives and look for the things at which we excel.

We can immediately see the dangers inherent within both of these approaches. In the first, attachment to momentary pleasure can confuse us. We are looking for a true joy here, one of the gifts of the Holy Spirit – the peace that "passeth understanding"; if we can't distinguish this from flights of fancy then we are in danger of concluding that we want to devote our lives to watching Netflix.

In the second case, because it is possible through will power and application to develop most skills to a pretty good level almost regardless of natural aptitude, unless we are careful we will always end up doing whatever we have been trained to do in the past. A process of discernment that always tells you to keep on doing what you have been doing up to now, is not much help. We want to be able to distinguish ordinary skills and abilities from *charisms*, special abilities that are gifts of the Holy Spirit.

When we use these charisms they will be directed towards the good for which we were given them. We will feel fulfilled and joyful and be effective in what we do. It will seem natural to us, so natural that we sometimes can't appreciate that other people can't do these things as easily and effectively as we can. But the effects will very likely be remarkable…quite literally – people *will* remark upon them.

When these gifts are directed towards a participation in the creative love of God which is made possible by supernatural transformation in Christ, then truly amazing, miraculous things can happen.

Participation in the creative love of God? Supernatural transformation? Partaking of the divine nature? What are we talking about here, I mean… really?

We *can* be divine… really!

God created us out of love and formed us to desire what is good for us. He is offering us himself in a personal relationship of love and the chance to share in his divinity. By this we are given the power to attain all the good things that we desire.

The noted author C. S. Lewis wrote of this in *Mere Christianity*:

> The command 'Be ye perfect' is not idealistic gas. Nor is it a command to do the impossible. He is going to make us into creatures that can obey that command. He said (in the Bible) that we were 'gods' and He is going to make good His words. If we let Him—for we can prevent Him, if we choose—He will make the feeblest and filthiest of us into a god or goddess, dazzling, radiant, immortal creatures, pulsating all through with such energy and joy and wisdom and love as we cannot now imagine, a bright stainless mirror which reflects back to Him perfectly (though, of course, on a smaller scale) His own boundless power and delight and goodness.[1]

This perfection is realized when we attain our destiny, which is to be in union with God in heaven in a perfectly realized personal relationship of love and happiness for eternity. Although not realized fully in this life, neither is it fully denied to us in the here-and-now. In this life the process of transformation is gradual and imperfect, but nevertheless real and noticeable, sometimes dramatically so. We can see and experience great change and wonderful things if we work for them and are prepared to believe that they can happen. Life will not be precisely as we wish, but that is not a bad thing. In fact, it will be much better than that because in our imperfections we cannot know perfectly what is good for us. The gifts we receive will be beyond our capacities to imagine. We might see 21st-century miracles every bit as spectacular as those that we read of in the lives of the saints or in the gospels.

What is the nature of that relationship with God?

By the proper meaning of the word, we can only have a *personal* relationship (which allows for the full mutual exchange of love) with someone who

---

[1] C.S. Lewis: *Mere Christianity*, pub. Macmillan, 1952, p. 174

has the same nature as us. (When two things share the same nature they are said to be 'connatural.') So, for example, because I have a human nature I cannot have a personal relationship with a pet, a dog or a cat however fond I might be of it and however affectionate it may be to me. They have canine and feline natures and so there is no intermingling of our spirits, so to speak. Trying to force it, to make it happen is like trying to mix oil and water. We can get close, the equivalent of creating an emulsion. In an emulsion there are oil droplets suspended in the water that are so fine that they cannot be seen with the naked eye, but they are always distinct from, never mixing with the water. We never get so close to a pet that we have a personal relationship, just as those droplets never dissolve into the water no matter how small they are.

Similarly, I who have a human nature cannot ordinarily have a personal relationship with God who has a divine nature. No matter how close the relationship, when the natures are different – human on the one hand and divine on the other – it will be akin to that of master and slave, albeit, a loving master and, perhaps, a loyal slave. There is always a distinction that means that we cannot accept the love of the other perfectly. We cannot enter into that *agape-eros* dynamic in the fullest sense. This full expression of love can only happen between individuals who are of the same nature.

So in contrast, when we have human interactions between two people of the same human nature, then it is possible to have truly loving interactions between them. We can have a loving relationship with the divine person, Jesus Christ therefore, by virtue of his *human* nature. Christ is a single person with two natures – he is both fully God and fully man – therefore we can have a personal relationship with Christ as man.

Once we are united with Christ, then because Christ is both God and man, we are subsumed into him and are transformed. We partake of His divine nature. By the undeserved generosity of God – grace – we become adopted brothers and sisters of Christ and therefore adopted sons and daughters of the Father also.

In the 2nd century AD St. Irenaeus put it this way: "The Word of God became man, the Son of God became Son of Man, in order to unite man with himself and make him, by adoption, a son of God."

Through this route (Christ calls himself 'the Way'), we enter into the mystery of the Trinity and participate in the dynamic of the perfect love that exists between the three persons, Father, Son and Holy Spirit. It is an extraordinary privilege that lifts us up above even the angels in heaven.

The Trinity – Lover, Beloved and Love

Each person of the Trinity is related to the others simultaneously as lover, beloved and the love that exists between the two, itself crystallized as a person, as described by St. Augustine in his *De Trinitate*:

> Now love is of someone who loves, and something is loved with love. So, then there are three: the lover, the beloved, and the love (Bk. 8 Ch. 10). If then, any one of these three is to be specially called love, what more fitting than that this should be the Holy Spirit? In the sense, that is, that in that simple and highest nature, substance is not one thing and love another thing, but that substance itself is love and that love itself is substance whether in the Father or the Son or the Holy Spirit, yet that the Holy Spirit is especially to be called love. (Bk 15 Ch. 17)

When transformed by grace we are united with Christ and participating in this dynamic of perfect peace that gives us joy. Our baptism opens up this privilege to us. It makes us part of the Church, the mystical body of Christ in which, paradoxically, all members are unique persons interconnected through their unity with Christ. This is attainable by degrees in this life. The 16th-century Spanish mystic St. John of the Cross put it as follows:

> For all things of his divine power, which are given to us for our life and goodness, are given through the knowledge of him who called us to his own glory and power, by which he has given us great and precious promises, that by these we may be made partakers of the divine nature. So the soul, in this union which God has ordained,

joins in the work of the Trinity, not yet fully as in the life to come, but nonetheless even now in a real and perceptible way.[2]

The worship of God in the sacred liturgy of the Church is the most direct way available to us by which we enter into the mystery of the Trinity. This relationship then guides us in all our activities so that all are harmonized to the grand ordering principle of the love of God. By it we are made sons of God and so as his son, drawing on the imagery of St. Augustine, we respond to the love of our Father in the love of the Holy Spirit that connects us. This is why the worship of God is the worship of the Father, *through* the Son, *in* the Spirit. You may have noticed that the prayers of the liturgy generally address the Father first and then close with the doxology (an expression of praise of God): '...*we ask this through our Lord Jesus Christ, who lives and reigns with you and the Holy Spirit, one God for ever and ever. Amen.*'

When we pay homage to God in the sacred liturgy we are raised up to so that we are united to the Son, adopted sons partaking of the divine nature, addressing the Father in the Spirit of Love, the Holy Spirit. Then we are dismissed to go out to our homes and communities and our interactions are infused with the creative love of the Father to the degree that we are transformed people.

You can have a life that is *greater* than anything you dreamed of

As we have said, while perfection is not possible in this life, partial transformation is. We can move along that Way of Beauty toward perfection and become an ever-better person. This means that we can have a life beyond our wildest imagination right here, right now. All we have to do is believe and do God's will, making his will our will. To the degree that our will is in accord with God's then great things, even miracles, will happen. What we desire and what we imagine can become truth.

In his book about heaven and what the Christian life offers us, the well-known Catholic philosopher and writer Peter Kreeft makes it clear that

---

[2]St. John of the Cross, *The Spiritual Canticle,* quotation taken from the Office of Readings, August 7th

the heavenly state that we hope for after death can be realized, by degrees, in the here and now:

> The puzzle of how to understand Christ's oft-repeated promises in the New Testament, such as 'Whatever you ask me, I will do for you' [Matthew *7:7, 21:22*; Luke *11:9*; John *14:13; 15:7; 16:24*] is easily solved. He means exactly what he says – no watering down, no evasion, no nuancing.[3]

He goes on to stress how this can happen in this life, it is not just a promise for life after death:

> Right now, therefore, if we believe we are in Heaven; that is if we accept the Divine gift, we have it. Right now, in our temporality we taste 'the powers of the age to come' [Heb. 6:5] unless we call the New Testament a lie or a fable. Right now, we can 'do all things' through Christ [Philippians 4:13] for He promised that 'He who believes in me will also do the works that I do' [John 14:12]. Like his claim to divinity, this is an offense, an embarrassment. We would prefer to avoid the choice to believe it or not. For believing it is 'strong meat' [Heb. 5:14] and disbelieving it is calling Christ a liar. We therefore often 'reinterpret' it, water it down, explain it away, reduce it to platitude.[4]

Then, continuing to draw on scripture, Kreeft lists four powers that will come to us as we partake of the divine nature.

First, we will lose fear of death because we have eternal life.

Second, we will be able to see as we didn't before: we will be given divine wisdom and knowledge and powers of prophecy and we will see as God sees, through the eyes of purity.

Third, we will learn to love as a gift, not as a need.

---

[3] Peter Kreeft: *Everything You Ever Wanted to Know About Heaven, But Never Dreamed of Asking*; pub Ignatius, 1990, p. 102

[4] Ibid

Fourth – *Zoë*. Kreeft gives the Greek word for it from scripture explaining that this "fourth power of Zoë is not a need but a glory, an extra. It is the power to work miracles, power over nature and its physical laws. This is the most empirical, most visible power of the four… but least often seen. Perhaps that is because it is the least believed… miracles are rare partly because we do not expect them. We fear the test will fail. We expect little so that our expectations cannot be disappointed. There are two reasons why miracles are rare. One is that our faith is much smaller than a grain of mustard seed. The other is that only when we are perfectly subject to God does God dare let nature be perfectly subject to us. To keep us from Hell, God limits our sample of heaven."[5]

Power to cause miracles and power over nature

Some may feel that Kreeft is stretching it a bit when he describes this power of *Zoë*. However, what he says is not new, but part of the tradition of the Church. To give just one illustration: while I was writing this chapter, the feast of the 6th century Italian saint, St. Scholastica happened to occur (the date was the 10th February). The Office of Readings for that day has a section from the Book of Dialogues of St. Gregory the Great. In it St. Gregory describes how Scholastica was visited once a year by her brother, St. Benedict (who wrote the monastic rule) and on one occasion he got up to go back to his monastery. Sensing that this would be their final visit together she asked him to stay longer: "Please do not leave me tonight, let us go on until morning talking about the delights of the spiritual life." Benedict, always conscious of the Rule, said that he had to return to his cell and couldn't. So St. Scholastica prayed to God and immediately there was a huge storm with such violent thunder and lightning and such heavy rain that it made it impossible for Benedict and his brothers to leave until the following day. Gregory remarks: "It was not surprising that she was more effective than he, since as John says, God is love, it was absolutely right that she could do more, as she loved more than her brother Benedict."

---

[5] Peter Kreeft: *Everything You Ever Wanted to Know About Heaven, But Never Dreamed of Asking*; pub Ignatius, 1990, p. 177

I say she must have loved God very well indeed, for Benedict (her twin) is a great saint himself.

Gregory the Great was writing not long after these saints actually lived in the 6th century. The Office of Readings where I found his account is the current edition recommended for most priests. Only the very highest and most important of readings would be included in the Liturgy of the Hours. We can safely say that in the eyes of the Church it is still considered valid and that this therefore demonstrates how the validity of this passage has not diminished over time. What lesson are we to learn from the life of the saint? Here is the closing prayer of all the Offices for that day:

> *Oh God, may we, like St. Scholastica, serve you with an unsullied love. Then our joy will be full as we receive from your loving hand all that we desire and ask. Through our Lord Jesus Christ, your Son, who lives and reigns with you and the Holy Spirit, one God, for ever and ever. Amen*

I suggest that the Church intends for us to be encouraged to lead a life of greater holiness, that we may share in the joy of living and may receive from God all that we desire and ask, as exemplified by the joy of St. Scholastica and this story of her cooperation with love's power over nature.

We can have all we desire when, as Peter Kreeft puts it, "we obey Him as perfectly as the Son obeys the Father," but when we do not and instead "succumb to the temptation to be like God in power but not in virtue,"[6] we are not given the same power. So, while it is true that we can, in this life, have much of what we want, and that the means by which God chooses to give such things to us are both supernatural and natural, it is unlikely that we will get *everything* we want.

We don't get all we want… it is much better than that

We are fallen people and even though deification can occur by degrees

---

[6]Peter Kreeft: *Everything You Ever Wanted to Know About Heaven, But Never Dreamed of Asking*, pub Ignatius, 1990, p. 177

in this life it is not complete. The part of us that is still self-seeking will sometimes succumb to the temptation to desire things that are not good for us or for others. When we ask for those things, God responds the way any loving parent would respond to a child who asks for something that is not good for him. The answer might be *Not yet, not until you are ready – in my time not in yours,* or *Okay but only because you will learn from this that there is a greater good than the one you ask for*, or, still more simply *No*.

We should therefore be as grateful when our prayers are not answered as when they are. For we can be sure that God is giving us something that is better for us than what we desired. Even more than a good parent, he knows best and will not let us come to any harm that we cannot, through grace, cheerfully bear. This is a win-win scenario. Through God's grace, our joy is always greater as a result than it would have been if our prayers had been answered as we had wished.

When viewed in this light we can see that our first wish list, the one we wrote out at the end of the introduction, is in fact, not the highest set of goods we can hope for, but the *least*. God gives us all that we want and if he denies us it is because he gives us – or allows us to receive – something greater for our good and the good of others.

Sometimes we do have great suffering that is not removed when we pray. Again, we must remind ourselves that although God is never the author of evil, sometimes evil is permitted so that a greater good will arise from it. We are never allowed to receive anything that, with God's grace, we cannot cope with and turn into an occasion for joy and God's glory. As we have said before, the fact of the great martyr saints in history provides evidence of that heartening truth.

I am fully aware as I write this that it is one thing to *know* we ought to be grateful for adversity and another to *feel* such gratitude. I get disheartened from time to time when things occur that are not on my wish list, or when they don't occur at the pace that I think would be good. Put more simply: if things don't go my way I don't like it. However, my experience is always that when I respond by putting into practice the prayers, spiritual exercises, and actions recommended in this book, I can reverse that first negative emotional reaction.

It is important to make the point here again that miracles really can occur as we are transformed and live the life of love. While acknowledging that we are not going to get everything we want, I am not intending that we should swing in the other direction and become pessimistic. *Everybody can find their personal vocation, and a life beyond our wildest dreams is available to us all.* It will happen, by whatever means necessary – whether mundane or miraculous.

If we wish to have this wonderful life, then we must take care not to succumb to the temptation, as described by Peter Kreeft, of seeking to be like God in power but not in virtue. To become virtuous, we must adopt the firm disposition to do good and develop the habit of doing so, so that our passions are ordered to the good in accordance with reason and faith. In other words, we must resolve always to try to do what is good, loving and beautiful. If we wish to be powerful as God is powerful, then we must be as virtuous as Christ who is the image of the Father. "Be ye perfect as your Father in heaven is perfect"[7] is the command. Only through cooperation with God's grace can we move towards this ideal. Nevertheless, if we aim for perfection always, and continue to work for it, remaining undeterred in our personal failures, through God's grace all good things are possible.

The *Catechism of the Catholic Church* tells us:

> The seven *gifts* of the Holy Spirit are wisdom, understanding, counsel, fortitude, knowledge, piety, and fear of the Lord. They belong in their fullness to Christ, Son of David.[109] They complete and perfect the virtues of those who receive them. They make the faithful docile in readily obeying divine inspirations.
>
> *Let your good spirit lead me on a level path.* 110
>
> *For all who are led by the Spirit of God are sons of God . . . If children, then heirs, heirs of God and fellow heirs with Christ.* 111[8]

---

[7]Mt 5:48

[8]CCC, 1831, quoting (in italics) 110, Ps 143:10, and 111, Rom 8:14, 17.

By cooperating with God's grace, we are transformed, and by our transformation we cooperate with God's grace ever more readily.

Now pray:

> *Bend my heart to your will, Oh God.*
> *I ask this in the name of my Lord Jesus Christ.*

6 Think and Grow Greedy

The problem with 'Law of Attraction' popular literature, why this book is different, and why Christianity delivers more than any of these books' promises

If you go to the self-help section of a chain bookstore you will see a whole section devoted to titles that promise you the fulfillment of all that you desire. These books tell us that they tap into the 'law of attraction' by which we 'manifest' our wildest dreams and live the life of 'abundance.'

As I went through the process that David showed to me I met and mixed with a small crowd of people who were like me, searching and on a journey. Some of these people introduced me to these ideas. Initially I was interested too, although I later became less enthusiastic, for reasons I will now explain.

The first book I read in this genre was *Think and Grow Rich* by Napoleon Hill – a famous title to which many of the other books acknowledge some debt. Published in the 1930s and still in print, it tells how we can tap into a great force that lies deep within ourselves which, once liberated, will allow us to 'manifest' all that we believe. Napoleon Hill said that his book contained information passed on to him by Andrew Carnegie, the Scottish-American entrepreneur and philanthropist, on the condition that he would pass it on to others. As the book contained the secret of Carnegie's great wealth, the argument goes, such wealth can be the reader's too.

False promises – too much positive thinking and too much desire for the wrong things

There are a number of common characteristics that run through books of this type, but the message that they all seem to push is that of positive thinking. If we want something to happen, we have to believe and believe *fervently* and with conviction that it will happen. We are supposed to have such certainty that what we want will happen, that it feels to us as though it already has happened – that what we wish for has been dispatched and is on its way to us. We might say, so to speak, that 'the supernatural check is in the mail.' We are told that there is nothing that we want or want to be that cannot happen if we desire it passionately enough. The universe will deliver these goods to us because our positive attitude attracts them in a way that is analogous to a gravitational pull. They say that the connection between cause (what I want in my heart), and effect (what I actually receive) is so well established that we can relate the two just like a scientific law. This is the 'law of attraction.'

I am not familiar with the historical roots of this philosophy of abundance. Many writers in the genre claim to be presenting ancient wisdom that is present in the great religions but I doubt that many adherents to the religions of the sacred texts which are referred to would agree. Certainly they do not represent any true teaching of Christ as I know it, although many of these law-of-attraction books quote the Bible regularly. One I read claimed to have great admiration for St. Francis of Assisi's vision of love and compassion and then went on to criticize the Church as a man-made construct and reject parts of Christian teaching and morality – seemingly unaware that St. Francis of Assisi's mission was to rebuild Christ's Church, that Francis was devoted to beautiful churches and liturgy, that he was orthodox in his adherence to church teaching, and would not countenance any other attitude to Church teaching in the Franciscan order.

This 'law of attraction' literature, if I can call it that, strikes me as a modern and Western form of paganism. Far from drawing on ancient wisdom, its cornerstone, the emphasis on the need for strong emotion and passion connected to what we desire is very much of the product of the modern age.

The wrong idea of God

Many Catholics will be, and quite rightly, profoundly suspicious of law-of-attraction books for a number of reasons. The conception of God varies from book to book, but most are flawed in that they are pantheist, claiming that "all is one" and "all is God," therefore "you are God." Some do not even use the word God, preferring phrases such as "spirit of the universe" or "divine order"; some reduce him directly to the inanimate law of attraction making no further reference to God at all.

It follows from this approach that all we have to do is unlock the divine power that already exists within us to invoke the law of attraction, and then we will get what we want. The way that we do it is by arousing and channeling emotion. The idea is to create a fervent desire and belief that "I am God" and that what I want "has already happened." Through the unlocking of my own divine power, the theory goes, this supernatural force can be harnessed and controlled for my own ends.

The inversion of the hierarchy of being – trying to make God subservient to me by lacking trust in God's providential care

This account of God falsely inverts the hierarchy of being, making me the 'god' and God my slave. It can only lead to unhappiness. At its root, it seems to me there is a lack of faith. If I believe that God loves me, then I am happy to accept what He gives and will not try to seek to control him by force of will, which is what these books seem to be trying to do. True happiness lies in giving myself to Him and allowing him to direct my will. Miracles can occur, but we can never depend on them for our happiness.

In addition, these books also push a false morality. They might advocate living a 'loving' life and leading a 'good' life, but rarely do they accurately describe what love and a good life are. They encourage people to be guided by emotion and feeling in what they do, rather than by faith and reason. When they get into the specifics of morality it is often on matters of sex and what they advocate is contrary to Christian teaching. Most reinforce post-1960s non-Christian, non-traditional sexual morality. Again, whatever immediate pleasures this may bring, it will lead ultimately to an unhappy life.

Although the writers generally do warn us that happiness does not come with money alone, and that each one of us should somehow determine what it is that makes us happy, the books are marketed to appeal very strongly to the desire to have our wishes fulfilled without any emphasis on conformity to an external authority who might regulate our desires and direct them towards the good. Given this packaging, it is very easy to see how the reader could, to use Peter Kreeft's phrase, "succumb to the serpent's temptation to be like God in power but not in virtue." When we do this, as Kreeft points out, "we reenact Adam's Fall."[1]

The writers are quite skilled at imparting optimism – I don't know if it is possible to use hypnotic techniques in writing, but if it is one must wonder if they are using them. As I read these books I felt a growing sense that I could achieve anything and have anything. When I first read them, I was energized, at least temporarily. However, I soon realized that this was a path that leads to misery based on a false promise.

The great marketing success of these books is to hook the reader into coming back for reinforcement when things don't work out. If, as the books say, the sole cause of my lack of success is that I am not positive enough, then the remedy is obvious: I must generate more optimism. So, I might read the book again, or if I've already done that buy a different book in similar vein, perhaps by the same author, and then after that I might even go to the author's live stage show. The cycle continues with more money going into the pockets of the authors each time.

But for all that there is *some* good in them

Although I would not recommend any of these books to anyone (always preferring to direct people to the Faith instead) I do think that there is something to what they say.

---

[1] Peter Kreeft: *Everything You Ever Wanted to Know About Heaven, But Never Dreamed of Asking*; pub Ignatius, 1990, p. 113

When I looked at those around me who read the books, there were some benefits. Generally, they did better in their careers and they did have an optimistic outlook and a strong sense of the potential of each human life. Setting goals and aiming high is something that is proven to work in all sorts of activities from sales to sport and it seemed to work with the people I saw. Generally, it made them better people to be around. It seemed to work best with those who seemed able to read them selectively and adopted those parts that seemed to be helpful and in conformity with a good moral code that was derived from another source. Furthermore, their claim that man is divine has a grain of truth to it although what they present beyond that is a subversion of Christian claims for man.

Why Christianity is different… and where it is similar it is better. Miracles *do* happen

A crucial difference between what Christianity offers and what the 'law of attraction' literature claims to do is that in Christianity man does not supplant God and become his master. According to the Church, the Christian can be raised up so that he partakes of the divine nature, provided that he always recognizes the supremacy of God. Another difference is an overemphasis in 'law of attraction' theory on the power of the will of man. In truth, no amount of willpower will enable someone to raise himself up from his fallen nature. It is not by asserting ourselves that we attain divinity; rather it is by giving up on ourselves and submitting totally to God. Then, by means of our cooperating with his grace, *God* raises us up.

Like 'law of attraction' theory, Christianity allows for the possibility of miracles and emphasizes the importance of personal faith in order for them to occur. For example, in Matthew's gospel (Mt. 17:20) the disciples have just asked Jesus why they couldn't cast out devils, when "He said them, 'Because of your little faith. For truly, I say to you, if you have faith as a grain of mustard seed, you will say to this mountain, "Move from here to there," and it will move; and nothing will be impossible to you.'" Again, in Matthew 21:22 we hear that "whatever you ask in prayer you will receive, if you have faith."

But the faith the gospels require, I would suggest, is broader and deeper than a simple emotional certainty that the requested miracle will happen. It is faith *in Christ*. And this faith cannot be separated from following the commandments of the Church or from what this leads to, the life of joy described in John 15:7-11. "If you abide in me, and my words abide in you, ask whatever you will and it shall be done for you. By this my Father is glorified, that you bear much fruit, and so prove to be my disciples. As the Father has loved me so I have loved you; continue in my love. If you keep my commandments you shall abide in my love, even as I have kept the Father's commandments and abide in His love. These things I have spoken to you, that my joy may be in you, and that your joy may be full."

For a Christian the search for God and union with him is the primary aim. All else that we do must conform to that. When we follow the teachings of the Church and we follow Christ in all that we do, we have a life of joy.

We do not need to worry, and we can be assured of what we need in order to do God's will if we seek God first and all other things in accordance with that primary aim:

> Be not solicitous therefore, saying, What shall we eat: or what shall we drink, or wherewith shall we be clothed? For after all these things do the heathens seek. For your Father knoweth that you have need of all these things. Seek ye therefore first the kingdom of God, and his justice, and all these things shall be added unto you.
>
> Mt. 6:31-33

When our wishes do not come true, the 'law of attraction' sees this as a failure, a fault to be remedied by reapplying ourselves to the practice of positive thinking. In contrast, Christianity sees such a development as something good. Though not what we would have chosen, not getting what we wanted is better than if our wishes had come true, because this development encourages us to realize fully that we are fallen people whose only true reliance is on a loving God. Christianity recognizes that no matter where we sit on the spiritual scale of perfection, every single one of us is capable of making choices that are bad because they are either foolish or selfish. It is the great wonder and evidence of God's love that even when we do choose foolishly or selfishly, provided we can acknowledge our own weakness, fallibility and need for him, God always offers us a way forward. No matter what mess our self-centeredness has landed us in there is always a path, with God's help, that will either take us out of adversity, or offer us joy in adversity.

This is not about positive thinking, it is about faith

How positive do I have to be for this to work? The answer to this question, if you are following the 'law of attraction' method is that you have to eliminate all doubt.

The answer, for the Christian, is more forgiving: we only need a 'mustard seed' of faith to make a start. Willingness is indicated by action, so in other words, we *do* need to have sufficient conviction to act as though what the Gospel says is true. This is the necessary 'mustard seed' of faith. But if we have this, we can 'move mountains.'

For example, I had many doubts that the process described in this book would work for me especially at the beginning. However, I had enough faith in it to *try* to do what was asked of me. So I always gave it my best shot. This was enough.

As my life got steadily better, gradually doubt receded and faith increased. But even then, along the way my first reaction to reversals could still be despondence. The great thing about this process, however, is that if I have just enough willingness left to take the necessary actions then this will allow me to overcome whatever is facing me, and to cease being despondent. Experiencing this repeatedly has reinforced my faith both in the process and in God's love for me.

It was a relief to me once I understood this. I am one of those people who is sunk if I am told that everything depends on confidence and positive thinking and that I must eliminate doubt. The very act of assessing how much doubt I have introduces doubt in my mind, and then that increases the doubt still further and a downward spiral to hopelessness begins. The way out of this spiral for me is to accept that I will always feel some doubt, but as long as my actions are in accord with some basic assumptions that rest in the truth, I will be fine.

Christianity offers more, and it is true

As I have described in this chapter, I believe that Christianity offers something more and better than 'law of attraction' theory can offer, even if you take that theory at face value. Furthermore, the means by which we obtain what is offered is both simpler to follow and more reliable.

This is not, however, the reason why I would suggest that people adopt Christianity. I would always direct people to the Church first because the Catholic Faith is true, and because only a life based in truth can offer joy. In other words, it doesn't really matter what a religion offers you if it is not true. Christianity delivers because it is true. And it delivers to all of us – ordinary people at times foolish, selfish, doubt-filled, or skeptical who are muddling along trying to do the best we can – who are ready to accept God's help.

Now, please pray…

Bend my heart to your will, Oh God.
I ask this in the name of my Lord Jesus Christ.

7 MISERY IS OPTIONAL

Christian joy is the greatest happiness and we can always choose it

Now it is our supreme delight to behold him and contemplate his divine splendor with the eyes of our spirit. When we participate in and associate with that beauty… we are filled with a joy that comes from God and endures through all the days of our earthly life. In the wise words of Ecclesiastes: *A man may live for many years, but he will experience happiness throughout his days. For all who gaze upon the Sun of Justice, he is their supreme delight.*[1]

St. Gregory of Agrigentum

St. Gregory's words make clear a truth that, sadly, seems not to be believed by all Christians. That truth is this: the Christian life is a happy life.

This is something David always used to tell me: that God's will for each of us is that we be happy regardless of what is happening to us. This should be a truth that brings hope to all unhappy people. However, it is not the case. In my experience many unhappy people resist this truth, not wanting to believe it. I personally saw quite a few people become

---

[1] St. Gregory of Agrigentum: *Explanation of* Ecclesiastes, taken from the Office of Readings, Saturday, Wk. 7, Ordinary Time.

extremely nasty and openly rude to David, often accusing him of lying about his own experience, when he tried to convey this truth to them. He would say 'misery is optional.' It seems that while this is good news for the person who desires to change, many people would rather not take responsibility for their unhappiness. They prefer to stay as they are and accept the sympathy of others.

I'm glad that David was courageous and didn't let his detractors stop him from telling the truth; otherwise I might never have heard the good news when I was ready to change.

Looking at scripture

The gospels and scripture are full of direct references to the joy we will have if we accept the Faith, a few of which I have already quoted. Here is one more example from scripture: "Hitherto, you have asked nothing in my name; ask, and you will receive, *that your joy may be full.*" (John 16:24).

What is this joy? What is really on offer, here?

To some it may seem strange that we even need to ask the question. But in my experience, these scriptural offers of joy are discounted by people who are trying to accommodate their own idea that life is miserable. Despite all that is promised they will say that being a Christian doesn't really promise us happiness.

For example, I have heard people distinguishing between happiness and joy in such a way that it sounds as though one could be unhappy but still have joy. Or perhaps they might nuance it slightly differently by stressing the difference between *being* joyful, *having* joy and *feeling* joy.

There may be some very useful reasons for making such distinctions; however, it always strikes me as a perverse sophistry to say that someone has joy but doesn't feel happy. My personal experience of the Faith so far is that misery indeed is optional. Misery results from choices I make and therefore I can choose not to be miserable. David was right!

And I can be happy *every day*, in the plain and simple way that most people mean when they say, "I am happy." This doesn't mean that we should expect to continually experience *perfect* happiness, not in this life at least. In a generally happy life there will be temporary periods of unhappiness. But I do maintain that there is always something we can do about the situation in order to become happy again.

Also, there are different degrees of happiness. Some forms of happiness are so superficial that we would more properly characterize them as pleasure, while others are deeper, more permanent and therefore more desirable. It is the latter sort of happiness that St. Gregory is describing at the beginning of the chapter when he refers to "supreme delight."

Again, we may be conflicted at any moment in time with the result that we are simultaneously happy at some level but unhappy in others. Although unhappy deep down I could be temporarily distracted by superficial pleasures, so that if pushed I might say that I am having fun, but I'm not happy. Conversely, I might be happy in my core, while experiencing anxiety and distress at other more superficial levels about what is happening to me today. When that situation occurs I might say that I am not happy about this or that event but still, 'in myself' I am happy.

I would also say, based upon my own experience, that happiness is something that is felt in different ways. Superficial forms of happiness can evoke emotional responses that are felt viscerally. Deeper, more permanent forms of happiness are experienced differently, producing a frame of mind or "mood" more akin to knowing than feeling but still able to be characterized as an emotion.

Thus, although some of these nuances are valid, the form of happiness that Christianity offers is not a mysterious happiness that we cannot recognize easily when we have acquired it or that we need a degree in theology to identify. It is happiness plain and simple, and it is open to all of us. It is not even possible to possess a form of joy, happiness or "supreme delight" that is so mysterious that we can't feel it as an emotion and know that it is good. I would further suggest that if holiness is

THE VISION FOR YOU

a prerequisite for the highest happiness, then the person who is holy enough to possess joy is also holy enough to feel and experience it. Holiness and happiness are both available to all.

This conviction is rooted in my own experience and the observations of people around me. My faith has given me happiness, just as promised. I don't believe that I am especially lucky in this; nor am I especially holy or good (just ask anyone who knows me). My only merit is to have had my pride so battered that I gave up on my own ideas and was willing to follow good advice. At various times I have had to face adversity and injustice and the consequences of my own foolishness and selfishness, but once I can see these things for what they are, as the *Vision for You* process has shown me, then I can be happy. In short, nothing I have experienced so far has undermined that gift of happiness.

I will freely admit, however, that at the moment when bad things happen I do not always react well, and my first response can be one of unhappiness or fear. But once I put the tenets of the Faith into practice my mood changes. I can choose to do this one split second after the event, if I want to, or I can stew in it until my pride is broken again, and I am forced to change. But once I do change, regardless of what happened to dump me into those unhappy or fearful depths, I have always felt protected and able to deal with the situation cheerfully, despite myself. Perhaps tomorrow I will be overcome by despair or depression, or face something so extreme that this is no longer true, but so far that has not happened.

I have found that the most important thing for me to understand in order to possess such joy is this: the problem always lies in me. When I am unhappy, I am the one who must change. Perhaps I have to change some other things too, but even then I will not be happy again unless I also change my personal attitude to what happened and to those I feel wronged me. Most importantly I must be rid of resentment and fear so that I cease to view the world through the distorting prism of self-centeredness and instead see it through the clarifying lens of truth and in the revealing Light of the Faith. Then I can see things as they really are and I know that life is good.

"Life is good" is a permanent truth.

The joy of the saints, the joy of the martyrs

Whenever I think that I have problems, I take heart from the accounts of martyrs and those saints whose suffering I know was greater than anything I have ever had to bear in my life to date.

For example, here is a letter from a priest named Emilian Kovch, who was imprisoned in a German concentration camp in Ukraine during the second world war. Writing to his daughters, he asks them not to try to secure his release.

> I thank God for His goodness to me. Apart from heaven, this is the one place where I wish to remain. Here we are all equal: Poles, Jews, Ukrainians, Russians, Latvians and Estonians. Of all these here I am the only priest. I cannot even imagine how it would be here without me. Here I see God, who is the same for us all, regardless of our religious distinctions. Perhaps our churches are different, but the same great and Almighty God rules over us all… I thank God a thousand times a day for sending me here. I do not ask him for anything else. Do not worry and do not lose faith at what I share. Instead, rejoice with me. Pray for those who created this concentration camp and this system. They are the only ones who need prayers. May God have mercy upon them.[2]

In a similar vein, St. Thomas More wrote to his daughter Margaret (also called Meg) from the Tower of London where he was being held shortly before his execution in 1535. This is taken from the Office of Readings for his Feast Day on July 9th:

> Although I know well, Margaret, that because of my past wickedness I deserve to be abandoned by God, I cannot but trust in his merciful goodness. His grace has strengthened me until now and made me content to lose goods, land, and life as well, rather than to swear against my conscience. God's grace

---

[2]Steve Smith: http://faithofthefatherssaints.blogspot.com/2006_01_01_archive.html

has given the king a gracious frame of mind toward me, so that as yet he has taken from me nothing but my liberty. In doing this His Majesty has done me such great good with respect to spiritual profit that I trust that among all the great benefits he has heaped so abundantly upon me I count my imprisonment the very greatest. I cannot, therefore, mistrust the grace of God.

By the merits of his bitter passion joined to mine and far surpassing in merit for me all that I can suffer myself, his bounteous goodness shall release me from the pains of purgatory and shall increase my reward in heaven besides.

I will not mistrust him, Meg, though I shall feel myself weakening and on the verge of being overcome with fear. I shall remember how Saint Peter at a blast of wind began to sink because of his lack of faith, and I shall do as he did: call upon Christ and pray to him for help. And then I trust he shall place his holy hand on me and in the stormy seas hold me up from drowning.

And finally, Margaret, I know this well: that without my fault he will not let me be lost. I shall, therefore, with good hope commit myself wholly to him. And if he permits me to perish for my faults, then I shall serve as praise for his justice. But in good faith, Meg, I trust that his tender pity shall keep my poor soul safe and make me commend his mercy.

And, therefore, my own good daughter, do not let your mind be troubled over anything that shall happen to me in this world. Nothing can come but what God wills. And I am very sure that whatever that be, however bad it may seem, it shall indeed be the best.

This seems to be an example of what St. Paul is referring to in Romans 5:1-3:

Therefore, having been justified by faith, we have peace with God through our Lord Jesus Christ, through whom also we have obtained our introduction by faith into this grace in which we stand; and we exult in hope of glory of God. And not only this, but we also exult in our tribulations, knowing that tribulation brings about perseverance.

Benedict XVI and the Catechism on happiness

And all of this corroborates what Benedict XVI appears to be saying when talking about the new evangelization[3] – that happiness depends upon one thing only, our relationship with Christ. When this relationship is sound, we are not only able to endure difficulties but even to see them as positive things for our own good. Furthermore, it is worth noting that when Pope Benedict talks of happiness he does not seem to see the need to explain in any great detail what happiness is or qualify it in any way. He seems to assume that we all know enough about happiness to know that we want it.

We can look to the Catechism for supporting evidence too. It tells us:

> "Heaven is the ultimate end and fulfillment of the deepest human longings, the state of supreme, definitive happiness." [4]

While this doesn't tell us too much about what happiness actually feels like, we can conclude also that we will be at least as aware of our happiness when we have it as we are aware of those longings that caused us to desire it in the first place. In other words, if we are able to recognize in ourselves a desire for happiness, we are able to recognize that we have achieved happiness when we get it, for at the very least, that desire will be satiated. The Catechism tells us, we are *all* aware that we long for something and that we desire to have that longing fulfilled:

> The Beatitudes respond to the natural desire for happiness. This desire is of divine origin: God has placed it in the human heart in order to draw man to the One who alone can fulfill it: '*We all want to live happily; in the whole human race there is no one who does not assent to*

---

[3] Joseph Cardinal Ratzinger: *The New Evangelization*, 2001, available from www.ewtn.com/new_evangelization/Ratzinger.htm

[4] CCC 1024

this proposition, even before it is fully articulated.' [5]

Again, nowhere is there any suggestion that happiness is a mysterious quality that we do not know. There is the clear impression that we know when we have it and we know when we don't. Certainly, there is plenty of disagreement in the world at large on the means by which we are to achieve happiness, but that is a different matter.

What of pleasure and superficial happiness?

Any happiness that arises from anything but the fulfillment of our desire for God will always be found wanting. It does not matter if that "happiness" is derived from the high octane thrills of extreme sports that might attract a teenager; or from what we might think of as the more elevated and cultured enjoyment of a string quartet performing at Wigmore Hall in London. Neither can satisfy our longing for God.

The hedonist, recognizing the temporary nature of any one of these experiences, responds by attempting to increase the intensity and duration of such thrills. We can easily see the poverty in this approach. Similarly, it hardly needs saying that if we seek to derive fulfillment through wealth, fame or power, our quest will fail. Whatever form it takes, focusing our longing on sensual pleasure will not deliver.

Even things that we perceive as always being good and of a higher order, for example the love that exists within a family or service to the community, are not enough in themselves to give us the joy we seek.

Only God can satisfy that longing for happiness.

This being so, one might respond, perhaps, that these lesser goods are all distractions that cause us to stop short of the ultimate good. If this is the case should we discard them and search only for God?

Some may say so, but I do not agree and would characterize that approach as an overly puritanical view. If we want to be happy we have to strive

---

[5]CCC 1718, quoting St. Augustine, *De moribus eccl.* 1,3,4:PL 32,1312

for *more* than these things certainly, but that doesn't mean that we need to disregard these lesser goods altogether. For most people, the happy life consists in striving for both spiritual goods and material goods. We are material beings as well as spiritual and are created to enjoy both. The question is, how do we strike the right balance?

God first, but not only God… in this life

The commandment we are given is not "seek ye only the kingdom of God" but rather "seek ye *first* the kingdom of God" (Mt. 6:33). It would be wrong to say that anything that is not God is bad and so the desire for wealth or the good things it can buy automatically sinful. Rather, to the degree that these things are good, then the desire for them is a good thing as well. Thus, a puritanical attitude that condemns all that is not God can be as destructive as the opposite extreme of envy and greed for material things. The goal is always to place lesser goods in right relation to all others so that each leads us towards the greatest good, which is the love of God.

The satisfaction of the hierarchy of needs: the body, the soul, and the spirit[6]

In order to understand what the right hierarchy of goods might be, it will be helpful first to discuss Christian anthropology. There are three relevant aspects of man to consider: body, soul, and spirit. St. Paul[7] refers to them, as does the writer of the Letter to the Hebrews.[8]

First the spirit. The spirit is the highest part of the soul. It is that part of the soul which is open to God, a portal for the grace that "transfigures" us. It is the part of us that, when we are pure, "sees" God (to quote the first Beatitude), and by which we relate to him.

The divinely created order of the human person is that the spirit, which

---

[6] For an alternative approach to the same question, readers might wish to look at St. Thomas Aquinas's *Summa Theologiae*, First Part of the Second Part, Question 2

[7] 1 Thessalonians 5:23

[8] Hebrews 4:12

is closest to God, rules the rest of the soul, which in turn rules the body. All move together in union and communion with God. This is how it would be in the ideal. However, perfect complementarity has been disrupted by the Fall and only with the help of God's grace can we move back toward that ideal.

When considering this tripartite anthropology one should be aware of something the Catechism makes clear: consideration of the spirit, which is non-material and spiritual in nature, doesn't introduce duality into the soul.[9] The spirit is an aspect of man's spiritual soul. It is the higher part of the soul or as I once heard it described, the "soul of the soul." So, its existence does not change the fact that man is a profound unity of *two* fundamental things, body and soul.

The hierarchy of operation of each part of us was beautifully described by 4th-century saint and Doctor of the Church, Ephraim the Syrian. In his *Hymns to Paradise* he writes:

> Far more glorious than the body is the soul, and more glorious still than the soul is the spirit, but more hidden than the spirit is the Godhead.
>
> At the end, the body will put on the beauty of the soul, the soul will put on that of the spirit, while the spirit shall put on the very likeness of God's majesty.
>
> For bodies shall be raised to the level of souls, and the soul to that of the spirit, while the spirit shall be raised to height of God's majesty.

When the human person is ruled by the spirit, then all lower aspects of the soul and the body are in harmony with it. All aspects of the person are then ordered to the love of God, and in this perfect order we have heaven for it satiates the most noble and deepest longing we have, which is for God. When we are fully transformed in Christ, this is how we will be.

---

[9] Cf. CCC 367

Not all our longings are for God – we desire food and sex for example – but our lower appetites, right down to the occasional desire for the fun of dancing the night away, can be ordered so that they are in harmony with our longing for God and so aid its fulfillment. When they are, then the gratification of these lower appetites is a good thing and the pleasure they bring adds to our general happiness.

When, however, the lower appetites are directed so that their gratification is in conflict with the longing for God, then the pleasure that they bring can distract us from God. When this happens, because of our sinful nature, we can still be inclined to believe that this pleasure is contributing to the fulfillment of our deepest longing and to our general happiness. Our consciences and the teachings of the Church will correct us, but again, because of our sinful natures, we might find that we want to disregard both, because we are attached to the pleasure of the sin.

The Christian life, which is a life well-lived, leads us to God and happiness. Sin leads us away from God and undermines our happiness because it is opposed to our ultimate purpose.

As we move towards the proper ordering of our own nature – the properly ordered spirit ruling the soul as a whole and the properly ordered soul ruling the body – then our passions will naturally become ordered to the good of the whole person and to the highest good, which is God himself. Sometimes, it is a helpful discipline to deny ourselves lesser goods so that we might focus more on the highest good and place it in its right place. But in general, this should not be the permanent rule. The joyful life is one that fulfills the ordered desires of the whole person, body and soul.

We can never control all circumstances in our lives, of course, so at times these lesser goods – including those that are necessary for living – may be denied to us. When this occurs, we do suffer. But, if we are united to Christ, then the grace that we receive will create a consolation that is greater than the unhappiness of the suffering. On such occasions I will experience conflicting emotions of happiness and unhappiness, but whichever belongs to the highest part of the soul will dominate in my general sense of how I am.

Sometimes such deprivation enables me to change my attitude so that I see the situation truthfully. If, for example, I was barred from attending classical concerts at Wigmore Hall, I would be annoyed to have that pleasure denied to me, but very quickly I would be able to see that this is one good I could do without very easily. If, however, I was not able to get food, that might be more difficult to come to terms with, but nevertheless possible to bear for even this earthly life itself is not absolutely necessary for eternal bliss, for there is life after death (still, I hope I never have to face that situation).

The people who show us how God can care for us even in cases of extreme suffering are the saints. Like the saints, when our happiness is rooted in truth and derived from a love of God with the spirit ruling our lives, then we can endure great physical and psychological hardships cheerfully. This is how the martyrs can sing hymns while burning at the stake, and how saints find great joy in the prison cell or concentration camp. To deny ourselves all goods other than God is a great evil that no one should choose willingly; it would amount to suicide. However, when we are forced through the cruelty of others to face this, as is the case with the martyrs, then our right attachment to the greatest Good will give us the grace to be joyful.

The one thing that no one has the power to deny us is our friendship with God and that is why there is always solace sufficient to overcome our difficulties.

Pope Benedict describes this principle in connection with the 6th-century philosopher Boethius. Like St. Thomas More, Boethius was wrongly imprisoned by his king (the ruler of Italy, Theodoric) after a long period of being his chief adviser. And like More, his faith was a consolation so powerful that it gave him joy. While in prison reflecting on this he wrote his great work, the *Consolation of Philosophy*. While he never mentions Christ and his arguments are, as the name of the book indicates, philosophical rather than theological, this book has always been understood in the Light of the Faith. Benedict spoke of it as follows:

> Through this work, *De Consolatione Philosophiae*, he sought consolation, enlightenment and wisdom in prison. And he said

that precisely in this situation he knew how to distinguish between apparent goods, which disappear in prison, and true goods such as genuine friendship, which even in prison do not disappear. The loftiest good is God. Boethius — and he teaches us this — learned not to sink into a fatalism that extinguishes hope. He teaches us that it is not the event but Providence that governs and Providence has a face. It is possible to speak to Providence because Providence is God. Thus, even in prison, he was left with the possibility of prayer, of dialogue with the One who saves us.[10]

Here, Benedict is stressing again how the theological virtue of hope for the future offers a profound consolation that transcends present suffering (a theme, incidentally, that he brought up in his encyclical *Spe Salvi: Saved in Hope*).

In order for our relationship with God to be personal so that we can call it a friendship we must be divine too. In Book 3 of the *Consolation*, Boethius argues that God not only gives us happiness, but that God *is* happiness. God is the highest good that can be imagined, he tells us, and given that perfect happiness is the highest good that men seek, we can say also that God is happiness. He then goes on:

> Since men become happy by achieving happiness, and happiness is itself divinity, clearly they become happy by attaining divinity. Now just as men become just by acquiring justice, and wise by acquiring wisdom, so by the same argument they must become gods by acquiring divinity. Hence every happy person is God: God is by nature one only, but nothing prevents the greatest possible number from sharing in that divinity.[11]

Although this is again a philosophical argument, as a Christian Boethius would have known that through Christ we do indeed attain divinity. We first establish a personal relationship with Christ as man and then through Christ, as God, we are transformed and participate in the divine nature

---

[10] Pope Benedict XVI: General Audience, Rome, March 12, 2008

[11] Boethius, *Consolation of Philosophy*, Bk. 3 Ch. 10.

too. As partakers of the divine nature we then enter into a personal relationship with each person of the Trinity.

You may not accept Boethius's argument, but it is striking that even given what he was facing he believed firmly that he could be happy because, as Benedict points out, the source of happiness could not be denied him.

While each of the saints described has suffered more deprivation than I would ever want, the examples of Kovch, More and Boethius each in their own way reveal to me the path to joy. My own experience gives me a sense of how the transformation might manifest itself. Before I went through "the process" and subsequently converted, there were moments of fun or pleasure, but if ever I was on my own without these distractions, feelings of hopelessness would crowd in on me and I would feel myself sinking into despair. The only way to escape this despair was that of the hedonist, to seek yet more distraction and superficial pleasure, which in my case involved drinking heavily. Now, having been through the process, the reverse is true: there are things that happen that I don't like and which might cause me to feel down for a while when they occur; but when I pause for a moment and reflect on the truth of my life, perhaps by counting my blessings, I have waves of gratitude and an appreciation of God's generosity. Then the happiness returns even if the situation has not changed.

What is the place of the heart in Christian anthropology?

There is another aspect of the human person which we have not yet mentioned, the consideration of which can help us even further. That is the human heart.

In the spiritual tradition of the Church the heart is the place at the very core of our being that represents, one might say, our human center of gravity. When all aspects of our thoughts, desires, emotions and actions are taken into account, some possibly conflicting with each other, the heart is where we really *are* as a person in relation to God. As the Catechism tells us, it is that place deep down inside us "where the person decides for or against God." If the spirit is the part that "sees" God and is in relation to him and prompts the soul to seek spiritual goods, so to speak, it is the heart that actually *chooses*, for or against.

Because we have freedom of will, we can go against what is right even when we know it to be right at some level. Even if the spirit draws us to do what is right, the lower part of the soul that is subject to the desires that arise, for example, from the body, can tempt us to pursue those lesser goods and in such a situation, the heart might choose against God.

The optimum situation is to have the spirit governing all the aspects of the soul and the body. Then there is no conflict and the heart and spirit are in complete harmony and we decide "wholeheartedly" for God each time. However, we can be aware at times that we are conflicted and that the decisions we make, whether good or bad, are not "wholehearted."

The spirit is that place that sees God and so hierarchically occupies the highest position; but in another way it can be considered also the deepest part of our soul, the furthest removed from the bodily senses and closest to God, who is "hidden" (as described by Ephraim the Syrian, above) yet can be "seen" by the spirit of those who are pure of heart. This is why it is often referred to as a "secret" or "hidden" place. The Catechism describes the heart in the following way:

> The heart is the dwelling-place where I am, where I live; ... The heart is our hidden center, beyond the grasp of our reason and of others; only the Spirit of God can fathom the human heart and know it fully. The heart is the place of decision, deeper than our psychic drives. It is the place of truth, where we choose life or death. It is the place of encounter, because as image of God we live in relation: it is the place of covenant.[12]

As we have said, in making choices we can consider the promptings of the spirit, but we can also consider the promptings of the lower parts of the soul which, in the disordered person (which we all are to a degree), can be in conflict with each other. Because we have free will, the heart is not unerringly right in its decisions and can be swayed so as to choose

---

[12] CCC 2563

badly. Hence, we have Christ instructing his disciples on the mountain: "Watch and pray so that you will not fall into temptation; The spirit is willing but the flesh is weak,"[13] and St. Paul writing: "I do not understand my own actions. For I do not do what I want, but I do the very thing I hate."[14]

I will say that for myself there is hardly ever a time when there is no conflict at all in my desires. I am always unhappy at some level about something. When you are as proud, greedy and impatient as I am and there are so many variables in life to control then this is inevitable, it seems to me. I can't remember a day ever when everything went right. But I can say that in every day when I have put the principles of the process outlined in this book into practice, I have been happy. I can remember myself saying, when asked the question "How are you?" that things weren't perfect but that *"in myself* I am well." And this was before I knew or cared about any of this anthropology stuff. I didn't realize it then but what I was saying was, in effect, that I had happiness where it matters: in the heart.

The happiness of the heart, the happiness that really matters

When the heart decides with the spirit and for God, we are happy. To the degree that heart and spirit are in harmony then at our very core we can say that we possess joy and we feel joy. Then the spirit is ruling the man, if not yet perfectly, at least sufficiently for us to say, I am happy. Regardless of what other suffering I might experience, I can say that while I am unhappy about this or that, or in pain about something else, but nevertheless *I am happy*.

When we make the right decisions and heart and soul are in harmony then that decision is in accord with our ultimate purpose as people, to love God. This is why the heart has become the symbol of love. The soul or more particularly the spirit can desire God, but the choice is the heart's. When the heart is pure and is close to God, our prayer is most powerful and effective. Quoting the Catechism again:

---

[13] Matthew 26:41; Mark 14:38
[14] Rm 7:15

> Where does prayer come from? Whether prayer is expressed in words or gestures, it is the whole man who prays. But in naming the source of prayer, Scripture speaks sometimes of the soul or the spirit, but most often of the heart (more than a thousand times). According to Scripture, it is the *heart* that prays. If our heart is far from God, the words of prayer are in vain.[15]

The great thing about this from your point of view, reader, is that this is me, ordinary David Clayton saying this. While I have always done my best, my adherence to these principles has never been anything near perfect and if my life is the measure of what is needed, I offer you a low bar to jump over. All that is required is for you to do this process as badly as I have or better and then you will get this too.

The next part of this book contains exercises for developing the habit of choosing God and thereby increasing our happiness. They are given on the premise that if we make the time to choose God in little ways, by developing habits of prayer and regular devotion, then we exercise the will and build up the power and the inclination to choose him in more profound ways.

Before we go on to the work, in the next two chapters we will discuss in greater detail different aspects of happiness. First will be one that doesn't sound like happiness at all, something called by mystics the 'dark night of the soul.'

Now, pray happily…

> *Bend my heart to your will, Oh God.*
> *I ask this in the name of my Lord Jesus Christ.*

---

[15] CCC 2562

8 The Dark Night of the Soul and Christian Joy

Is one contrary to the other?

We have written of these blessings so that when souls become frightened by the horror of so many trials they might take courage in the sure hope of the many advantageous blessings obtained from God through these trials.[1]

St. John of the Cross

Blessed [i.e., happy] is the man who has set his hope in the Lord.[2]

Psalm 40(39):5

The phrase "the dark night of the soul" comes from a book written by the 17th-century Spanish mystic and Doctor of the Church, St. John of the Cross. It refers to an emotional state experienced by contemplatives which is characterized by intense desolation. The phrase has come to be used as a generic term to describe a part of the spiritual journey whereby the sources of consolation previously relied upon, which may well be good in themselves, are removed. The natural reaction of the contemplative person when he experiences this is to assume that he has done something wrong and has sinned in some way. In most accounts

---

[1] St. John of the Cross, *Dark Night of the Soul*, Bk. 2, Ch. 22. Section 2.
[2] Psalm 40(39):5, Coverdale translation

I have read the person then talks to his spiritual director who informs him that he has not sinned, but rather that this indicates that he is at a particular point on his spiritual journey and that it is a good thing. This knowledge gives the afflicted soul hope, and this hope transcends any anxiety that persists.

Contemplation (as we will describe more fully later in this book) is a passive state in which God communicates with the spirit directly without mediation from the senses. It is a gift from God and while the person can *meditate* as an act of will and these exercises in meditation can lead the mind to that state of readiness whereby it is ready to receive God, nothing can guarantee that *contemplation* will actually happen. We cannot order up God on demand. His manifestation of presence and the nature of that manifestation is always subject to his will. His reasons for choosing to be present to us or not in this way or that are beyond our comprehension.

When people refer to contemplative prayer, therefore, they are not indicating the contemplation is performed as an act of the will of the one who prays. Rather, they are referring to a program of prayer that is intended to take that person to the point where they are more open to experience contemplation, should God decide to bestow it upon them. A contemplative (or a mystic) in the sense that I use it here is one who engages regularly in contemplative prayer. In this sense every one of us is meant to be a contemplative to some degree and to be open, at least, to this profound deepening of the mysteries of the Faith. However, some are meant to devote more of their time to it than others. Often in spiritual literature when someone is described as a contemplative, they are referring to people whose particular charism is contemplative prayer – for example Carmelite monks and nuns.

The goal of contemplative prayer is to develop the faculty of being receptive to God and to his Word at all times, most especially during our participation in the Sacred Liturgy, with the ultimate goal of union with God in heaven. The heavenly state is a permanent contemplative state and all that we do on earth ought to be done with heavenly contemplation in mind. In this life, however, the aspiring contemplative may never actually experience true contemplation, but that does not mean he has failed. If he has applied himself well to contemplative prayer, then his participation in the Sacred Liturgy will be deeper in all ways desired by God.

Also, strange as it may seem, contemplative prayer as a programmed activity is not necessary for contemplation to occur in this life (although it seems to help). God is not restricted or controlled by our actions of prayer and he can reveal himself to whomever he chooses whenever he pleases, even to non-Christians, as he did to St. Paul on the road to Damascus before he converted.

Techniques for contemplative prayer are described in the next section of the book and more information on contemplative prayer itself is given there. In regard to this chapter and our discussion on joy, we return now to consideration of the 'dark night of the soul.'

God is teaching the mystic a new mode of perception of his gifts

When someone experiences the dark night, it is a consequence of an act of God.

The intellect which hitherto has relied on information and experiences mediated by the senses is being led into a mode of perception that relies on direct communication with the spirit by God, unmediated by the bodily senses. Initially, the sensory part of the soul is incapable of grasping the goods offered to the spirit directly and so is deprived of information – it is in the dark, so to speak. Because God does not communicate information that relates to him through the senses as he did before there is no discursive succession of thought by the intellect, which is accustomed to responding to information fed to it via the senses. Therefore, the intellect has no past memories of anything similar to draw upon and the imagination is completely dark too. This is why it is called a 'dark night.' The internal senses of the intellect are in the dark in regard to their normal mode of operation.

There is an even more intense dark night after this, which John of the Cross also describes, in which the intellect steadily changes its nature from human to divine and "no longer understands by means of its natural vigor and light, but by means of the divine wisdom" to which it is united. What is happening is that the manner of loving changes in the process of divinization.[3] St. John says:

> United with the divine love, it no longer loves in a lowly manner, with its natural strength, but with the strength and purity of the Holy Spirit; and thus the will does not operate humanly in relation to God.[4]

In each case, the darkness – the denial of the old mode of reception – is experienced as a form of suffering before the intellect adapts to the new mode of expression, and we have joy. At first, therefore, it might seem that perhaps the dark night is an exception to the premise that joy is part of the gift of the Faith regardless of one's personal circumstances. However, my reading seems to suggest that this is not the case. The experience of the dark night is analogous to the Christian's bearing of physical suffering. The Christian life does not necessarily remove it, but rather it offers a consolation that is more powerful than it so that the person experiences at once both the suffering and the greater consolation that arises from it. I do not have any personal experience to relate here because I don't think I have experienced a dark night (certainly not as dramatically and intensely in the manner of John of the Cross at any rate).

During this second type of dark night the person is transformed supernaturally so that rather than relating to the human nature of the person of Christ, he relates to Christ's divine nature. As he gradually partakes more and more of the divine nature, the person enters into the mystery of the Trinity, since his divine nature can relate to the other persons of the Trinity directly now too. This is what all Christians are promised and so in itself is not unusual, although it is unusual to have this degree in our earthly lives.

---

[3]Divinization – partaking of the divine nature – is, remember, available to every person and happens to all Christians to the degree that they conform to the sacramental life.

[4]St. John of the Cross, *Dark Night of the Soul*, Bk. 2, Ch. 4. Section 2. (para. 2)

What is particular in the dark night it is the negation of consolation from all but the highest good given to the person. Ordinarily, all goods and the pleasures derived from them co-exist. In the proper order there is pleasure from all goods from the lowest to the highest and each contributes in harmony to the general happiness of the person. In the dark night, the pleasure of the lower goods is denied and if the person tries to partake of them it might be experienced as totally lacking in the old pleasure – dry and unfulfilling – or even painful. The darkness and the distress of this denial is great because much that was previously seen as good and godly now appears not to be so. This is not the purging of sin, but rather the steady purging of a reliance on lesser goods so as to accelerate the development of the faculty of grasping the highest good. Again, this absence of goods is perceived as a profound darkness:

> Since the wisdom of this contemplation is the language of God to the soul, of Pure Spirit to pure spirit, all that is less than spirit, such as the sensory, fails to perceive it. Consequently, this wisdom is secret to the senses; they have neither the knowledge nor the ability to speak of it, nor do they even desire to do so because it is beyond words.[5]

These words of St. John of the Cross are in accord with those of St. Paul who wrote in his Letter to the Corinthians: "We teach what Scripture calls: the things that no eye has seen and no ear has heard, things beyond the mind of man, all that God has prepared for those who love him. These are the very things that God has revealed to us through the Spirit." [6]

The person now becomes steadily more accustomed to looking at the Light of God. The natural inclination is to turn away from this blinding light, but God has removed all pleasure derived from looking anywhere else and that combined with the fact that the desire for God is so great means that he keeps looking until his eyes become accustomed to what previously dazzled.

---

[5] St. John of the Cross, *Dark Night of the Soul*, Bk. 2, Ch. 17. Section 4. (para. 2)
[6] 1 Cor. 2:9-10, taken from the scripture reading for Vespers, Friday Week 14 in Ordinary Time.

As the person has free will he could have chosen to be free of this particular suffering by stepping out of whole cycle and rejecting God. However, the holy mystic does not reject God but willingly bears the anguish until God decides to remove it, because he is fired by the love of God whom he desires more than anything else.

However, even while this acute distress is felt, which — make no mistake — is real and profound, the highest and deepest aspect of the soul, the spirit, feels a companionship that is so great that in his heart he is happy. For even in these great afflictions the spirit is aware of God's love for the person. John of the Cross puts it thus: "In the midst of these dark and loving afflictions, the soul feels a certain companionship and an interior strength." [7]

The best analogy to this that I have heard is that of parents of a large family who are suffering sleep deprivation, worry about financial difficulties, and children who are rebellious and difficult. On top of this they have to get up in the middle of the night to attend to a screaming baby. None of these things are pleasant or comfortable and at this moment all the difficulties will be concentrated in the mind of the fatigued parents in reaction to this latest screamed demand, made without "please" or "thank you." The parent could be rid of all these problems if there were no children, but would never consider trading for that option. Love for the child means that they get up and offer themselves, and deep down that love is what makes them happy, despite all the difficulties.

The dark night is like this except more so in terms of depth of the anguish and the love respectively.

The dark night is usually temporary and short-lived. But not always. Wikipedia mentions the exceptional case of St. Paul of the Cross who suffered a dark night for 45 years. The recently canonized saint of our own times Mother Teresa of Calcutta, according to private writings made public after her death, also endured a dark night lasting many years

---

[7] St. John of the Cross, *Dark Night of the Soul*, Bk. 2, Ch. 11. Section 7. (para. 2)

during which she took consolation in believing that she was sharing supernaturally in the sufferings of Christ.

However long the dark night lasts, the wait would seem to be worth it. St. John of the Cross describes the period after his purgation as one of unambiguous spiritual delight that went beyond all he had previously imagined.

The danger of reading *The Dark Night of the Soul*

Contemplation of the exact variety and intensity that St. John of the Cross describes is, as I have already mentioned, rare and so would only apply to a small minority of the faithful. However, *The Dark Night of the Soul* has consistently been a bestseller among spiritual books since it first came out in the 16th century. This means that many more people have read about the spiritual state than have actually experienced it.

When I first saw the book on the shelves of the spiritual bookstore in Covent Garden, I was in the early stages of the *Vision for You* process. I couldn't resist buying and reading it. The effect on me was that I started to imagine that I was scaling the spiritual heights and concluded that any period of anxiety or unhappiness I happened to be going through was my own divinely bestowed dark night. When I mentioned this to David, his response was pretty quick: "Don't flatter yourself, lad. You're not that holy yet." He had no interest in discussing it further and closed the conversation by telling me offhandedly to write a gratitude list and do a review of conscience so that I could snap out of my self-pity (guidance that will mean more to you after you read the next section of this book). Then he told me to go out and be of service to others.

I found out later that I was not unusual in my reaction to reading this book. Nearly everyone I have discussed it with reacted in exactly the same way. Perhaps some of the others were genuinely going through a dark night; I don't know. But I can speak with greater certainty about myself and I now think that what I was trying to do was avoid taking responsibility for my unhappiness by convincing myself that I was a spiritual guru in the making. I imagined that even my self-pity, the very worst of me, was in fact experiencing a special holy self-pity and a gift from God. This was great, I thought, because it meant that I could now justly demand that people indulge me in it and take pity on me and treat me better. This was a self-centered reaction which almost certainly indicates that this wasn't a dark night of the St. John of the Cross variety.

There was another form of self-flattery that I was indulging in. Some passages I had read when reading further about the dark night suggested that it involved suffering connected to a participation in the undeserved suffering of Christ, a sort of spiritual equivalent to the stigmata. ("stigmata" is the name given to the actual physical appearance of the wounds the suffering Christ endured in saints such as Padre Pio and Francis of Assisi.) In addition to physical suffering, Christ experienced great *spiritual* suffering during His Passion as well. We can begin to imagine this by reflecting on the relief of spiritual suffering in the form of fear and resentment that we experience after a single good sacramental Confession. In one historical event, by contrast, Christ experienced all the pain of all the sins ever to be committed in the whole of human history before or since. That is misery indeed. What's more, he himself never sinned; we did the sinning and he took on the pain. That is an act of love beyond imagination.

Some mystics have participated in this immense spiritual suffering out of love of Christ and for the good of man, experiencing that past historical event in the present by supernatural means as part of the mystical body of Christ. St. Teresa of Calcutta went through this, as we now know from her diary and letters published posthumously. So, here's what happened to me when I read the *Dark Night of the Soul*: in my conceit I thought of myself one of this select group. Perhaps, I thought, even higher than Padre Pio and St. Francis because where they only took on the physical suffering of Our Lord, I am accorded the privilege of taking on his spiritual suffering. How good is that?

If David had allowed me to continue in this vein of thought (and vanity of thought) then it would have undermined all possibility for future happiness for it would have distracted me from the true cause of my unhappiness: sin. I am glad he knocked me off my pedestal so sharply.

In fact, the natural initial response to a genuine dark night is the exact opposite of mine. It is one of a humility (not my personal forte) that assumes first that the cause is one's own sin. This is because the experience of the holy person up to that point is that all unhappiness *is* caused by sin. Even spiritual giants like John of the Cross thought this at first until they were told that it was not the case.

This idea of a 'holy depression' is so attractive to some that it seems to have caught the public imagination and found a place even in contemporary popular culture. Every New Age guru worth his salt, for example, will describe going through his own dark night as a badge of honor. We hear about it in pop songs and even the Batman flicks directed by Christopher Nolan seem to be making an allusion to it. The misunderstood and suffering-but-virtuous hero is called the Dark Knight. The allusion is accentuated by an almost complete lack of daylight in the films.

Most of the popular portrayals of the dark night that I have seen seem to do a good job of emphasizing the idea of the suffering of the good man on behalf of others, but what seems less often appreciated is that the dark night is at its very heart a form of *happiness*. In the deepest place, where he decides for or against God, the person is happy for he chooses God. At every other level there may be distress and anxiety, but because at the deepest level there is joy the sufferer can still say, hand on heart, that life is good.

As in Benedict's description of Boethius facing execution in prison, the virtue of hope is the antidote for the dark night for St. John of the Cross. Hope provides solace, and is especially suited to dealing with a present suffering, because it brings into the present, in our minds, the good which is assured to us in the future. As St. John says:

Hope has this characteristic: it covers all the senses of a person's head so they do not become absorbed in any worldly thing, nor is there any way some arrow from the world might wound them. Hope allows the soul only a visor that it may look toward heavenly things, and no more. This is the ordinary task of hope in the soul; it raises the eyes to look only at

God. ⁸And again:

> Hope empties and withdraws the memory from all creature possessions, for as St. Paul says, hope is for that which is not possessed [Rom. 8:24]. It withdraws the memory from what can be possessed and fixes it on what it hopes for. Hence only hope in God prepares the memory perfectly for union with him.⁹

St. John then goes on to explain that the reason he wrote his book, *Dark Night of the Soul*, is so that those experiencing this dark night might understand what it is they are going through and might have the consolation that transcends their current trials, which is that theological virtue of hope:

> What was more important and the reason I undertook this task was to explain this night to many souls who in passing through it do not understand it, as is pointed out in the prologue. The nature of this night has now been explained to some extent. We have also discussed the many blessings this night brings to the soul – though in a way that makes them seem less than what they in fact are – and how great a grace it is for one who passes through it. We have written of these blessings so that when souls become frightened by the horror of so many trials they might take courage in the sure hope of the many advantageous blessings obtained from God through these trials.¹⁰

The words of the psalmist come to mind here: "Blessed [i.e., happy] is the man who has set his hope in the Lord."¹¹

Dealing with the dark night if you go through it

I am not aware of having gone through anything so extreme as the sainted Doctor seems to describe – unless the principles of *the process* are

---

⁸St. John of God, *Dark Night of the Soul*, Bk. 2, Ch. 21. Section 7. (para. 2)

⁹Ibid Bk. 2, Ch. 21. Section 3. (para. 2)

¹⁰Ibid Bk. 2, Ch. 22. Section 2.

¹¹Psalm 40(39):5, Coverdale translation

so effective in dealing with it that I have dealt with it and it has dissipated before I was aware of being in it. However, this is what I hope I would do if I experienced a dark night.

Clearly the first thing would be to seek a spiritual director, ask for advice and then take heart because regardless of what I feel emotionally in the moment, I can be assured that God is with me and my hope will not be in vain. For some people, such as Mother Teresa, it seems that at times hope was all she had. But her hope was strong and her Faith never wavered, as evidenced by the fact that it led her to strive more, not love less.

How do you practice hope? It seems to me that this comes back to the same thing that David told me right at the start: to act as though there is a God and as though all of this is leading somewhere even if I don't 'feel' any certainty of this at that moment. I must persevere in my prayers, good works, and spiritual exercises even if the actions themselves seem empty and unrewarding. Rest assured, I was told, they will still be adding to my general happiness, and things will improve, in time. Developing the habits of doing these things in the face of slight discouragements, will help to ensure that I will continue to do them in the face of greater discouragements, such as, should God decide it in his wisdom, an intense dark night.

Reading accounts of the spiritual life written by people other than St. John of the Cross, it appears that people more commonly suffer aspects of the dark night by degrees than in such an intense and dramatic way. Some of these degrees are so gradual that they almost seem to be just the natural process of growing up and maturing that we all ought to go through – 'growing old gracefully' as we might say.

My grandpa was a lesson in this for me. When he was a young man, he was a very good rugby player (almost at international level). My granny told me that after his 30th birthday he just suddenly decided to stop playing rugby and instead took up tennis and golf, which were less physically demanding sports. He played tennis for the local tennis club and got his golf handicap down to 5 at one point. Then twenty years later at the age of 50 he decided to give up golf and tennis and took up beekeeping as his main hobby. He became active in the local beekeeping society and even wrote a regular column for the local newspaper (in rural Northumberland in England). He was still beekeeping at the age of 83 when he died. I only knew him during the beekeeping phase of his life.

If Grandpa had any regrets about not playing rugby or tennis or golf any more, I never heard him express them. The sense I got was that he felt he was about ready to do something different when his capacity to derive pleasure from the old pastime activities began to diminish. He understood that for a man of 70, for example, rugby was a lesser good than beekeeping and when he did what was right for a 70-year-old man, he derived greater pleasure from life.

I used to play a lot of sports as well and enjoyed them immensely. I played soccer until I was 33, tennis until I was 42, and now I enjoy country walks – something which I have always done since I was young, but it is one activity I can still maintain now. I am different from my grandpa in two ways. First, I wasn't as good at sports as he was (which was something I had to come to terms with). Second, I was a lot less graceful in my transitions from one activity to another. I was slower to recognize that I was changing and that soccer, for example, was now a lesser good than tennis. I went through greater periods of frustration and self-pity about getting older and not being able to do things as well as I used to. In the end the change was imposed on me when recurring minor injuries forced me out of each sport. It took me a while to get used to the idea that I couldn't do them any longer. After the period of transition was over, during which I had to use the methods of the process that David had given me, I reached a point that I no longer regretted the change and was glad that I had been forced into it, because I was happier in the place I had been taken to. This process has been mirrored in a development of my other interests, in that I gradually moved into things less physical and more academic. Steadily, painting and writing have occupied more and more of my time.

Interestingly, when my grandpa died the local paper in Hexham, Northumberland ran a small article about him under the headline, "Sports Hero Dies." It was a well written and respectful piece. It spoke for the most part of his achievements in rugby and how under his leadership the local rugby club at this small market town in northern England had become prominent nationally for a while in the 1930s. When we saw it, my granny remarked: "Isn't sport overrated! When I think of him now there is so much more about him than his rugby achievements, which seem such a minor part of our life together."

This pattern of a seamless transition from lesser things to greater and a natural progression in life ought to characterize the person's entire journey to God, it seems to me. Just as in my Grandpa's hobbies, we should expect to see changes from lesser goods to greater goods in our spiritual lives too, following the progression described by St. Paul: "When I was a child I talked like a child, I had the intelligence and thoughts of a child. Since I became a man I have outgrown childish ways. At present we are looking at a confused reflection in a mirror; then we shall see face-to-face; now I have only glimpses of knowledge; then I shall recognize God as he has recognized me."[12]

In matters of prayer and the sacramental life, it may not always be that I should change the outward activity; rather, I am being nudged onward by God so that my participation in these activities is progressively richer and more elevated. I have to make spiritual progress that will affect change in the way I approach such activities at a level deep in the heart.

For example, I have experienced emptiness and dryness of prayer and worship, something that many describe. At times even participating in a Mass with wonderful chant or polyphony does not offer the same emotional experience that I had when I first stumbled into the Brompton Oratory. Fortunately, I have never doubted that the Mass is good for me regardless of how bored or disinterested I might feel at times when there. I know that being present at Mass contributes to my general happiness and that it is the right thing to do.[13]

---

[12] 1 Cor. 13:11-12, Knox translation

[13] This may not be quite at the level of the holy mystic who suddenly found that at communion, previously a moment of great joy, the Blessed Sacrament gave physical pain to their mouth; but it is, perhaps, a participation in something similar that gives me a hint, at least, of what a holier person might be going through.

Similarly, with prayer: there is often a renewed enthusiasm with some new introduction or discovery of a technique of say, contemplative prayer. I look forward to doing it and afterwards feel as though I am walking on air. Then the novelty wears off. The tendency at this point is to want to drop it or to introduce a change to reinvigorate it with some fresh novelty. Other things being equal, the answer is not to change the experience, but to accept that these are still the things that will take me forward regardless of how I feel emotionally during the experience. It is the effect on my life generally that I should be examining, rather than how I feel during or immediately following the period of prayer itself. It is like riding a bicycle. I haven't changed my pedaling technique since I first rode without stabilizers when I was very young. In order to keep moving forward I do what I have always done, pedal. The thrill of riding without stabilizers is not what it was when I was five, but I keep pedaling nevertheless, and that keeps me moving forward.

I do sometimes experience moments of anxiety or fear in which I feel that God has deserted me or is perhaps punishing me. Paradoxically, this fear is only possible when I have some faith, because if I had no faith in God I couldn't possibly be bothered by the thought that God had abandoned me! What I need therefore is even greater faith. In confession once, the priest told me to repeat the prayer, "Oh God, I believe; help me with my unbelief," (Mk. 9:24) as a response to this feeling. Over time I have found that a fear that God has abandoned me is always linked to my self-centeredness. When I am thinking about myself to the exclusion of God I become fearful. Again, the cultivation of gratitude is the great cure for this, as well as the exercises for eliminating fear that I will describe in the next section.

St. Teresa of Avila remarked after seeing God in her ecstatic experience (as portrayed so dramatically in the famous sculpture by Bernini) that all of this life, even the greatest parts, seemed irrecoverably dull by comparison. I have never had an experience like hers and cannot even imagine what it must be like. In some ways this gives me an advantage over St. Teresa, in that I still find that I am able to derive pleasure from this ordinary life a little more naturally than she was able to at that point.

The most powerful way to dispel fear and return to God is love. It always comes back to love. When all else fails, working to be of service to others will raise my spirits even when mental exercises alone fail.

In the next chapter, we put the dark night into the general picture of happiness. But first, pray joyfully…

Bend my heart to your will, Oh God.
I ask this in the name of my Lord Jesus Christ.

9 Blessed Are the Poor in Spirit, For They Shall See God

More about happiness – looking to the Apostles and Saints

One wonders if the dark night of St. John of the Cross is an intense version of what Our Lord was talking about when he gave us this Beatitude in the Sermon on the Mount. Pope St. Leo the Great writes:

> What kind of poverty, then, is blessed? The kind that is not in love with earthly things and does not seek worldly riches: the kind that longs to be filled with the blessings of heaven.

> After our Lord himself, the Apostles have given us the best example of this greatness of heart in poverty. When their Master called, they instantly left behind all that they possessed, and from catching fish they turned swiftly to fishing for men. Their example inspired many to emulate their faith and so become like them: it was at this time that these first sons of the Church were of one heart and there was one spirit among believers. With all their possessions stripped away they received the riches of eternal blessings, and through the Apostles' preaching they rejoiced at having nothing that the world could give and possessing all things with Christ.

> So it was that when the blessed apostle Peter was going up into the Temple and the cripple begged him for alms, he replied *I have*

> *neither silver nor gold, but I will give you what I have: in the name of Jesus Christ the Nazarene, walk!* *[Acts 3:6]* What could be higher than this lowliness? What could be richer than this poverty? He cannot give the support of money, but he can give the gift of a restored nature. From the womb his mother brought him forth a cripple; by a word Peter raises him up to health. He did not give the image of Caesar stamped on a coin but he restored the image of Christ in the man himself.[1]

This appears to illustrate my point that the poverty of spirit which is a great longing for Christ is itself a state of blessedness (that is happiness) for we are told, without equivocation, that we will see God through supernatural transformation in Christ. The outward healing of the physical ailments of the cripple is a blessing in itself also, of course, and is also symbol of the inner healing that is open to all of us as we seek restoration of our true nature through the Church.

David described two powerful experiences that, when I think about them now, could well have been contemplative. At the very least they were moments of grace in which there was a strong consolation – I will leave it to the theologians among you to work out exactly what was going on.

The first incident I heard him relate only once in the nine years that I knew him. He described what he called "some sort of spiritual experience" in which he had a very strong sense of the presence of God, not because he saw or felt God directly, but because of the consolation it gave him. He said it was characterized by a great calm and the perfect conviction that everything was going to be fine, even when all was falling apart, God was with him. Furthermore, he said, he simply knew that would be true also for anyone else who placed their trust in God. I do not know precisely what he was describing but I always felt that this experience was crucial to his ability to pass the process on to others. When he first told me, for example, that he believed that what he was passing on to me would benefit every aspect of my life, he said it with a conviction that was infectious. He made me believe it too.

---

[1] Pope St. Leo the Great on the Beatitudes, taken from the Office of Readings, Friday Week 22 in Ordinary Time.

The other occasion he spoke about more often. In order to illustrate how powerful the process is, he used to tell people about the experience of his third heart attack (it was the fourth, some years later, that killed him). As I write this, I can't remember the full story, but I do remember David describing how he was ignored for quite a long time while lying on the roadside of the very busy Wandsworth High Street in London. He was gasping for breath and unable to speak, with traffic rushing past and all the pedestrians stepping over him because they thought he was drunk. He wasn't absolutely sure what was happening to him physically, but he knew it was not good. He said that he couldn't think of anything to do but say the Serenity Prayer to himself repeatedly (see next chapter for the text of that prayer). As he did so he said that, as in his other experience, he became calm and knew that whatever happened, he was being looked after. He still thought he might die, but now he did not fear it. Eventually someone must have realized what was happening and called an ambulance and he survived that heart attack.

St. Ignatius of Loyola on temporary pleasure and joy

I mentioned previously the importance of distinguishing between superficial pleasure and true happiness or joy. A way of characterizing the difference between the two comes from an account of the founder of the Society of Jesus (the Jesuits) in the 16th century, St. Ignatius of Loyola.

Ignatius was Spanish, of a Basque noble family. As a young man he was not a man of faith. He was a soldier and at one time was injured in battle and was recuperating. He was given to reading "exaggerated accounts of illustrious deeds by the famous" the equivalent today, one imagines, of watching Hollywood feature films that portray tales of derring-do.

When Ignatius had read all that he could find he asked for more books of that type. None were available, so he was given two spiritual Christian books called *The Life of Christ* and *Flower of the Saints*. Reluctantly he read them. As an account of his life relates:

> He noticed a difference in how he felt as read the two sorts of book. With those of the first type, in which he was intent on worldly

pleasure and fame, he felt great pleasure at the time, but whenever he wearied of them and gave them up he felt dejected and empty. On the other hand, when he thought of the austerities which the holy men practiced, not only did he find joy in the account of them, but when he stopped thinking of them his joy remained unabated.[2]

Look at the general effect – applying the Ignatian test

Some temporary pleasures add to my joy, others will undermine it. The task is to try to differentiate between the two. When judging the good of something that I experience I must distinguish between any temporary pleasure that it might bring and the overall effect that it has on my life. Narcotics can bring great temporary pleasure but have a detrimental effect on my life overall. Similarly, sometimes there are things that are bitter medicine – not pleasant in themselves yet the effect they have outside of the experience of actually taking the medicine is good. The purpose of something unpleasant may be one of directing us to a particular response so that a greater joy comes out of it.

Therefore, we cannot judge the good of something on the temporary feeling alone. It is not always true that if something immediately feels good or is pleasurable or enjoyable it is good. Neither can we say the opposite, that medicine must always be bitter. The rule 'no pain, no gain' may apply in some situations such as physical exercise (perhaps), but as a general rule for life it is profoundly false. Rather, we should disregard the temporary and judge the good of a thing on how we feel in general.

Also, when considering whether or not we wish to do something, we can save ourselves a lot of bother if we look to the testimonies and experience of others. We can look at the overall effect that such an act has had on the lives of others who have done it. For example, we don't need to try heroin to decide that it is bad. No matter how pleasurable the temporary experience of taking it promises to be, we look at the general picture of the lives of heroin addicts.

---

[2] *Acts of St. Ignatius taken down by Luis Gonzalez* from the Office of Readings, July 31st, Commemoration of St. Ignatius.

As a rule, it is natural for us to seek those things that are both enjoyable or pleasurable in the moment and have a beneficial effect in the long term. The good news is that that there are plenty of those as well. Furthermore, as we develop the habit of doing the right thing, we associate the long-term effect more and more strongly with a particular action or experience that might in itself be unpleasant. At this point, we see the whole picture, which is good, and that transcends the feeling of the moment. In time this can develop to the degree that the experience itself is truly joyful even though superficially unpleasant. This is what happens as we develop a taste for what is good.

In deciding what is right and good, be guided by good authority

In order to guide us in our activity, the Church infallibly draws on the Revelation that comes to us in Tradition (with a capital 'T') and this includes Holy Scripture. In those matters in which the Church is an authority, matters of faith and morals for example, it is particularly important not to be guided by temporary feelings, but rather by the teachings of the Church. When our personal enjoyment of liturgy, for example, is at odds with the teaching of the Church on what is right in the liturgy, we should always persist in choosing to attend liturgies that are in accord with Church teaching.

Over time, appreciation of what is truly good can develop within us to the degree that we find pleasure even in a superficially unpleasant experience, because of its association with the general effect of good that we know it brings. This is how holy people can genuinely enjoy the fasting and penance of Lent, for example. It is by fixing our sights on the overall or future good that we develop the motivation that disciplines us to do what is right in life.

This idea is reinforced by one of the biblical readings for the Liturgy of the Hours during Lent: *"This day is sacred to the Lord your God. Do not be mournful, do not weep. For this day is sacred to our Lord. Do not be sad: the joy of the Lord is your stronghold."*[3]

---

[3] Nehemiah 8:9,10 from Lauds of the Fourth Sunday in Lent.

We can also look to tradition (with a lowercase 't') for guidance. This is the positive experience of the past that has been passed down through the generations. The writings of the Church Fathers, for example, are not infallible but nevertheless worthy of great respect. As a general principle, a respect for things that have been effective over an extended period of time for many people is an attitude that is going to help us.

If all this is true, why aren't all Christians happy?

If all this is true it does raise the question, why aren't more Christians obviously happy, or at least happy enough to attract others to the faith? Clearly, in writing as he did about the new evangelization Benedict XVI believed that there weren't enough Catholics showing those outside the Church "the art of living joyfully."

Here is Peter Kreeft again on the subject:

> [Christian joy] is not an ideal, but a given reality. It is given not only to saints and mystics, but to all Christians… for it is God. God does not give joy. God is joy. And he gives Himself (and therefore joy) without limit…
>
> Nor do we feel it, but feeling is only another kind of seeing… Once we believe this – that we already have the joy we want even if we do not feel it – the feeling follows. It is like earthly happiness: grab after it and it escapes you; forget the feeling and seek the good instead of happiness, and feelings and happiness come unsought.[4]

We need eros to feel joy

The goal here is to consummate the 'possession' of joy into a joy that is known and felt. When we feel it, to put it simply, we feel happy. I would put Kreeft's point slightly differently by adding one detail: I would say that a joy that is not yet felt is not yet fully possessed. At this point it is still for us, in part, unrealized and potential joy. It is unrealized because, although as Kreeft rightly points out, God has given himself to us, but

---

[4] Peter Kreeft: *Everything You Ever Wanted to Know About Heaven, But Never Dreamed of Asking*; pub Ignatius, 1990, p198

we have not yet accepted that gift; that is, we have not taken possession of it fully and offered ourselves in return. What is lacking is our *eros* – the ordered acceptance of the gift in response to God's *agape* and then our own *agape* – the giving of ourselves in love. We *feel* that joy when we *know* God; when we *see* him; or when we *believe*, in the fullest sense of the word.

Knowing, seeing, believing – each can all be partially realized as well as fully realized. We can *know* of someone or all about them, but we do not truly know them until we have encountered them personally. We may *see* dimly as though through cataracts or with clouded vision as though at a "confused reflection in a mirror," but we cannot see clearly until we become pure in heart. We can *believe* in the existence of God yet hate him just as the devil does, but we do not truly believe in God unless we *love* him.

Love is the key. Each of these faculties is completed by the love of God – his love for us and our response and acceptance of it. We know fully, see clearly, and believe firmly when we do so in love… and then we feel joy. Indeed, the Catechism tells us that joy is one of the fruits of love (charity).[5]

If we want to feel joy, therefore, we must grow in love. And if we want to grow in love we must practice love as a habit until it becomes our natural *modus operandi*. This is exactly what everything in the process David outlined was directing me to.

Our spirit and the Holy Spirit – joy is a fruit of the Spirit

When we encounter God, our spirit is engaged first with the Holy Spirit. The Holy Spirit draws us to Christ, who pours out the Spirit in abundance. Through cooperation with the Spirit in the *agape-eros* dynamic we accept the gift of the Holy Spirit. This gift is Love. God is Love and love is his first gift, containing all others. The other gifts that are contained within that love that is poured into our hearts through the Holy Spirit are known as the seven gifts of the Holy Spirit. These are: wisdom, understanding,

---

[5]Cf. CCC 1829

counsel, fortitude, knowledge, piety, and fear of the Lord. These *gifts* bear fruit through continued cooperation with grace yielding the twelve *fruits* of the Holy Spirit: love, joy, peace, patience, kindness, goodness, generosity, faithfulness, gentleness, modesty, self-control, and chastity. These benefits are not given to us directly by the Holy Spirit, but are derived, by our cooperation with grace, from what is given. Through the power that the Holy Spirit gives us we grow in virtue and become like Christ. St. Basil tells us: "Through the Holy Spirit we are restored to paradise, led back to the Kingdom of heaven, and adopted as children, given confidence to call God 'Father' and to share in Christ's grace to be called children of light and given a share in eternal glory." [6]

The fruits of love belong in their fullness to Christ.[7] And as with all else, it is through the liturgy that we participate in this superabundant love. We engage personally with Christ as man and through Christ as God we see the Father. The Spirit is the Love between each of us and Christ, and the Love between each of us, now deified, and the Father. We adore the Father, through the Son, in the Spirit, and the worship of God in the Sacred Liturgy draws us up to the consummation of all that is Good.

The Holy Spirit never speaks to us of himself and rarely speaks to us directly. His presence is not felt emotionally. We know of Him by his effects, such as his revealing of Christ; through the gifts he gives us, the fruits that ensue, and the effects of prayer; and through Revelation. He speaks to us also through secondary and inspired sources such as the Church, the saints, scripture, the liturgy and so on. This is worth noting, as the importance of emotion as a direct indicator of the workings of the Holy Spirit tends to be over-emphasized today. It can be dangerous to rely too heavily on either the strength of a conviction or the intensity of an emotion when judging whether or not God is speaking to us.

The exercises, prayers and meditations given in the next part of this book describe what David told me to do. This is the process by which I might be transformed and become a better lover. As you will discover as you

---

[6] St. Basil, De Spiritu Sancto, 15, 36

[7] This section on the nature of the Holy Spirit is drawn from the CCC 688, 733-736, 1830-1832

go on to do these things, each one addresses a different type of failure to love God and be joyful. David directed me toward the habitual practice of love through the love of my fellow man by asking me to commit myself to the service of others. My faith and my hope are reinforced by daily asking God for help and then counting the blessings that he gives me each day so that I can see that he really does answer my prayers as a loving God would. My ability to 'see' God is enhanced through the spiritual exercises whereby I examine my thoughts, feelings, and actions systematically and wherever at fault ask for his forgiveness. Finally, there is a chapter on contemplative prayer, by which we develop the faculty of being receptive to the Spirit.

The pattern of prayer and meditation that David gave me echoes the Sacred Liturgy, and as such gave me the most powerful and effective means of encounter with God that was possible for someone not yet Catholic. It pointed me to the Sacred Liturgy and primed me so that when I did finally attend a Mass I responded instinctively and this, ultimately, led to my conversion.

Even since my conversion I have continued the discipline of practicing the prayer, meditation and spiritual exercises that David gave me. My experience is that right here, right now, if I love God by doing my best to follow these directions and the commandments of the Church, then *immediately* I will have joy. A joy that is felt.

I hope my readers who do not feel joy now might be helped to do so by this book.

Now pray peacefully…

Bend my heart to your will, Oh God.
I ask this in the name of my Lord Jesus Christ.

Part 2

CHAPTERS 10 - 12

In the next three chapters I describe what we actually do to get the life that is on offer. There are several stages to the process.

The first is the foundation of a simple routine of daily prayer.

When this has been adopted and has started to develop as habit then the next stage is a systematic examination of our moral conduct. This involves, a process of guided and deep reflection by which we look at our past and analyze our thoughts and feelings and account for the causes of any unhappiness we feel. This is the process that finally enabled me to understand precisely how my defective reactions to events and circumstances made me unhappy. It is the acceptance of this truth that gave me a new freedom – a life free of all resentment and fear.

After the completion of this self-examination, we adopt the techniques learned as part of our daily routine of prayer and meditation. This ensures that as more resentments and fears occur (which they inevitably will) we continue to recognize them and allow God to remove them.

After that there is a brief introduction to contemplative prayer that will help to deepen the relationship with God that has resulted from the work done so far.

With this new openness of spirit we have as the result of these prayers and spiritual exercises, we are then ready to move on to the final stage of the process: **Part 3** of this book helps us discern our personal vocation and work towards its realization.

10 A Routine of Prayer, Meditation, and Good Works

A Daily Routine of Prayer and Meditation

Here is the routine of prayer as given to me by David. He wrote it on a paper napkin in a café in London. When I had first come to him I was an atheist, and he was aware of this, so before giving me this prayer routine, he checked that I was willing to believe in a power greater than myself, and that I was ready to take certain actions consistent with this willingness. If I had already been a believer when I met him this would have been unnecessary – he could have taken me straight into the routine of prayer.

The daily routine of prayer and meditation is as follows:

Prayers morning and night

Kneel as you pray to God and say the following:

> **Morning**: *Please God, look after me today and let me do your will so that I might be of service to you and my fellows.*
> **Night:** *Thank you for looking after me today.*

It is important I was told, to get on my knees when saying these prayers because kneeling is an action of humility. When I do this it ensures that both words and action are consistent with the idea that I am appealing to One who is greater than I am. When body and soul are in harmony with each other then the whole person is engaged in prayer, and this is the ideal we strive for. Furthermore, the unity of body and soul is so profound in the human person that sometimes the action can influence the thought. So even if at first my attitude is not one of humility before God, if I kneel as I pray, that can influence my attitude.

Reactive prayers during the day

Anxious or fearful?
Repeat the Serenity Prayer until the anxiety dissipates:

> *God grant me the serenity to accept the things I cannot change, the courage to change the things I can, and the wisdom to know the difference.*

Angry or annoyed at someone?
Pray for the person, through gritted teeth if necessary, and repeat it until you feel better about the person:

> *Please bless [name] and let him have everything I would wish for myself.*

These are prayers that I can use to respond to different situations during the day. Sometimes I think them while I am dealing with others or doing something else. However, if I can find a place to kneel for five minutes and say these prayers repeatedly and in a focused way, it will be very powerful. For example, if someone makes me angry I might excuse myself and go to the bathroom. Then once the door is shut behind me I can kneel in prayer and repeat the prayer until I feel better. Even five minutes is not so long that my absence is likely to cause problems, but it is a long time for repeated prayers. It might be 500 prayers. It is rare that I need that many repetitions to remove any anger or anxiety.

This really works. I know of many people who suffer from anxiety attacks and/or panic attacks who have used the Serenity Prayer in just this way to calm themselves successfully.

There is a school of thought that says that it is good to express your anger. That is not my experience. Anger clouds my judgment and so if I indulge in angry outbursts, I am likely to create more division and difficulty. It is usually better to remove the emotion of anger using the techniques of the process, and then take the course of action in response to the situation that I think is appropriate.

Reflection

Read an ideal for living

I was told to choose a text, or series of texts, that articulate principles of good living and read a little bit each day, even if it is just a couple of paragraphs. The choice you make depends upon where you are on the spiritual journey. Some choose a simple prayer that seems to encapsulate that ideal and read it daily – for example the prayer sometimes called the *Prayer of St. Francis* which begins, 'Lord, let me be an instrument of thy peace…'

In my case, I began by reading the following every day. It was good for me because it had a generic, non-religious feel to it, so it didn't arouse my prejudice. It is called the *Just for Today* card and the text ran like this:

- *Just for today I will try to live through this day only and not tackle my whole life problem at once. I can do something for twelve hours that would appall me if I felt that I had to keep it up for a lifetime.*
- *Just for today I will be happy. Most folks are as happy as they make up their minds to be.*
- *Just for today I will adjust myself to what is and not try to adjust everything else to my desires. I will take my 'luck' as it comes and fit myself to it.*
- *Just for today I will try to strengthen my mind. I will study; I will learn something useful; I will not be a mental loafer; I will read something that requires effort, thought and concentration.*
- *Just for today I will exercise my soul in three ways: I will do somebody a good turn and not get found out; if anybody knows of it, it will not count; I will do*

at least two things I don't want to do, just for exercise. I will not show anyone that my feelings are hurt; they may be hurt, but today I will not show it.

- *Just for today I will be agreeable. I will look as good as I can, dress becomingly, talk low, act courteously, criticize not one bit, not find fault with anything and not try to improve or regulate anybody except myself.*

- *Just for today I will have a program. I may not follow it exactly, but I will have it. I will save myself from two pests: hurry and indecision.*

- *Just for today I will have a quiet half hour all by myself and relax. During this half hour, sometime, I will get a better perspective on my life.*

- *Just for today I will be unafraid. I will enjoy that which is beautiful and will believe that as I give to the world, so the world will give to me.*

Others might prefer to pick a holy book and read part of it daily and work through systematically – the Bible would be the ideal. Or you could focus on part of the Bible daily, for example the gospels or the Letter of St. James or the Book of Psalms. An alternative to the Bible might be the Rule of St. Benedict. You can change the book you read and move from one to the other. Whatever you decide on, read it.

Those who know about the ancient way of reflection on a text called *lectio divina* can do this. For any who do not know how to do it, my book, *The Little Oratory* contains a description.

Count your blessings – write a gratitude list

Write a list of the good things that are in your life today and then, on your knees, thank God for giving them to you. Actually pick up a pen, don't just do this mentally.

When David told me to do this I protested to him that I had nothing to be grateful for. So he wrote my first 'gratitude list' (as he called it) for me. He said first, 'You are alive' then he paused and looked at me and said, this is true isn't it? When I said yes, he wrote 'Alive' on the list; then he asked me 'Have you eaten today?' again when I said yes he wrote down 'Food'; in similar vein he asked me if I had a bed to sleep in tonight, and a roof over my head, clothes to wear and so on. Each time he wrote down a word that encapsulated this blessing. My list looked like this:

Alive, food, bed, roof, clothes.

Then he stopped and looked at me and said, "At this point you are ahead of a significant proportion of the world's population. There are billions of people who don't know where their next meal is coming from. These are the necessities of life. You have told me that it is true that you have every item on this list today. So here is written evidence that God is giving you what you need to day and that when you prayed this morning and asked God to look after you, he answered your prayers."

Then he asked me if there was anything that was good or that I liked about the day that I could add to the list. He encouraged me to think of even little things that I could take pleasure in or could see were good – a sunny day, a funny joke, a pleasant exchange with a stranger, a relaxing cup of coffee. Things that were peculiar to that day:

Sunny day, laughed at funny joke, friendly conversation, cup of coffee, kind word from my boss

Now, David told me, the fact that I was given these blessings today showed that God gave me more than I needed today. These things were more than the basic necessities of life and so they were luxuries. I had thought that my life was miserable and had nothing to recommend it, and in five minutes David had showed me that God had answered my prayers that morning by giving me all that I needed and more. Furthermore, I could now see that he had been looking after me ever since I was born, even during those periods when I rejected him altogether. God is indeed generous. This was helping me to see properly the truth of my life: life is good.

Then he said something that sounded tough but is one of the most valuable truths I have ever been told and for this I will always be grateful: "This tells you that regardless of how you *feel* about the day, you *are* having a good day. God is giving you great blessings and has been for years. Therefore, I don't want to hear you complaining about your day again. The task now is to feel good about the good day which we know you are having. That is what the rest of this process will do."

Then he told me to write a list like this one comprising both basic necessities and luxuries, and on my knees thank God every day for the blessings he had given me. It was important, I was told, to actually write them down. Writing forced me to crystallize them in my mind. Similarly taking the act of humility and gratitude was as important as the words, so it was important to thank him when kneeling. If I took these actions, soon I would move from the state of acknowledging that I ought to be grateful, to actually feeling grateful, he said.

And he was right. Very quickly, within a few days, just as he predicted, I began to feel genuinely grateful for the blessings that God was giving me. Once it becomes a habit it takes just a minute or two daily each day. I can scribble ten words or phrases down onto a piece of a paper and thank God for them. Then I just throw the paper away and use a fresh piece the next day. Post-it notes are almost purpose-made for daily gratitude lists.

More items to go on the gratitude list: bad things that happen to us, and people we don't like… I'm serious

David told me along with the good things, he always put the bad things on his gratitude list. He said that although he couldn't always see the reason, he knew that God permitted bad things for a good reason; and so to help him see that and accept it, he always thanked God for those things too. I started to do this too and have found this to be a very powerful tool in helping me to accept that in all that happens God really is looking after me.

The same is true for those people whom I dislike and for whom I have to pray in any day. If I am resentful at them, I should pray for them until I feel better, I was told, then put that name on my gratitude list and thank God for allowing that person into my life. This doesn't mean that I should allow people to walk all over me or take advantage of me unfairly – I must still make judgments as to right and wrong in each situation and act accordingly. But, when I am resentful at the person and the event, then God is giving me the opportunity to be tolerant of a different view and compassionate even if I am taking firm action to change things.

Of course, it is good to pray for those we love and for whom we have good feelings too. This prayer is not limited to those we resent.

Write a 'to-do' list

Each morning, I was told to sit quietly for five minutes or so and run through what I planned to do that day and write it down. I was told not to let this list become a rod to beat myself with, rather it was something to guide me and encourage me to do what is front of me each day. If by the end of the day there are things I haven't managed to do, then I can decide either just to let them go altogether or put them on tomorrow's list. Many of the items on such a list are the mundane activities in life that we must attend to: paying the electricity bill and so on.

From time to time I might be inspired during this period of reflection and have grand ideas of things I can do. Should this happen, I should take care not to presume that everything that comes to me is inspiration from God. Such a presumption can lead us to do the silliest things based upon the misconception that it is God's will. Remember, it is still possible to have bad ideas too. Before taking any drastic action on thoughts that occur it is good to take time to consider whether or not what I propose to do is sensible. If I am doubt, I ask someone else whom I trust for advice.

Reflection and meditation are the same thing… and I thought meditation was about the elimination of thought.

I have used the word 'reflection' to describe certain exercises. I could have easily used the word 'meditation.' I avoided using it because the word meditation has certain connotations today that can cause confusion.

Some time before I began the process, when I was at university, I became interested in meditation. I even paid to learn one technique. This was a form of meditation that came from India and involved the repetition of a mantra and the elimination of all other thoughts until finally the mantra was released and there was mental stillness.

When I heard that reflection and meditation were encouraged as part of *The Vision for You* process, I asked whether I could restart daily meditation using the method I had learned at university. At this point I was told what these words – meditation and reflection – mean in the Western tradition, and how they mean something different in the Eastern tradition. The Western tradition of meditation comes out of Christian mysticism. To meditate in this context means literally 'to think' or alternatively 'to reflect.' Thinking is an active process, not a passive one. To meditate in this context is not to eliminate thought, but rather to direct thoughts to good things and ultimately to God.

The form of meditation that involves the elimination of thought comes from Eastern religions and as was popularized in the Sixties when figures such as the Beatles took guidance from Maharishi Yogi. It was one of these Eastern techniques that I had learnt a few years earlier. There is a form of passive prayer in the Western tradition too, similar in some ways to the Eastern technique. But it is not called meditation. In the Western tradition it is called *contemplation*. Contemplation is something quite distinct from meditation/reflection.

As mentioned, the Christian tradition of contemplative prayer is more like that Eastern form of meditation that I had learnt, but with a critical difference. The goal is not the absence of thought, but rather a state whereby God makes himself known to us and the sole thought occupying the mind is the presence of God. While we can prepare ourselves for this, we cannot make it happen, for it is God's choice whether or not he makes himself present to us in this way. The practice of *lectio divina*, mentioned earlier in this section is one of meditation and prayer that prepares the person for that final stage of contemplation – *contemplatio* – which will happen only if God chooses to make it happen. God's ways are a mystery to us and even if it happens, we cannot interpret its occurrence as reward due to the holy one who is skilled at meditation. Neither can we interpret the denial of it as a punishment. God wills for our benefit and it may or may not involve contemplation.

For those who wish to know more about this, a later chapter goes into the subject of Christian contemplation in more detail.

Good works

One of the conditions that David attached to being taken through the process was to ask that I promise that I would be ready to pass on what I was learning from him to anyone else who wanted it. I have since been privileged to take several dozen people through this process. Each time I did so, I would attach the same condition to it for them.

In addition to this David told me that I had to develop the habit of being of service to others by making a regular sacrifice of time. And ideally it should include service for people with whom I otherwise have little personal connection. If I was helping my friends or family, he said, then that is a wonderful thing, but it is still helping myself indirectly. Things come back to me because they are *my* friends and *my* family. He was not belittling the importance of caring for friends and family, of course – it is important to be ready to do the loving thing with them at all times. Rather, he was saying that it is important to try to be of service to those who are unlikely ever to give back me directly, too. This he said, was closer to the ideal of giving without thought of return and so would be most powerful in transforming me into a better lover. My experience was that as I did my best to do this, I changed as a person and I noticed that other relationships improved as a result. Without always know quite how, it seemed that my contribution to them was to be more loving. The way that I noticed this was as follows: the more I did the process, the nicer everyone else became.

You can decide what form of service you wish to do and it can change over time. Over the years I have volunteered for groups that dealt with homeless people, alcoholics and drug addicts, and people with mental illness. In my case, working with people with drinking problems has been particularly important. Some people (it is not the case with everybody) have particular problems or habits that are so severe that they become barriers to their being able to do these exercises effectively. In my case I had to stop drinking altogether before I could develop spiritually. I found that trying to control it just didn't work for me – I couldn't seem to stop once I started. Sometimes I could stop for a day or two on my own, but after that I would usually start again. I found that by including in my daily routine a request each day to God that he give me the power to stop drinking; and by volunteering to be of service with groups of people who themselves had drinking problems I was able to stop drinking and not start again. In my case, drinking is such a barrier to a happy life that I have always included a prayer for help with my drinking problem in my daily routine.

There will be many organizations in your area for whom you can participate and be of service in a way that you can be most helpful. Ask God, in your daily reflection how you can be of service to your fellows and he will show you.

A possibility for you if you have no obvious place to be of service is to find others who are interested in working through the principles contained in this book. Perhaps you could start your own weekly group that offers workshops and is available for new people to attend.

This routine primes us for its consummation in the worship of God

Although not everybody is ready for this when they start the process (I certainly was not), this pattern of daily personal prayer and spiritual exercises is preparing me for the worship of God in the sacred liturgy of the Church. If you cannot see this right now I pray that one day you may discover the life of greatest joy, which has the worship of God at its heart.

Although the daily routine does not involve worship directly, it is patterned after the liturgy in the following way:

The prayer in the liturgy takes four basic forms: atonement, supplication (or intercession), thanksgiving, and adoration.

Atonement means reparation for harms done; in the context of the Church's sacred liturgy this means for sin. If we ask for mercy for our sins in the sacrament of reconciliation and participate in the sacrifice of the Mass then that is the fullest expression of it. The examination of feelings, thoughts and actions is a participation in this process of reconciliation with God. When we know how to analyze our bad feelings

– resentments and fears – in the way described, then this brings an aspect of atonement into our daily routine.

Supplication, otherwise known as intercession, is asking for things from God so that we might be able to love him and our fellow man better. It is easy to see how this is present in this routine.

Similarly, it is easy, with the daily gratitude list, to see how the routine is priming me for *thanksgiving* in the context of the liturgy too.

Adoration of God is an aspect of worship that is not so obvious in these exercises, but it is there. St. Thomas Aquinas stated:

> Adoration is primarily an interior reverence for God expressing itself secondarily in bodily signs of humility: bending our knee (to express our weakness compared to God) and prostrating ourselves (to show that of ourselves we are nothing).[1]

David did not quote Thomas Aquinas when he told me to 'hit my knees' when I prayed. He just said I should do it and it was a sign of humility. But he was drawing on this Catholic tradition.

This sort of action is right when done for God, but not for anyone else. *A Catholic Dictionary* defines adoration thus:

> Adoration is the word used to express those acts of divine worship which are directed to God only, and of which the characteristics are recognition of His perfection and omnipotence and our own complete dependence upon Him.[2]

Consistent with this, I can remember David telling me that he bowed and kneeled in adoration before no one but God.

The same outward sign – for example, a bow – can indicate a lesser interior act than the worship of God, too. We English curtsy or bow in

---

[1] St. Thomas Aquinas, *Summa Theologiae*, 84.2.
[2] *A Catholic Dictionary*, Donald Attwater, editor, TAN, 1997

the presence of the Queen out of respect for her office. In this case the outward sign does not indicate adoration, but respect and humility and this would be understood. Similarly, when anyone we respect comes into a room, our natural inclination is to stand. These are natural signals of respect for others appropriate to their place relative to our own. How much more natural it is to us, therefore, to show respect to God through both actions and words.

All of this points to the fact that when we do our daily prayers, it is important to kneel in prayer. The posture speaks of what we believe as much as the words.

A summary of the action points from this chapter is contained in the appendices. I suggest that you look at this now and as a daily reference once you start these actions and until they become habits.

Now pray:

Bend my heart to your will, Oh God.
I ask this in the name of my Lord Jesus Christ.

11 A Spiritual Exercise: An Examination of Feelings, Thoughts, and Actions

Part One – Rooting Out the Cause of Our Unhappiness

> 'Happy are you when men hate you and say that you are evil, because of the Son of Man.
> Even if you should suffer for doing what is right, how happy you are!'
>
> Luke 6:22

> **Rejoice when that day comes, and dance for joy, for then your reward will be great in heaven, alleluia.**
>
> Responsory from the Office of Readings, Easter Thursday

A recap: God alone satisfies our desire for happiness. Indeed, that desire for happiness has been planted in us by God to draw us to him through love so that we may be perfectly happy, in full union with him in heaven. In this life our joy is never complete, and we will always have a longing for that greatest joy. However, that does not mean that in this life we are doomed to unhappiness. The Christian life lived to the full is, generally speaking, a happy life. As we move along the road toward our final home and are transformed supernaturally by degrees it is one of ever-increasing joy.

Movement away from God is the cause of unhappiness

Life is a process of change. Time moves forward inexorably and we are aware of this because we and the world around us change constantly. Therefore, whether we like it or not, in this life we are constant travelers, moving forward to our final resting place, which will be in the next. The direction of our motion is critical in this respect. It is always either towards God or away from God. That direction depends on the degree to which that motion is informed by love. When we are moving closer to God then our lives are moved by love and we are happy. We are on the joyful path, the Way of Beauty.

Nobody can remain on the Way of Beauty all the time. The pattern for all of us is one of continual deviation and correction. It is the practice of love, which we call virtue – doing the right thing – that keeps us on that path, and a lack of love that causes us to deviate.

Sin is another word for these freely willed deviations from the good road. Once we sin, we are put into a state of sin – a state of separation from God that results from a deviation from the path he intends for us. We cannot bridge the gap and go back on to the Way of Beauty except through God's grace.

The Catechism puts it as follows:

> To try to understand what sin is, one must first recognize *the profound relation of man to God*, for only in this relationship is the evil of sin unmasked in its true identity as humanity's rejection of God and opposition to him.[1]

It is only through the Church, which was entrusted with and preserves the full truth of divine Revelation, that we can know what sin is, and therefore recognize our own sin; and it is only through the Church, the mystical body of Christ, that we can re-form that relationship with God to the purity that will bring us joy.

---

[1] Catechism of the Catholic Church, 386

Quoting the Catechism again:

> Without the knowledge Revelation gives of God we cannot recognize sin clearly and are tempted to explain it as merely a developmental flaw, a psychological weakness, a mistake, or the necessary consequence of an inadequate social structure, etc. Only in the knowledge of God's plan for man can we grasp that sin is an abuse of the freedom that God gives to created persons so that they are capable of loving him and loving one another.[2]

When we are unhappy, in order to be happy again we must be aware of our sins so that we can highlight the causes of our state of separation from God and then through grace be re-formed.

The conventional way to highlight such causes is compare our conduct against the measure of moral law by asking the question, 'Have I sinned.' If you look at suggested reviews of conscience they will take you through an examination of the thoughts, words, and actions, usually with a series of directed questions in order to highlight where moral law has been contravened. Practicing Catholics will be used to this in one form or another, and if they are not, they probably should be. For Catholics, such an examination of conscience and then confession of the sins in the context of the Sacrament of Reconciliation is vital in the re-establishment of a pure relationship with God, and hence of a happy life.

For those with well-developed consciences and faith, a simple reflection in this manner will highlight all sin, their confessions will be thorough and their lives will be as happy as one can hope to be in this life.

However, for some (and I am one) this common practice is not enough. If I relied on this question alone – have I sinned? – I would still be unhappy for I am not able to recognize my own sin fully by such an examination.

---

[2]Catechism of the Catholic Church, 387

Fortunately, David showed me another way to do a review of conscience which opened the way to a greater happiness. This is the examination of conscience we will describe in this book.

If sin is the cause of all our unhappiness, then this suggests that there is another way we can examine our consciences. In addition to asking ourselves the question, "Have I sinned?" we can ask ourselves the supplemental question: "Am I happy?" For if I am unhappy then I am in sin. This suggests that a further analysis of our unhappiness will reveal to us what those sins are. If we now confess those sins, too, then through the grace of God we will be forgiven, and we can be happy.

If I am unhappy, what exactly am I unhappy about?

David also suggested an additional exercise to help me answer this question if I needed to. He told me to get a pen and paper and write at the top:

I am not happy, joyful and free because…

Then, he told me to write down in ordinary terms what was bothering, for example:

> *I am worried that I am unemployed; I am still hurt by the way that a friend of mine treated me - he ignored me when I waved at him, and I think he doesn't like me;*

> *I hate the office politics and especially the way Mike makes sarcastic comments about my work. It annoys me and makes me think that it might stop my chances of promotion if it continues;*

> *I still feel guilty about something I said to my friend even though I know I didn't do anything wrong, I think I might have hurt his feelings;*

> *I am still suffering because of the way I was treated as a child, which was…*

Some of these things are grave things that have affected us for years. Some are petty things that happened this morning and we know it even as we write it, but it is important that we acknowledge to ourselves how we really feel about such things however petty or childish we think it makes us.

What such an exercise is doing is revealing a whole range of negative emotions that are related to the things I have done, to what has happened to me, and what I think might happen to me in the future. In the case of things I have done, it gives rise to a lingering guilt; in the case of things done to me, I am still unhappy about the way that others treat me or about my circumstances, it is called resentment; and in the case of things that I am worried might happen to me, we call that fear.

In order to be free of this unhappiness I had to recognize that in each case, what was causing me to feel in this way was not so much what happened, but rather it is my emotional reaction to it. This emotional reaction I discovered is self-centered (although I often hadn't seen it as such until this time) and therefore sinful; and therefore, it increases my unhappiness.

It is especially important to recognize this truth in regard to those bad feelings about circumstances beyond our control and the things that others do to us. Here it is again: the problem, in the sense of the fundamental reason for my unhappiness, is not what has happened, *but my reaction to it*. And this is sinful, although I don't usually use that word in this context.

This is not to say that there are not external influences or predispositions that incline us to a sin so powerfully that they might reduce culpability. Nor is it to say that we are the cause of all injustice, harm and suffering that comes to us. Rather, regardless of whether or not we are responsible for what happened, when we are unhappy about past events, then ultimately it is always our reactions to them that is causing our unhappiness, not the circumstance or person we are reacting to.

I am probably not a great saint (although I still hope to be). A saint accepts adversity with perfect equanimity because he knows that what has happened is either willed directly by God or permitted by him, and each is for the good of his soul.

My unsaintly *modus operandi* in the face of adversity is to resent what is happening and to blame other people (or fate, or God) for mistreating me. I might manage to control my behavior so that my actions are not governed by such resentment, but even so I am not happy about it inwardly. A great saint on the other hand has compassion and love for those who persecute him unjustly or mock him or unfairly restrict his liberty in some way. He might take evasive action – sometimes strong action, and in the case of soldiers or policemen, even violent action. But if acting justly and in virtue, he does not do so resentfully.

My first instinct, on the other hand, is to wish to see those who make me suffer, suffer too; and at least as badly. Again, on a good day, I might manage to ignore my angry feelings so that they don't govern my actions – perhaps because I know that it is right, or perhaps it is self-preservation because I fear that there will be worse consequences if I do. But regardless, in order to be at peace I must both do what is right and be free of any resentment while doing it.

Sometimes when we have negative experiences we move forward quickly and it is forgotten. But on other occasions these experiences can reside in the memory for years, building up and festering and causing us greater and greater unease. We can't always predict which memories will fester and which will be forgotten quickly. Sometimes the grudge from quite minor events can cause us the greatest discomfort for the longest time. Do you ever find yourself running over and over imagined conversations in which you finally deal emphatically with someone who detracted you 20 years ago? That is resentment!

This self-centered reaction to the events around us, however natural or human it might be, is an example of the abuse of freedom that the *Catechism* refers to in the earlier quotation. So even in the case where we are victims of injustice, if we are resentful about it we can say that it is our sin that is causing our unhappiness. Even if we are sure that we are behaving as anyone else would in the face of such adversity that doesn't change the truth of it – we are still the cause of our own misery.

Because of the Fall and our concupiscence, we all sin so we should not be surprised that we react in this way. When we feel bad the way out is to recognize that this is the cause of our unhappiness and joyfully take the way out. Rather than resisting the idea that we might be responsible for how we feel, we can look upon each resentment as an opportunity to acknowledge our sins and ask for forgiveness so that we are no longer bound in this state of sin and can lead a happy life once more.

For those who do not like the word sin

A note at this point to those who react against the word 'sin.' When I went through this process I did not understand what sin really was. The use of the word 'sin' would have triggered a negative reaction. David did not use this word at all when he was showing me the process. Instead he described a series of self-centered impulses for which he used a variety of generic collective names, such as 'character flaws' or 'character defects' or 'shortcomings.'

This was wise. It helped me to grasp the underlying principle and start to take responsibility for my misery.

It was later in my journey that I came to realize that the Church (or anyone else for that matter) does not make people feel guilty by pointing out sins to them. We feel guilty because of the sins themselves: our disordered and selfish thoughts, words and deeds. All the Church does is point us to the cause of what we already feel, in the hope that we may be free of the guilt. To blame the Church for my guilt is shooting the messenger and it will not help me.

Please take note of the following: no one should feel guilty about being unhappy. This is just doubling your misery – if you do so, not only are you unhappy as a result of some external event, but because you feel guilty about being unhappy you feel unhappier still. Rather, we should humbly look to recognize the truth of the state we are in, whatever that may be, and where we see fault seek to root it out. This is the way out that all can grasp with great joy.

An examination of our feelings in the way that I was shown offers us the possibility of a greater freedom, a deeper happiness, and a purer relationship with God than we previously had. This is the whole purpose of this chapter – the intention is not to rub your nose in your unhappiness, but rather to explain how we can identify the sinful causes of our unhappiness so as to be free of them.

The impact will always be positive, but the extent of it will depend on where we are spiritually before we begin the process. I was deeply unhappy and had never done any sort of confession prior to this process. The impact on my life was dramatic. My whole worldview was turned upside down in a way that improved just about every aspect of my life. It began the journey that led to my conversion to Catholicism.

There are others for whom things are going pretty well, but who have a sense that it could be even better. Although your change may not be as dramatic as mine was, you will feel a difference if you follow the directions of this chapter.

If you are generally happy and are living out the Faith such that you feel no need for improvement, then you have least to gain from this, for you already have a well-developed spiritual life and a conscience that is well-formed and sensitive to your own wrongdoing. However, this process is still worth doing, since by this technique of self-examination you might be able to offer others who are suffering a way out of their misery.

Think of this as an opportunity, not a punishment

For anyone who is unhappy, we are offering you good news. If external circumstances really are the cause of unhappiness, then we are going to be the victims of what happens to us for the rest of our lives. We cannot change the past, so we would be stuck with our resentments forever. However, as we will discover, we can do something about our reactions to those events as we feel them today. We can change our feelings with the help of God.

If you harbor grudges or painful memories, rather than just bearing such resentment and waiting or praying in the hope that at some point you will eventually forget the incident and it will go away, the technique for analysis that we describe in this chapter tells you how to be free of them very quickly. It shows us how we can pinpoint the precise nature of the self-centered reaction which gives rise to the negative emotion. No matter how understandable it may be, it is our focus on ourselves to the exclusion of God that causes us to be unhappy.

Once we have accepted the principle and we go through this process we can change how we feel. It offers the chance to lead a truly happy life.

Swallow your pride and take responsibility for your happiness… and your unhappiness

The greatest barrier to anyone doing this is pride. For the proud there is a high price to pay. I know, because I am one who had to pay it.

Before things could change, I had to change. I had to admit that I was the cause of my own misery. I still have to do this today when I react unhappily to events around me. If I cannot or will not accept this, then I will be stuck with my misery. It is not my circumstances nor other people, no matter how difficult or unjust or malicious. It is not God, neither is it fate, bad luck, the government, members of my family, or church nor anything else. Just me. And even when I accept that it is something in me causing me to feel as I do, I have to go further still. I am responsible because I abused the freedom given to me by God. It is not, to use the examples given by the Catechism, a developmental flaw of mine, a psychological weakness, a mistake, the necessary consequence of an inadequate social structure, nor any other aspect of me that I cannot help.

No. I am unhappy because I have sinned.

Some people, I know, will not accept what I am saying because they are determined to hang onto the belief that the only way they are going to be happy is for circumstances or other people to change as we wish. I know this because I went through this myself for years before I met David.

I felt that given the injustices or misfortunes that I was going through, I had a right to be unhappy. Unhappy as I was, I was reluctant to take responsibility for my feelings because it would require an acknowledgment of two things: first, my ignorance of how to deal with life; and second, that *I* would have to conform to the world around me rather than expect the world to conform to my ideas of how it ought to be.

I was burdened – sometimes I would go as far as to say crippled – by a false belief that everything would be fine if only certain things were different. It was only when I finally accepted that I could never control these things to my satisfaction, no matter how much I might try or wish things were different, that things began to change for me.

On the first day I met David, without further explanation at that point, he handed me a small sticker with the following words on it: "You are now looking at the problem." He told me to put it on my bathroom mirror so that I would see it every morning when shaving and its meaning would sink in. As I went through this process, I realized that in one respect I had been right. I did have a *right* to blame people and circumstances if I wanted to. But the point was that I was not obliged to exercise that right. Here was one right that it was better to waive and exchange for a happy life.

Accepting all of this doesn't mean that we don't try to change difficult or unpleasant circumstances if we can. Rather, it is saying that we cannot depend on being able to do so if we want to be happy.

And when we try to change things we should aim to be free of all resentment as we do so. You don't have to be motivated by anger in order to wish to remove injustice. For example, believe it or not, you can be motivated by love.

Resentment and fear

We have used the word 'resentment' to describe some of our negative feelings already. In the context of our unhappiness it has a particular meaning that we will use.

As it was explained to me, nearly all negative emotion can be classified as either fear or resentment. Resentment arises from hurtful memories of our past (from as far back as our earliest childhood memories right through to just a split-second ago); fear arises from an anticipation that something might happen in the future that we are not going to like.

A resentment is *any* bad feeling relating to the past. Sometimes the very recent past, and sometimes going right back to early childhood. Resentments can be directed against different things. Resentments against people, for example, give arise to the feelings of anger, irritation, dislike, and antagonism that we feel towards someone. We can also have resentments against institutions, such as the Church or the government. These feelings can range in intensity from mild irritation to burning anger.

Resentments can also be directed against ourselves: these are the feelings that we would describe as the guilt, shame, remorse, and regret we have for our actions or for things we have failed to do. Any negative sense about our appearance or our bodies is also arising from resentment against ourselves (for example, I might wish I was better looking) and will often be compounded by resentments against others whom we blame for this (for example, our parents, or God). All resentment arises from a self-centered reaction to these things.

Most fear arises from self-centeredness, too. When I am afraid, I am usually anticipating things that I think I will resent once they happen. My anticipation of something happening is usually a reaction to present circumstances. This means that fear and resentment meet where the future and the past meet: in the present. A single event can sometimes spark both: I can be resentful about what someone has done to me, and fearful that it might happen again in the future. For example, imagine that I leave a message for someone inviting her out for the evening, but she never returns my call. Then I will resent her for doing this. But if I am even more emotionally invested in that person getting back to me, perhaps because I have romantic aspirations, the fact she doesn't get back to me also creates the fear that she is *never* going to go out with me… and if she won't, perhaps *no one* is ever going to go out with me because I am unattractive, and if that's the case I am going to be on my own forever…

The self-centeredness that fear and resentment engender separates us from God. It impairs our faith and our inclination to respond to grace, increases our inclination to sin more, and leads in turn to more resentment and fear, and therefore even greater unhappiness. It can become a downward spiral. This is why resentments and fears are to be taken very seriously. As St. Paul says: 'Do not let resentment lead you into sin; the sunset must not find you still angry. Do not give the devil his opportunity.'[3]

When we are free of resentment, we are calm and at ease in even the most difficult situations, and we are better able to deal with events around us because our ability to reason is higher. That is why St. Peter tells us not only to vigilant in looking out for pitfalls that threaten our faith, but to be *calm* as well – that is, free from resentment: 'Be *calm* but vigilant, because your enemy the devil is prowling round like a roaring lion, looking for someone to eat. Stand up to him, strong in faith.'[4] It is interesting that the Church places both of these readings in Compline in the Liturgy of the Hours. Compline is the last prayer before bedtime and often done in conjunction with the daily review of conscience.

Some of you may say, even if we accept this partially, surely on some occasions it is right to be angry about certain things, otherwise we would never right a wrong; and surely fear is a necessary emotion in some situations because otherwise we would not avoid genuinely dangerous situations. We will address that question in a later section called 'Common Objections and Questions.'

We can't help our initial reactions, but we can change how we feel after that

We cannot help how we react initially to the events of life. Fear and resentment are natural responses, in the sense that they arise from deep

---

[3] Eph. 4:26-27; quoted in Wednesday Compline in the Divine Office
[4] 1 Pet 5:8-9; quoted in Tuesday Compline in the Divine Office

within us at a preconscious level. However, once we are aware of our initial emotional reactions, we do have a choice as to whether or not we want to remain resentful or fearful, or change how we feel. As I was once told: 'You can't do anything about the first thought that enters your head, but you can do something about the second.'

Happiness in life, we might say, is all about making the right choices in regard to that *second* thought.

Keeping it real

At the root of happiness is a grasp of what is true and good. I say, therefore, that someone who is happy has a grasp of reality. I know this is not a universally held view. There is a modern outlook that says the opposite – that the true characterization of the reality of life is a description of what is going wrong and what we are unhappy about. People who have this outlook will encourage others to be 'sincere' or 'to keep it real' by describing to others exactly how bad they are feeling. If someone decides not to burden others by complaining or moaning about something that is not going their way then this, so the argument goes, is unhealthy because they must be 'suppressing' their unhappiness.

This is, in my opinion, a falsely pessimistic view of life. True, misery *is* the emotional experience for those who do not have God, but that does not mean that unhappiness is inevitable. God is there for everyone. As we have stated continually, the Christian message is one of joy even in difficult circumstances. Happy people, I discovered, do not lead problem-free lives. Rather, they know how deal with their problems. They do not suppress or bottle up their bad feelings; they deal with them. But they do so not by declaring their feelings publicly to anyone who happens to be within earshot, or to a group in therapy.

It does not give a true picture of what our lives are like if we sift through our emotions and selectively highlight those that are negative and then describe them to other people as an indication of 'what is going on with me.' The true situation of our lives is what is good about it, and we can see this when we look at our lives objectively through the eyes of faith. This will always be an optimistic and joyful message for this is intrinsic to life itself.

This is not a false optimism. It is rooted in truth. If what we were proposing was an arbitrary changing of feelings that had no basis in truth, it would be a delusional approach to life. This, like taking drugs, might work temporarily, but in the long term it will lead to great unhappiness. But this is absolutely not what is proposed here.

Resentment and fear are the result of delusion. It is a delusion caused by self-centeredness.

Fundamental to our new approach as outlined in *The Vision for You* process is the idea that the world is good and God's intention for us is to be happy. Freeing ourselves from resentment and fear leads us to a clearer vision of the world and its events *as they really are*. It is the person who looks at the world this way who is closer to the person that God intends us to be. The real David Clayton is the one who is happy and joyful. This is what 'keeping it real' ought to mean.

Now I will explain how we analyze our resentments and fears.

An Examination of Feelings, Thoughts, and Actions

Part Two – Writing Down Our Resentments, Our Fears, and an Analysis of Our General Conduct

The technique

Here's what I did under David's direction. I listed all resentments and fears I had at the time of writing and all those I could ever remember having in the past – right back to my earliest memories, and then looked for the cause for each one.

I bought a school exercise book and listed all the people, institutions, principles, and ideas with whom I was resentful. I surveyed the whole of my life up to that point. I then used this list as a basis for recalling all the resentments I had. Against some people I might have many resentments. Some of these resentments were imagined – I assumed that people's actions were driven by their attitude to me when I couldn't know that this was the case. I was told that all *perceived* wrongs and slights, whether real or imaginary, must be taken into consideration. This means that I might suspect that something is done and not have real evidence, but if I feel uncomfortable about it, it is a resentment that should be analyzed.

How David taught me the process

I made an appointment to visit David at his flat and went to see him one Saturday afternoon. He explained to me the general principles that I gave in Part One and then he took a pad of paper and a pen. He told me that he would ask me some questions so that I could articulate some of my resentments. Then he would write them out as though they were his own and he was feeling these resentments.

The first thing he did was ask me to think about the time when I was growing up. He asked me if I had any resentments against my parents. My first reaction was to say, no. I thought, wrongly, that the idea was to bring up only very serious life changing cases of neglect or abuse that I thought might have a deep psychological impact, but I couldn't think of any of those.

David reiterated that this wasn't about psychology, it was a spiritual exercise and it was simply one of locating instances of self-centeredness. He pushed me a bit and asked me if I had agreed with everything they ever did to me. Had I ever been scolded or told off? If so, had I been happy about this at the time? Even the resentments caused by minor events might be important because they separate us from God and cause unhappiness.

I was able to list things my parents did to me that I didn't like, and he wrote them down and showed me how to analyze them according to this process. As he did so he emphasized that we were not looking for any psychological explanation of my feelings beyond the analysis he was giving me. Spiritual and psychological approaches are quite different, he told me.

Furthermore, he emphasized that if I had resentments against my parents it didn't mean that I didn't love them. In fact, those whom we love the most are often those whom we have most resentments against because we have spent the most time with them. It is rare that people we spend time with don't do some things, or have some traits, even if quite minor, that we don't like at some level.

My first example was something like the following:

I am resentful at:	The resentment:	Components of selfcenteredness that give rise to the resentment:
Mum and Dad	They sent me to a high school several miles from home, so I didn't have many friends near where I lived. They kept me there even when I asked to go to another school	Pride, self-pity, acedia, self-centeredness, arrogance, dishonesty, hypocrisy, sloth
Mum and Dad	They sent me to an all-boys high school so I didn't know how to relate to girls. This is one reason I can't get a girlfriend	Pride, self-pity, acedia, self-centeredness, arrogance, dishonesty, hypocrisy, lust

THE VISION FOR YOU

| *Birkenhead School* | *It ruined my social life and made me inept in social situations, so I can't get a girlfriend* | *Pride, self-pity, acedia, self-centeredness, arrogance, dishonesty, hypocrisy, lust* |

Notice first how the same grudge is really a little cluster of resentments. This is very common.

Once David had written them down he started to ask me some questions. I can remember that he was very compassionate in the way that he asked them, but nevertheless it seemed tough because these questions were leveling my pride and forcing me to look at myself in a way that I hadn't before.

Here are the questions he asked me: what is the purpose of going to school primarily? Is to make friends? Is it to meet girls? Or is it to be educated? Of course, I told him it was the latter. Then he asked me if I'd had a good education at this school. I couldn't deny that I had because as a result of it I had gone on to Oxford University. Then he asked my how many boys were at my school. About 800. Did all 800 have problems getting girlfriends, he asked? Of course, the answer was no. So, he said, I couldn't really blame the school for my girlfriend problems or my lack of friends. Therefore, I was being dishonest in doing so.

Then he pointed out to me that my parents had done what they had done because they loved me and the wanted me to have the best education I could have and so I should be grateful to them for sending me to this school.

I knew as soon as he said it that this was true and told David so. Nevertheless, even though I knew that I was being childish and ungrateful, I had to acknowledge that part of me still, all these years later, blamed my school and my parents for this aspect of my current unhappiness. The fact that I could remember being resentful at some time about these things relating to my high school meant that at some level I was feeling it again.

The word resentment is derived from the Latin *sentire* meaning 'to feel' so it means literally 'to feel again.' At some level I was feeling this sentiment again – it was a 'resentment.'

Accordingly, when I left him and put aside time in the following week to do the full examination, I wrote down all resentments that I remembered having, even if I didn't feel it very strongly by this time and applied the same analysis to them as all other resentments that were strongly felt.

Then David wrote down the words that are in the final column of the diagram above – the self-centered impulses – telling me why he put them there as he did so (I'll get that part in a moment). The recognition that these caused the resentment was the most important part of the whole thing, he told me.

As we got into the process he started to ask me some very pointed questions about my personal life mentioning specific things that I might have done or thought. It is not appropriate for me to write these down here, he was coaxing out of me thoughts that had crossed my mind that I would never have admitted to anyone prior to that point. These were my deepest, darkest secrets. This took me unawares and I squirmed quite a lot but answered honestly. David then told me that he had done and thought pretty nearly all of those things too. This was a huge relief. For each one we wrote them down as resentments against myself (we have some hypothetical examples later on).

He then asked me what was the thing that I had done in the past that I was most ashamed of? What is the thing that flashed across my mind when I was asked the question and that I least wanted to reveal to anyone? Here is a chance, he said, to be free of the guilt. I told him, and we wrote this down in the three-column format too as a resentment against myself (i.e., with Self in the first column).

Although this was not an altogether comfortable experience, I am glad David homed in on my greatest shame early in the process. Since the most personal and shameful things from my past were out at this early stage, I had very little fear about writing down the rest of my resentments later. When I left his apartment in Chelsea in southwest London with a sheaf of papers in my bag (and firmly out of view) I knew I had a lot more work to do, but I was no more afraid of it that I was of doing school homework.

More about the selfish impulses themselves and how we decide which ones go in the final column

Here is the list of selfish impulses by which we can account for every resentment and self-centered fear. There are 17 in all. They are: *pride, self-pity, self-centeredness, acedia, dishonesty, hypocrisy, envy, jealousy, greed, selfishness, gluttony, lust, anger, arrogance, intolerance, impatience, and sloth.*

The meanings of all of these words are given at the end of this part of this chapter.

I didn't know it when I was shown them, but they are the seven deadly sins with some others derived from them. You don't have to use this exact list of selfish impulses, as long as you recognize that when you feel bad we blame other people, places and things for how you feel, and then we acknowledge that in some way it is because our sense of well-being is threatened and you react selfishly. Usually it is because our personal reputations, relationships or our economic security are threatened in some way. Whatever words we use, it is the various components of that self-centered reaction to these threats to our well-being that we must put in that final column.

This is easier to learn if someone can show you how to do it, rather than relying on just reading this book

If you are lucky enough to have somebody who has already done this process who can explain to you how to do this analysis of resentments and fears, then this is the ideal way to learn this technique. Then this chapter is not redundant, but rather can be a reference that helps you after you have had that personal explanation.

If you do not have the benefit of someone with experience to show you, then I suggest that as you work your way through the examples given in this chapter you refer to the list that defines each self-centered impulse so that you can understand why they have been used.

I have met people who have been through the 12-steps of Alcoholics Anonymous who tell me that this process is very similar to one that they use in their 4th step, which they call 'taking moral inventory.' If you know anyone who has been through a 12-step program, they might recognize what you are doing and be able to help you. They should at least understand the underlying principles.

This seems like a complicated process at first, but most people find that once they get the hang of it, it is like driving a car – when you are learning there are too many tasks to do at once, but once you have a bit of experience it becomes second nature and the car almost seems to drive itself. So it is with this process of self-examination. Once you get used to assessing which character defects are causing the resentment it becomes almost automatic.

In the end each person must work out for himself how his sins combine to create the resentments and the fears that he feels. The examples that follow are designed to illustrate the principles used. Some are genuine, and some are hypothetical. They do not correspond precisely to any particular situation or person. This is done to protect anonymity of people involved. However, they are still absolutely typical of the resentments that people have.

The reader should be aware that knowledge of how people think and the sort of resentments that commonly occur is based upon my own examination and by hearing others read out all their resentments. This work has largely been with other men. This is because David drilled into me early on that it is generally better for men to help men and for women to help women. This means that the examples I give are more typical of a man's experience. My discussions with women about this have been, necessarily, more general and superficial. Nevertheless, women tell me that while some of the particulars vary, all their resentments and fears can be accounted for in exactly the same way.

More examples

Imagine the writer is worried about certain things that are happening at work. He might write them down as follows:

I am resentful at:	*Resentment:*	*Components of selfcenteredness that give rise to the resentment:*
My boss, Richard	He threatened to sack me because of what my colleague Fred told him, and didn't give me a chance to give my side of the story.	Pride, self-pity, acedia, self-centeredness, hypocrisy, dishonesty, sloth, greed, arrogance.
Fred	He stole money from the till at work and told my boss that I did it.	Pride, anger, self-centeredness, dishonesty, hypocrisy.
Self	I should have been more clever and seen this coming and got Fred first. I am a pushover.	Pride, self-pity, acedia, self-centeredness.

In regard to the three resentments shown above, notice how specific to the situation they are and how, again, we have a cluster of resentments associated with the same incident. Very often this is what happens —we resent all parties involved in the situation, and on top that we resent ourselves for not dealing with it better. In this case, the writer resents Fred for spreading lies, the boss for believing him and reprimanding him, and himself for being outsmarted by Fred and not having the courage to stand up to him.

Common combinations, or sins that hunt in a pack – more about how you choose the selfish impulses for the final column

This is an analysis of our negative emotions. Our starting point therefore is the unhappy feeling that we have. In each case I found that it was characterized by *self-pity* or *anger*. These are the two self centered impulses out of our list of 17 that we feel directly; unless one of these is present we can't have a resentment, because a resentment is by definition is a felt emotion. Moving on, any resentment is always created by an undue focus on ourselves to the exclusion of God (*self-centeredness*) and the rejection of the love of God and his authority (*pride*). The melancholy or *self-pity* is derived from *acedia* and so the two defects go together. Acedia is an old word that describes an inertia against doing what we know to be right. It is at the root of nearly every resentment we have because, in order to react badly, we must first reject the prompting of grace that is always there through the generosity of God and is directing us to do what is right and good. It arises from a lack of faith in divine providence and is characterized by a feeling of hopelessness or melancholy – 'what's the point?' It results in despair and a lack of activity, or ironically, the opposite: frantic overactivity as we seek distraction through superficial pleasures – lesser goods that distract us from this melancholy. Any activity that originates in creating a distraction from what we ought to do, like drug abuse, drinking, or even workaholism can all arise from acedia.

Since in nearly every case there is some sense of shame associated with the resentment, this is characterized by the thought "what do people think about me?" Or, "what would people think about me if they knew that I was thinking or doing this?" These are other aspects of *pride*.

Therefore, I always see one of these two groupings at the heart of every resentment:

Pride, self-pity, acedia, self-centeredness and if we feel indignant or charged up in some way, we are feeling *anger*.

In addition to the usual meaning of lying, cheating, and stealing, *dishonesty* has a specific use in this analysis. If I am blaming someone else or an institution for making me feel bad, which is always the case when I resent someone or something other than myself, then I am being dishonest. In this example when Fred or my boss Richard is in the first column, I also put dishonesty in the final column.

Similarly, in the context of this analysis we use *hypocrisy* for those situations where I resent someone else for something that I have done myself. We then extend that idea further: even if I have never done what I had resented him for, but might have done had I been in his shoes and lived his life up to that point, I put it in. In fact, in almost every case I can say: There but for the grace of God go I. In other words, if the positions were reversed and I had been through everything that person had been through in life, then I could say there is a potential hypocrisy. This reflects the idea that is commonly expressed as, "don't make judgments about others unless you have walked a mile in their shoes." Therefore, like dishonesty, *hypocrisy* is at the core of those resentments where the name is someone's other than mine. There are occasional exceptions in the case of hypocrisy, sometimes you can't apply it – to God for example. You cannot ever walk a mile in God's shoes.

To return to the examples given before, for the resentments against Fred and Richard, *dishonesty* and *hypocrisy* appear in each case.

To summarize, at the core of every resentment that I have written, there is one of the two following combinations:

- *Pride, self-centeredness*
- *Pride, self-pity and acedia, anger, self-centeredness*

When I have someone <u>other than</u> Self in the first column I will usually add dishonesty and hypocrisy to the cluster, giving two possibilities:

- *Pride, self-pity and acedia, self-centeredness, dishonesty, hypocrisy*
- *Pride, anger, self-pity and acedia, self-centeredness, dishonesty, hypocrisy*

Other self-centered impulses can come into play as well, depending on the particular situation. For example, *sloth, greed, and arrogance* are in the first of the three resentments too. *Sloth*, because I know that if I lose my job it is a lot of hard work to find a new job and I don't like the idea of it; *greed* because I am worried about what I will do for money if I lose my job. This is a natural fear but if I had perfect trust in God I would know that He would care for me, job or no job and realize that I have enough money to get through today; and *arrogance* because regardless of the justice of the situation, my boss is in authority over me in such matters and I should not resent his exercising that authority. If you struggle to accept this last point, then there is a more thorough discussion of the principle in this book in the last part of this chapter where arrogance is defined.

We have both *acedia* and *sloth* in this list

If you look up the meaning of the word acedia in a dictionary, it is likely to tell you that it means sloth. This can be confusing, so we have included both words here in our analysis. We use acedia to describe the spiritual inertia – a rejection of God's grace which give rise to other sins. It is not common to use the word sloth to describe this, but technically it could be used too. We keep the word sloth for those other occasions for which sloth is more commonly used today – good old-fashioned procrastination and laziness.

Why is this happening to me? Dealing with bad luck or fate

Here's another sort of resentment. I was very resentful about what I felt was my bad luck. I thought 'fate' or 'chance' acted against me. On reflection I realized that to hold such a resentment, part of me must have felt that some*one* was controlling fate, otherwise there would be no one to blame. God is the word for the person who controls fate. I realized I had to write down resentments against what I felt was an unjust God. When I wrote down the resentments where I was angry at 'fate' or 'lady luck,' I therefore wrote them down as resentments against God.

God	*He didn't give me a good job when I needed one. As a result, I am not attractive to women because I am poor.*	*Pride, acedia, self-pity, self-centeredness, arrogance, anger, lust, greed.*

This was interesting to me for the following reason. When I first took this resentment, I would have told you I was an atheist. This analysis of my resentments revealed to me that I had believed in God all along (if not the full Christian understanding of him). When I read out the first of these resentments against an unjust God to David, he told me with a twinkle in his eye that I was lucky that God was unjust. Given my behavior and attitudes, he said, if God was rigidly just, I would have been a lot worse off than I was now. Then putting joking aside, he told that of course God is just, but he is also loving and merciful. It was because of his love and mercy that I was in a better situation than that which justice alone demanded for me. I had no cause for complaint, David said, and in fact I should be grateful for His mercy.

What I wrote down in the above resentment is what I had to admit to feeling when I looked at it honestly. I would not have acknowledged to anyone my insecurity about money and the feeling that poverty would stop my getting a girlfriend. I thought that this was a childish point of view – I always said to people that I felt that it didn't make any difference to a woman who matters who will love me for who I am regardless. The fact that I had this resentment reflects my real feelings and it was imperative, however childish I thought this made me, that I acknowledged the fact.

Here are some more typical examples:

Dad	He made me go to bed at 8pm on a light summer evening when my friends were still allowed out.	Pride, self-pity, acedia, self-centeredness, arrogance, dishonesty, hypocrisy.
My two friends	Their parents let them stay out later.	Pride, self-pity, self-centeredness, envy, jealousy, dishonesty, hypocrisy.

In this case I was eight years old when the occasion happened. I was 26 years old when I made the moral examination of my feelings. By this time even I understood that my Dad had done what he did out of concern for me. But because I remembered this incident I assumed that part of me still felt the resentment and wrote it down. There were a number like this, where I was embarrassed to acknowledge that I might still be feeling resentful at all.

Looking at the final column in regard to these resentments: *arrogance* is there because I am not accepting the authority of my father; *envy* is there because I am envious of their extended time playing; and I am *jealous* that their parents 'love' them more than mine loved me and so indulged their wishes.

My girlfriend XX	She bossed me around in front of my other friends – she made me look like I am weak and afraid of women.	Pride, self-pity, acedia self-centeredness, anger, hypocrisy, dishonesty, lust.
Self	I didn't want to create a scene, so I was weak and just allowed her to do it without complaint. I wish I had been quick and clever enough to have said something.	Pride, self-pity, acedia, self-centeredness, lust.

In the above example, *lust* is down because it was my selfish desire for her and the fear that I would lose her that was causing me not to stick up for myself. I was afraid that if I stood up to her, she would abandon me.

Tortured imaginations

I had a lot of resentments against myself, including worries about the secret thoughts that I had. I wrote these down too, they might look something like this:

Self	I am balding and overweight (I fear that no woman will look at me).	Acedia and self-pity, self-centeredness, pride, sloth, lust, gluttony.
Self	I have thoughts about ———.	Acedia and self-pity, self-centeredness, pride, lust, etc.

Before entering this process, I was troubled by the thoughts that occurred to me. I suffered from guilt about what I thought were my distorted desires. I had never divulged these to anyone and had never heard anyone else admit to such things. As a result, I had assumed that I was the only one who ever had such thoughts. These are not the sort of feelings that people normally acknowledge to anyone and not the sort of thing that one can be specific about in a book such as this.

These secret thoughts were so shameful that I wondered if the fact that I was capable of imagining such things indicated some terrible deviance in me. Even though I had never come close to acting on the thoughts, I was afraid nevertheless that their power might grow, and I might in the future. Clearly, it happens to some people who do bad things.

I wrote these down as resentments against myself, because I felt guilty about them. Later, when I later read them out to David, he told me that he had thought the same or very similar thoughts himself. He also said that almost every single person whose examination of conscience he had heard had had thoughts of this type and many had worse than me (although he didn't go into any detail or break any confidences). What is unusual, I was told, is not that people think them, but that they admit to it. This is why having such thoughts can isolate us in our shame and why it is important to tell someone about them in order to be free of the discomfort they cause us. David explained to me when I did so that that what is important is that I don't act on these thoughts and I try not to indulge them – that is let my imagination run with them. What I had to do now was to write my guilty thoughts down as resentments against myself. It was vital if I wanted to be free of them. I had to write down exactly what it was that was bothering me. As David put it to me, I should acknowledge all those thoughts that I would not want my mother to know about, or I would not want on the front page of the newspapers.

| Self | I had fantasies about _____. | Pride, self-pity, acedia, self-centeredness, lust |
| Self | I had violent thoughts about _____. | Pride, anger, self-centeredness |

If we are not used to acknowledging the thoughts that occur to us, it can be very difficult to admit to anyone that they even exist. For those of you who hesitate to say what is on your mind for fear of what it might reveal about your character I remind you of what I was told in regard to resentments – 'You can't do anything about the first thought that enters your head, but you can do something about the second.'

The true measure of the person is not the thoughts which cross his mind, which he cannot help. It is the reaction to those thoughts. Nevertheless, until I had shared with David the thoughts that occurred to me, I could not let go of the feeling that the person who had disturbing thoughts was the real me, and the person I presented to others was a facade. In fact, I now believe that it is the reverse. The true me is the good person I seek to become in my best judgment and wishes to be virtuous. If I live a life less than this, I am being a version that is less than who I really can be.

Dealing with extreme injustice such as violence and child abuse

I did not experience any of this kind in my life, but I have talked to people who, very sadly, have. Some of these people were still dealing with resentments connected to mistreatment of the most extreme kind by people who were in authority over them and against whom they were powerless to resist, perhaps because they were young children.

This process can be a powerful help. There is no suggestion here that it replaces any other counseling or other appropriate treatment. Nor does this process replace the justice system. Where crimes have been committed, the criminal justice system may well have a part to play.

The point is that even in these extreme situations the ideal we strive for is an attitude of forgiveness and an acceptance that we cannot change what has happened. With God's grace we can forgive and move forward even from these situations and cease to be prisoners of our past.

St. Peter tells us in his first letter:

> Slaves must be respectful and obedient to their masters, not only when they are kind and gentle but also when they are unfair. You see, there is some merit in putting up with the pains of unearned punishment if it is done for the sake of God but there is nothing meritorious in taking a beating patiently if you have done something wrong to deserve it. The merit, in the sight of God, is in bearing it patiently when you are punished after doing your duty.[1]

This is not an endorsement of slavery as an institution, rather it is talking to the people of his day who were suffering the gravest injustice and

---

[1] 1 Peter 2:18-20

offering them a way out of the torment of the situation which they were, for most part, powerless to change.

This analysis of resentments is a tool that can, with much prayer, help us to bear a beating (and worse) patiently when we have done no wrong. The writing down of the resentments will be simple and quick, but nevertheless powerful. I thought about putting some hypothetical examples down here but was not able to come up with any. All of those examples that were specific enough to be useful in instruction are inappropriate for print.

Here are a couple of additional points that might help: first, in this analysis we have no interest in the subconscious. The resentments, thoughts, and memories we are looking at are those that we are conscious of and so are already bothering us. Anything that we can remember we write down. If we can't remember it, we can't write it down. We do not try to dig deeper than by using the natural process of remembering things from the past that we have described.

Second, in this process it is not necessary to fully relive the emotion of the past event when recalled. All we need to do is remember the event in order to write down the analysis and then move on. So, beyond re-feeling it to the degree that we remember we were resentful, it is probably preferable that we don't seek immerse ourselves emotionally the memory of the experience. Having said that, it is unavoidable that some of these events will be painful in the recalling. If that is the case, write it down and move on.

Third, this point has been made already but is worth reiterating. Put down any resentments you have against yourself too. For example, it can be very difficult for victims of great injustice to acknowledge that sometimes and perversely they felt as though they were complying with what was going on, often through fear of what would happen if they did not. By this or other means it can lead to a misplaced guilt that somehow, they were responsible for what was done to them. Difficult though this may be to acknowledge it will help if it is acknowledged as guilt. Put this down as a resentment with 'self' in the first column and put this thought

'I was responsible for what happened to me… etc.' in the second column. Then, importantly, add *dishonesty* to the cluster of selfish impulses in the final column reflecting the fact that it is not true.

Recall that only a holy saint would not be resentful if he were the victim of great injustice. Nevertheless, though resentment is understandable in these situations, it is still a lack of love that causes that resentment. The fault, if we can call it that, that gives rise to this along with our core cluster of self-centered impulses is one of the rejection of the natural authority, such as parents have, even when acting unjustly. We use the word *arrogance* for that. We must stress here, that in this context the use of this word has this technical meaning of not accepting the authority of those who are in a rightful position of authority over us (as defined at the end of this chapter). You would not use this word in its common meaning – that of an overbearing and self-important attitude – to describe any victim in this situation. And again, this is not excusing injustice from those who are in authority. It is showing us how to be free from emotional trauma once we have experienced it.

Once the resentments connected with this trauma have been written down, they should be read to the confessor as we shall describe. Sometimes it can be a good idea for matters as serious as this to write them down the presence of the person whom they are to be told to and say them immediately. This way it is out and dealt with and does not sit in the consciousness of the victim for a long time without resolution. In addition, the victim should be ready to pray daily for the perpetrators until he is able to forgive them. This may mean many days of prayer.

Keep your document out of sight of others

In the light of this, one can see the importance of keeping any personal written documentation of resentments and fears out of sight of those who might misuse or be hurt by the information. In the ideal no one other than the confessor should know the detail of this examination.

The contents of this could easily be misunderstood if read by a spouse or family member. Even in the most loving marriage there will be resentments against our spouses to acknowledge. Although the whole point of this is for us to look at our part in the generation of resentments, someone who does not understand the process who read a resentment against themselves could easily misinterpret it and be deeply hurt. Furthermore, we are acknowledging thoughts and impulses that we generally do not disclose, and these could easily be shocking for people who have never seen this before.

It is always a balancing act with those we are close to. We do not want to be secretive, but at the same time we do not want to disclose things needlessly that would only hurt them. An approach that seems to work in most cases is to explain in general what you are doing and, assuming the good intentions of the spouse, say that this will not be a good thing for her or him to read, requesting cooperation.

What about things that I know are wrong, but I don't feel bad about? Developing ideals for conduct

For those who are used to doing confession this will not occur. You will be aware of your transgressions and have a well-formed conscience that informs you when you do something wrong and you will be able to connect all your unhappiness or guilt to the cause.

However, my experience was that when I went through this process, although by this time I did have a faith in God, I was not a Christian and was certainly not a highly moral person. I had never been to confession. My natural inclination, until I started to take direction from David was to neglect what my conscience was telling me if it was constraining me from having the pleasure of some selfish and immoral behavior. For example, I didn't want to acknowledge that any sexual immorality was making me feel bad because I wanted to keep on doing it. So, I tried to blame other things for my bad feelings and pronounced myself 'depressed.'

I realize now that what I was trying to do was create a morality of my own that reflected what I wanted to do so that I could justify my actions. My conscience was pricking nevertheless, so I was doing my best to attribute this discomfort to other causes so that I could keep indulging in the wrong, but temporarily pleasurable, behavior.

As I went through this process, David helped me to develop ideals for conduct, working first on sex conduct because this was the area in which the pleasure was greatest and my inclination to try to justify it was greatest.

Once the ideal was articulated, I measured my conduct against them and listed all the occasions I could remember falling short of this ideal *as though* I felt guilty, recording them as resentments against myself. I was told that this was because I almost certainly did feel guilty, but I was not yet connecting the feeling of self-pity to its true cause at this stage.

| Self | I (write down exact nature of act) | Pride, self-pity, acedia, self-centeredness, lust, etc. |

Depression… or self-pity?

Before starting the process with David, I had diagnosed myself as suffering from 'depression.' I now realize it was *self-pity* by another name. I discovered that this was another instance in which I was the cause of my own misery. In order to avoid taking responsibility for how I felt, as I have explained already, I was trying to break the connection between the true cause of my discomfort, which was immorality, and the effect, which was a bad conscience and self-dislike. So I blamed my 'depression' on other causes, this usually meant pointing the finger at other people and their treatment of me for the way I felt. They were responsible, I would say, for my 'low self-esteem.'

Someone told me as I was going through this process that what people call low self-esteem is really just a modern phrase for what used to be called a guilty conscience. Certainly this was true for me. David told me directly that one way to raise my self-esteem is to start doing things worthy of high esteem. 'You can't escape your own conscience and the only way that you can feel good about yourself is to do good things,' he said. An even better solution, he explained, is to stop thinking about yourself altogether, and start taking an interest in others.

A Review of Sex Conduct – Why It is Needed and How to Do It

As I was going through the process of analyzing past conduct, the link between cause and effect, action and feeling, was gradually established in my mind. I started to notice that even in this area of sex conduct I did feel some regret and shame for those things that I had done that were truly wrong. Through this I was able to start to move toward the development of a better ideal for behavior in the future. This was a significant step in leading a happy life.

However, because my conscience still could not be considered a reliable indicator of right and wrong in the area of sex (because of my desire to justify the pleasure of such immorality), this is the one area more than any other where I looked at my conduct and measured it against an objective standard of morality regardless of whether or not my conscience was pricking. I listed all those areas where my actions or thoughts fell short of my ideal. I realized some time later that the more I tried to match my behavior against the standard of love (I shall describe this in more detail in the next paragraph) the closer that my own conscience moved toward a morality that matched that taught by the Catholic Church.

By what standard do we measure our actions and thoughts regarding sex conduct?

Obviously, Catholics or other Christians will use Christian morality as their reference standard here. I was not religious when I did it and would not have accepted a Catholic morality or that of any other religion. My friend David, who was showing me this technique knew this and approached it in a way appropriate for someone in my situation. David allowed me to develop an ideal for behavior in sex by appealing to my natural sense of what was right and then leading me on from there.

He appealed to my natural sense of what constitutes a genuinely loving approach in this context, suggesting first that my sex conduct should always be in accord with love. I agreed to this. Consequently, David said, I should strive, as an ideal, to eliminate all behavior and motivation that is self-centered rather than loving. So, he said, as a general principle, where I was motivated by pleasure for myself only, without regard for others, then that was selfish and therefore wrong because I was using another for my own pleasure. This went against the ideal of love, because I was objectifying both sex – as just another source of pleasure – and the person (the object by which I can obtain that pleasure). A loving motivation does seek pleasure too, but pleasure that is bound up in the dynamic of two people giving themselves to each other in love. Although I was somewhat reluctant to do so, I did accept David's proposal as a theoretical concept. I agreed not to get involved with anyone romantically until I was through the process, and so at this stage all the acceptance of this principle affected was what I wrote down. It was only later, I had to admit, that I accepted this idea to the degree that I was prepared to let it govern my conduct.

In accordance with this, I looked in my past for all those occasions when my sex conduct was motivated by selfishness, rather than love, and recorded each one in the form of a resentment against myself, regardless of whether or not I felt guilty about it, as already described.

How did I use these principles to examine my sexual conduct? With David's help I started to apply the ideal of love to all the different situations I could imagine finding myself in. As David pointed out to me, for example, heterosexual sex always involves the possibility of conception, that is, the creation of new life. No contraception method is 100% effective.

This point was driven home to me when watching a comedy show, *Frasier*. Roz Doyle, Frasier's unmarried and openly-promiscuous-and-proud-of-it work colleague announced that she was pregnant. "But Roz," Frasier said. "I thought you indulged in safe sex?" [2] "I do," Roz protests. "But that is only 99% percent reliable. How am I ever going to beat those odds?"

Whatever my views on the legal status of abortion – and at this stage I was pro-choice – there was no way, once conception had occurred I could consider as a loving action the willful destruction of a person (or even a person in the making). When put in this way I couldn't reconcile abortion with love.

So as I thought about it, it came down to this: if contraception doesn't

---

[2] 'Safe sex' was the euphemism for using artificial contraception.

work and abortion is wrong, that means that every time I engage in sexual activity, I entertain the possibility of having a baby. Once I allow for this possibility, then if I am motivated by love as I wish to be in the ideal, I must ask myself, "have I taken the right steps to look after this baby after it is born?" A loving family is the best environment for a child to grow up in. Therefore, all sexual activity outside a permanent and loving relationship, which is the basis of a stable family, is self-centered and therefore wrong. In this context a 'permanent' relationship is defined as one which I could reasonably expect to last at least as long enough to nurture it and care for it to adulthood; that is, 21 years after the birth of the youngest child. This being so, it was unloving for me to indulge in sexual relations if I have any personal doubts that the relationship will last less than 21 years.

This being so it begs the question: how can you tell that a relationship is going to last that long? Assuming that I can picture myself being with my lover for this long, it is not reasonable to expect that it is permanent unless I have taken steps to find out if that this person sees me in the same way as I see her. In other words, we need to have discussed this and agreed that this is how we feel. I could see also that a courtship in which we test compatibility before engaging in this activity is vital if we are to make such a decision in an informed manner. And then how can either of us know that we can really trust the intentions, as well as demonstrate sincerity? The strongest way to do this for each of us is to promise each other solemnly that this is our intention. And to make it even more binding, make a solemn public declaration in front of witnesses that this is what we intend to do. The common word for this solemn public declaration is marriage.

David had taken me through a process whereby I had systematically built for myself a moral code of conduct in regard to sex that corresponded to a traditional approach to sex, marriage and the family. All this came from the starting point of the idea that I ought to act lovingly and to avoid acting selfishly. David had guided in me in such a way that I made my own conclusions without any reference to the Bible or any other religious book or teaching.

Now I had my ideal for sex conduct. I could return to my moral examination and give an account of my sexual conduct. I listed all the occasions, in the form of resentments against myself, when I had acted outside this standard of behavior.

I don't want to give the impression that my conscience was totally ignored before I did the process. There were many things associated with my sex conduct about which I felt guilty or deeply embarrassed and clearly these went down in the review of resentments. In fact, it was in this area of sex that many of my most shameful thoughts occurred. The point is that I had to go further still, acknowledging the possibility of a conscience that is not properly formed.

When, later, I shared all this with David, he remarked simply that despite what I thought, this was all pretty normal stuff and in fact I was a pretty average guy.

Fears

For the final part of this examination of conscience we look at our fears. We should review our fears thoroughly. When we do this we classify them in two ways: self-centered fears and phobic fears. Self-centered fears are fears about things that will happen to us while we are alive and have components of self-centeredness as their ultimate cause; phobic fears on the other hand are irrational fears of death and physical pain (heights, spiders, flying, etc.).

Self-centered fears: many of these are connected with resentments and might have been covered when we wrote our resentments. For example, if I have a resentment against my boss for shouting at me there is a fear about my job security at its root. I resent him because part of me thinks that his shouting at me indicates that he might sack me.

Some self-centered fears will not have a person associated with them — if I just have a fear of losing my job, there might not be anybody to put into the first column. In this last case we insert the word 'Fear' in the first column instead so that we understand what it is we are analyzing when we read it out to our confessor later.

My boss	He shouted at me (I was afraid that he might sack me).	Pride, self-pity, self-centeredness, arrogance, hypocrisy, dishonesty, greed, sloth.
Fear	I have a lingering worry that I may lose my job and not be able to keep paying my mortgage.	Pride, self-pity, acedia, self-centeredness, greed, sloth.

Phobic fears:

The fears we have detailed before considering phobic fears all relate to anxieties about meeting our needs while alive. We call these self-centered fears and they are all caused by the same self-centered impulses that cause resentments.

Phobic fears are different. These are the irrational fears of death (spiders, catching cancer, heights, crowds, open spaces, etc.). Not everyone has phobic fears.

Phobic fears are not listed in the same form as resentments and self-centered fears because they have a different cause. We write the fear out as shown below putting in brackets afterwards the ultimate fear that is at its root. In many cases the root fear will be a fear of death. For some people (not all) the ultimate fear is not death, but what will happen to us after death — hell. For others there is a fear of extreme physical pain. Whatever that ultimate fear is, we need to state it in order to be thorough. Self-centered fears cannot apply once we are dead. Therefore, they do not cause the phobic fears, which are inordinate fears of dying. Because of this, phobic fears do not appear in the three-column form.

Fear	I'm afraid of spiders - death (hell)
Fear	I'm afraid of catching cancer - physical pain, death (hell)
Fear	I'm afraid of heights - I'm afraid that I will fall, or jump and then die painfully (hell)

Is there a particular order in which the resentments and fears should be written down?

To reiterate a few points that often crop up: there is no significance in the order that fears, resentments and details of our sexual conduct actually go down on the list. We write them down as we remember them. Beyond the analysis already given, we do not make any psychological interpretation of patterns of behavior. Accordingly, and as already stated, we do not worry about the role of the subconscious in our behavior. We write down what we can remember. If you remember it, write it down. If you can't remember it, you can't write it down and there's no need to worry about it.

Many of us carry a notepad with us during the period when we are doing the moral examination of the feelings of our past. Then, as a memory occurs while on the train, say, we can jot it down briefly and then add it in full inventory form later on.

The 17 component forms of self-centeredness used in this examination of conscience

These are the definitions used for the moral examination of feelings. It is worth noting that these are not always the definitions that are used in everyday and conversational language. They may also differ from the precise definitions that an expert in moral theology might use. I pass this on in this way because it works. I have found that every resentment and self-centered fear that I have ever had could be accounted for by piecing together combinations of the defective character traits as described below.

What we are trying to do here is to put in words the self-centered impulses and feelings that cause our resentments and fears. Sometimes in order to do this the meaning of the word is stretched a little to fit it and sometimes it can be applied in different, if associated ways. Arrogance, for example, is one of these that when used in everyday conversation has a broader meaning than the particular use that we make of it in this analysis.

In the end you are not bound to use this set of 17 defective character traits. If you feel the list is inaccurate, incomplete, or too cumbersome you are free to write your own, to modify, add to, or prune the list. The important thing is to account for each component part of the self-centeredness that causes your resentment and fear.

The 17 'sins' I used are: *self-centeredness, self-pity, pride, acedia, dishonesty, hypocrisy, envy, jealousy, greed, selfishness, gluttony, lust, anger, arrogance, intolerance, impatience, and sloth.*

Self-centeredness: thinking of myself excessively and not giving due regard to others. This is a form of pride and is the umbrella defect so to speak – all the other 16 impulses listed below can be considered self-centeredness manifested in one form or another.

Self-pity: feeling down about my own situation. This is a defect that we feel directly. Because we feel it, it's one that lets us know that we have a resentment — 'poor me!' is how I feel. Self-pity is the manifestation of melancholy or despair associated with a sin called 'acedia' (see later).

Pride: the rejection of the love of God and his authority. An unreasonable and inordinate self-esteem: worrying about what people think of us — what would they think of me if they knew? How could he do that to the great me? This includes occasions where we are boastful of our achievements (which used to be known as vainglory).

Acedia: is the neglect to take care of something that one should do. It can be an inertia or spiritual sloth whereby because of a lack of faith and hope we do not reach for what is good and feel down. It is translated to listlessness, depression, and feelings of self-pity. If we sit with our self-pity it can become intense and in today's language would be described as depression. The true antidote to feelings of self-pity are virtuous actions and the cultivation of joy, such as those described in this process. However, it can be a temptation to seek solace instead in lesser goods in order to distract us or to escape from our self-pity. These may not be bad in themselves, but they can only be a temporary fix for self-pity and so if misused in this way can lead to our seeking happiness through them fruitlessly, and neglecting our obligations. This is a root of addictions, workaholism, hedonistic lifestyles, giving in to the temptation to look at pornography and so on. Acedia describes the inertia towards doing what is right, while self-pity describes the emotional aspect that is felt.

Dishonesty: not being honest (i.e., lying, cheating, stealing).

Hypocrisy: in simple terms this is accusing others of faults that we have done ourselves. We can extend that further, so even if I have never done what I had resented him for, then in almost every case I can say: There but for the grace of God go I. In other words, if the positions were reversed and I had been through everything that person had been through in life, then I have to acknowledge that I might have done as this person did, and there is a potential hypocrisy. This reflects the idea that is commonly expressed as, don't make judgments about others unless you have walked a mile in their shoes.

There are certain situations where this would not apply: we cannot ever put ourselves in God's position. So, other things being equal, if we resented God we would not include hypocrisy.

Envy: wanting what rightfully belongs to others (i.e., their possessions and abilities). For example, I might be envious of Fred's Mercedes and his good looks, but in this case I am still jealous of him as well because Mary fancies him and not me).

Jealousy: resenting affection that is given to others in preference to me — I am jealous of Fred because Mary fancies him and she doesn't fancy me.

Greed: when I have what I need yet I want more. Refers to material possessions.

Selfishness: not being prepared to let others have some of what is mine (i.e., material goods, time). Although in common parlance selfishness and self-centeredness are interchangeable, in this context we use them slightly differently. If we are just thinking of ourselves, that is self-centeredness and not selfishness. Selfishness is about not being free with goods we possess or are in control of for the benefit of others, and is similar to greed.

Gluttony: greed for food and drink (including alcohol).

Lust: an inordinate (i.e., disordered) desire for carnal pleasure. Usually used in association with sexual pleasure.

Anger: is an inordinate and uncontrolled feeling of hatred toward the person who perpetrates injustice, and is characterized by a desire for vengeance. It is something that is felt, viscerally, and is – like self-pity – a fault that lets us know that we have a resentment. If self-pity makes us feel down, anger fires us up. It is particularly grave if a lack of self-control leads us to indulge in our anger to the degree that there are external expressions of it and others are on the receiving end of actions or words driven by it. It is to be distinguished from righteous anger, which is a desire to right wrongs and is a hatred of vice rather than a hatred of the person who is causing the injustice. Righteous anger is compatible with the love of God and reinforces rather than undermines our inner peace.

Arrogance: knowing better than my equals (not minding my own business, telling people who have not asked my opinion and over whom I have no authority, what to do); or thinking I am the equal of my betters (not accepting the authority of those I should — parents, bosses at work, teachers when I am at school). Also making judgments on the morality of people's behavior is arrogance because ultimately only God is entitled to do that. This is a form of pride. St. Peter characterized a right approach to injustice from natural authority figures as follows:

> "Slaves must be respectful and obedient to their masters, not only when they are kind and gentle but also when they are unfair. You see, there is some merit in putting up with the pains of unearned punishment if it is done for the sake of God but there is nothing meritorious in taking a beating patiently if you have done something wrong to deserve it. The merit, in the sight of God, is in bearing it patiently when you are punished after doing your duty."[1]

Note, this is not an endorsement of slavery, neither is it saying we shouldn't do something to stop it if we can (or any other injustice which might exist). It is telling us a general principle of how to be free of resentment against authority figures, regardless of whether that authority is exercised justly or unjustly.

This is a high ideal – taking an unjust beating patiently – but with God's grace we can move towards it. In the Lord's prayer, we ask God to 'forgive us our *trespasses as we forgive those who trespass against us.*' I found that acknowledgment of arrogance helped me to move towards this ideal of forgiving those who have perpetrated an injustice against me. This is the whole point about forgiveness: if the act against us is not unjust, then there is nothing to forgive. Its very essence is all about freeing ourselves from the resentment we bear in the face of unjust persecution.

---

[1] 1 Peter 2:18-20

Intolerance: not putting up with qualities in others that they cannot help — he is ugly; I don't like her accent; I don't like the English; I don't like the working/middle/upper class; I don't like his or her skin color/race/nationality. Intolerance is not used for when we don't like someone's behavior (see 'arrogance').

Impatience: I am fed up with waiting (i.e., bus stops, "she hasn't returned my telephone call yet," etc.).

Sloth: I am being lazy or procrastinating about taking action for ordinary activities. Although in many commentaries sloth and acedia are used interchangeably in this context, I was directed to use acedia for a spiritual sloth, not doing something that arises from a lack of love; whereas sloth here is used for more conventional way – i.e., being lazy, lacking energy for work, and so on.

An Examination of Feelings, Thoughts, and Actions

Part Three – Confessing Our Self-Centered Impulses to Another

Now that you have this written account of your resentments, fears, and sex conduct, you must read it out to someone.

Who do we read it to?

Catholics will want to say this to a priest. However, this is likely to be a document that will take a lot longer to read than the time given to most visits to the confessional in church. Also, the form in which our lists were written is not the usual format of confessions: 'I am resentful at XXX: he did XXXX; pride, self-pity, self-centeredness, envy,' etc... So if we ask a priest to hear this in the Sacrament of Confession, it is worth explaining what is going on so that he understands the process and has the time available to devote to it. An appointment may need to be made and this is not done during a regular church confession time.

In most cases he will not have the time, so it is unfair to ask a busy man to hear every item you have written down. It is better to be selective and read out the most strongly felt resentments – the most personal and the most embarrassing – and then refer to the rest in a general fashion, for example: 'On many occasions I was fearful of XXXX.' Then keep the document so that you can read the rest of it out when a suitable confessor does appear. Although this does not need to be a priest, as I will describe, you do need to find *someone*.

When I did this process I was not a Catholic (that was still about 5 years away) and had never said confession before to anyone. I read out everything to David who was a layman. I went to see him every Thursday evening for 2 hours –10 weeks running – until I had read out more than 200 pages of an exercise book filled with resentments, fears, and sex conduct.

I had to have great trust in him – I revealed to him many thoughts and actions that I had never revealed to anyone before. Quite apart from my worries about being able to trust someone not to pass on such thoughts to others, I have to think of the person who hears it as well. Much of this might have be shocking for someone who is not used to being exposed to the worst secrets of private thought and imagination. I trusted David because I knew that he had been through this too and would not be scandalized by what he heard.

David listened to me, for the most part, without comment. Occasionally he suggested that I might have missed some of the self-centered impulses from the third column of a resentment. If my description of the event was long and rambling he would stop me and tell me that he didn't need to hear all the detail, he just needed to know the essence of it in a couple of sentences – what exactly was I resentful about?

When I read out resentments against my family and especially my parents, he did stop me and gave me some feedback. He told me that I must not blame my parents in any way for how I am or for my unhappiness. Even if on occasion I have been mistreated by my parents, he said, we must remember that nobody has perfect parents. If we really did have to have a perfect upbringing in order to be sane, he said, then no one would be sane. Rather, I should pray for them, forgive them for any injustice and understand that they were doing the best they could. Also, I should be grateful to them for bringing me into the world, and for all the sacrifices they made on my behalf. If I had any trouble being grateful then I should list all the good things they had done for me.

In my case I could see very clearly that I had been brought up well and in a loving home. I could blame no one, least of all my parents for any shortcomings I might have; and, again referring to my personal situation, that my family was dysfunctional for the most part only to the degree that *I* participated in it. Certainly, the only dysfunctionality that I could change was mine.

There was so little response from David that at times I even thought he was dropping off to sleep. I would stop reading and he would come to life again. 'Carry on lad,' he would say.

When you have finished reading it out, ask God for forgiveness and resolve to live up to the ideal of love

Once all had been read out, I was told to go home and pray to God for forgiveness, asking him for the strength and grace so that I might move towards the ideal of love in all areas of my life. I was told that if I found that I still had some lingering resentments against individuals or was still anxious about anything, I should pray for them daily until the resentments are no longer there.

I was told also to ask God to remove my fears and direct my thoughts towards a better end in accordance with his will.

This really works

The point I am making here is that even though it was not a priest who was hearing my confession, the process had a profound effect on me…

… in time! The *immediate* sense I had upon completion was one of anticlimax. But, at some point a few days later I was sitting with a group of people at a social function and noticed that I felt connected to them in a way that I never been before. For the first time that I could remember I no longer felt lonely. The sense of isolation that had been with me almost as long as I could remember, had lifted. My resentment and fear had gone! This was miraculous.

Furthermore, going through this process had given me a moral code that I was prepared to live up to. Previously, as a nonbeliever, I did not subscribe to any moral authority. I had rejected Christian teaching, or what I knew of it at a young age. But now, I could see that whatever I might have wanted to believe, the pattern of my resentments showed me that I felt bad when I contravened the Christian moral law.

This was even more obvious to me after the process than during it. I could connect the sense of guilt with a single action much more directly once hundreds of resentments that I had been carrying with me for years were cleared away. This change made it much harder to justify bad behavior from hereon. Similarly, it was now much more difficult to blame something else or someone else for how I felt (although I often am tempted to have a try!). Now, when I sin, I feel it and I know what the cause is.

Some might argue that I had been conditioned in some way by my parents or by a Christian society to believe in a Christian morality. I do not accept this. My parents were good examples to me, certainly, but I had never been taught Christian morality in detail and so had never known it in detail. In nearly every aspect, any choices I made as I was growing up were made without any reference to Christian morality. It was reason (albeit badly applied) and selfishness that had led me to bad behavior, just as it was reason (properly applied with the guidance of David) and my conscience, which I couldn't help, that led me to a right behavior that I had never known before.

The nature of the transformation that I experienced from this part of the process convinced me it was supernatural, that is, one that involved God. I no longer believed that it could be explained away as psychological or intellectual. I say this because I had understood and had accepted fully the premise that my self-centered reactions were the cause of my unhappiness very quickly during the writing process. But understanding the principle did not give me the relief that I was to experience later. That only came once I had read it out to 'God and another person' as David put it. Furthermore, during the reading of it, as I have described, David added very little during the process of my reading it out – so I didn't learn very much during that part of the process. All that I did, for the most part, was read it out while David listened. The change that came afterwards, and which I have described, was so profound and so good that in my mind I knew that someone else was involved. It was not just me and David. God was there too and that was why the change was so profound.

When I became Catholic I did wonder how this 'unofficial' confession process was related to the official Sacrament of Reconciliation. In my first confession to a priest I decided to do what I suggested at the beginning of this chapter – a confession that was, as far as I was aware, closer to the level of detail of what someone who had never been through the process would have done. So, I confessed the big things one by one and then confessed to the minutiae by describing only general patterns of bad behavior, thought, and speech.

I still do that today. On a daily basis I consult my conscience in the way that the process describes and then, ideally, somewhere between weekly and monthly, I go to confession with a priest and confess to things within the sacrament more generally.

I wondered, how a non-sacramental process of confession before I ever became a Catholic could work so well? I also wondered what the official attitude of the Church to this non-sacramental confession was. When I asked questions, no priest that I spoke to was hostile to it; quite the reverse, they were very encouraging and pleased about the effects that it had.

I found out also that the Church approves of a very similar process to the one I have described, and which takes place in Alcoholic Anonymous and other 12-step programs such as Cocaine Anonymous and Narcotics Anonymous (many of these meetings even take place at Catholic Church halls). These are support groups that treat addiction through what they call a 'spiritual' program. This is very effective and works without any help from professional counselors or ordained ministers. When they do go through a similar process of self-examination to the one I was shown (which they call a 'moral inventory') it is simply one alcoholic or addict helping another alcoholic or addict. The effect on them is profound, too – people recover from alcoholism or drug addiction. It is still, as far as I know, the most effective treatment for alcoholism that exists, even with all the wonders of modern medicine and psychotherapy.

My belief now is that these lay-run processes cannot work apart from the Church. Even though those involved are not cooperating with the Church as an institution, they participate in the Sacrament of Reconciliation through this process and it derives its power from the presence on earth of the Church. The change in people is real; the Catechism tells us that it is only through the Church that such a re-formation can occur. I believe, therefore, that what is happening is similar to that process by which the whole world – including non-Catholics and even non-Christians – benefit from the presence of the Church in the world. God is not limited by his sacraments, and is so generous in that He offers the gift of re-formation even to those who are not Catholic. Nevertheless, this is still taking place through Christ, and therefore by virtue of the presence of his mystical body – the Church – on earth.

I always think of this when I read the letter of James:

> And the prayer of faith shall save the sick man: and the Lord shall raise him up: and if he be in sins, they shall be forgiven him. Confess therefore your sins one to another: and pray one for another, that you may be saved.[1]

This could refer to the conventional process of confession where one of those people is a priest, but it could also refer to precisely the sort of process I went through, with one layman confessing to another.

---

[1] James 5:14-16 (Douay Rheims)

An Examination of Feelings, Thoughts, and Actions

Part Four – Making Restitution for All Harm We Have Done to Others

In going through this examination of feelings it will probably become apparent that we have harmed others. If this is so, then after we have finished the first three stages of this Examination, we must make amends for the harm done, and usually (but not always) this means making a direct approach. When we do this we should always have the well-being of the other person at the forefront of our thinking. We are careful to consider whether or not such an approach might cause more distress than it alleviates, particularly if the situation means that we have to bring others into the process who would be damaged by any disclosures of wrongdoing that we make. If this is the case, we must at the very least seek their permission first, and we might decide that it means we can't approach at all.

It can easily be seen that good judgment is needed here, and those who wish to make amends for harms done are urged to seek counsel if they are in any doubt about the right thing to do. This is one area where a priest or experienced spiritual director would be very helpful.

When I did this stage I did not know any priests and wouldn't have gone to one anyway. I stuck with David. I will relate some aspects of how my discussion with him went and how he told me to make amends. My thought here is that it might be helpful to some who do not have anyone to consult. In doing this, I would stress that no two personal situations are identical and there are always nuances that come into play that differentiate even those cases which on paper seem alike. Therefore, if in doubt, wait for someone to talk to about your particular cases. If you have no one to talk to whom you can trust then pray to God each day until the right person comes along.

Another writing exercise, I'm afraid

The first thing I had to do before I could even think about approaching anyone was to consider carefully exactly how I had harmed them. David suggested to me that I write down on paper another three-column analysis. This time, in the first column was the person or group of people I had harmed. In the second column I put the harm done. In the third I wrote down how I would have felt if I had been in this person's shoes and had the same experience.

<u>The Harm</u>

Person	a) What I did	b) Emotional damage – how I would have felt if I had been this person?
My old girlfriend, Mary	I cruelly made fun of her in front of her parents and family on the day she introduced me to them. I laughed at her and called her stupid. She loved me, and I was about to break up but hadn't had the resolve to let her know yet. Then a week later I dumped her.	Unloved and unlovable, betrayed. Humiliated. It would look to my parents that I couldn't choose a good boyfriend - did I have some psychological flaw? It would make me wonder if there was something wrong with me that a person I loved would treat me like this.

The harms we put down are likely to be emotional harms, debts, and, in some cases, criminal acts. It will include people who are close to us. The harms will include both things we have done and things we have failed to do – sins of omission as well as sins of commission. I found, for example, that I was guilty of neglect of my family; this is a sin of omission.

Put the thought of approaching people out of your mind as you write this list

Sometimes we can hesitate at this point because we are afraid of approaching those we have harmed. In some cases these may be people who have the most reason to dislike us and we are afraid of how they might react. I was advised at this point to put all thoughts about approaching people out of my mind. All I am doing here is writing a list and considering the harm done. At a later stage, David said, God would give me the strength to do what was right, but I didn't need that strength yet.

This showed me how self-centered I really was

If I had begun to get some sense of how self-centered I can be, when I was in writing down my resentments and fears, I knew it now. This part of the process revealed to me that I had never been someone who empathized with others and this was why I found it very difficult to imagine how I would feel if I was in that situation.

This meditation revealed to me a side of myself that wasn't so pleasant. Previously, the closest I ever came to this was to consider how my actions would affect how people felt about *me*. In other words, I had thought about how I could manipulate people, but not how I could affirm (or undermine) their own sense of their human worth.

My first attempt at the written exercise for this part of the process was not well done. When I wrote down the example like the one shown above, initially I would have phrases such as 'cross,' 'annoyed,' and 'fed up' in the third column. David told me that if you annoy someone or make them 'fed up' you are not causing them harm. He asked to think about what a mother feels, for example, when her son treats her as I did. If what I had done was serious enough to cause harm – and he told me he thought this was – then she would feel not only unloved by me, but also in some way unlovable, or unworthy of love. It was after this that I revised my final column so that I could see much more clearly the harm I really did cause.

THE VISION FOR YOU

In this way I began to get true sense of how I had harmed others and I began to have a genuine remorse for what I had done. This, in turn, influenced me so that I was more willing to approach others and make reparation.

This part of the process helped me greatly in all my relationships. I could now begin to consider how my future actions might affect others; not so that I might be able to manipulate them, but in order to consider how my actions might reinforce their own sense of human worth. I am still liable to be selfish and inconsiderate or coarse in my dealings with others, but at least now I could begin to move away from that and start to be a better person.

Just because people do not like me doesn't mean I have harmed them

Sometimes, where I regretted having fallen out with people, I wanted to approach them and re-establish the connection. I put these people down on the list, thinking that this process of making amends would be a great opportunity for me to do so. I think I hoped that with my newfound insights into leading the good life, I would make a much greater impact this time. This desire was particularly strong in the case of women for whom I had once held a torch, so to speak.

With some of the examples, David put the second column under scrutiny. He kept on asking what harm I had done. When I repeated the action that I had taken, he said to me that this would not have harmed the person. He said he could see that it was selfish, silly, or foolish and probably explained why this lady didn't admire me as I wished, but it didn't constitute harm.

It was very likely that she hadn't given me a second thought since the last time I saw her. He told me, 'I'm sorry to say this, lad, but you'd probably be offended if you realized just how little and infrequently most people actually do think about you.'

I just had to accept that some people had decided they didn't want me as a friend, and that was their privilege. If I wished to establish contact with them then I was free to approach them, but not under the guise of making amends in order to try to justify the approach – making it look as though I was doing it for their benefit. This was in fact a slightly more sophisticated form of what I always used to try to do – manipulate people to make them like me.

There were some occasions where the reason that people didn't like me was because I did the *right* thing. These were less common, I have to admit, but nevertheless they did exist. As David had often pointed out to me since I had begun the process, doing the right thing doesn't make you popular. In nearly all of us there is, to some degree, a trait by which we do not like to see people doing good things because good behavior is an example that shines a light on our bad behavior, causing our consciences to twinge. If people don't like us because we try to do the right thing, then no matter how upset those people are with us, I was told, we have not harmed them. All we have done is displease them, which is something different. In this case we don't apologize and don't change.

We do not put ourselves on the list

Some who go through this process want to do this. They say that the main person we have harmed is ourselves, so we must make amends to ourselves too. On the contrary, I was told, absolutely not! This is just another form of self-centeredness that would undermine my happiness. This part of the process is all about the consideration of the good of others. It is true that as a result of harming others we harm ourselves too, but being gentle with ourselves is not the answer. The antidote is to turn our pattern of thinking around so that we cease to think about ourselves for moment and start to think about others. Then paradoxically, we do help ourselves, but now indirectly, for this concern for others transforms us in love.

My final list was a lot shorter than I thought it was going to be

By the time I had given it my full consideration, guided by David, this list which began with many names on it was now much shorter. I had perhaps 15 people whom I had harmed emotionally. Most of these were close family whom I had neglected. The pattern was that the list became shorter, but my sense of the harm done to those who remained was much more acute.

In addition to those whom I had harmed emotionally, my list included a string of people and institutions to whom I owed money, or from whom I had taken it without their knowing. In my case it was a list of petty offenses – largely expense fiddling, fare dodging and so on, but all were recorded on the list.

Now we have the list, how do we repair the harm done?

So far we have been thinking only about the harm we have caused. Now for the first time we can start to think about actually approaching people and repairing the damage.

We don't approach everybody

As a general principle. We do not approach people if to do so would cause greater harm or implicate others when we have no right to do so. Also, if doing this would imperil our ability to meet our financial obligations to others we might decide to not go ahead. For example, to declare your wrongs in some situations might hamper your ability to earn a living, and if you are the main breadwinner in a family then you might hesitate.

Another common example where this consideration comes into play is when we want to make amends for harms done to old girlfriends or boyfriends. Our sudden re-emergence might cause embarrassment and difficulties to current relationships and we have no right to do that. So unless we are sure they are single and that it will not cause distress or embarrassment we do not approach them. Even then it is often wise to be cautious and to seek advice. Sometimes the hope of reawakening romantic adventures with former heartthrobs can be so great that it can distract us from proper consideration of their well-being.

However, it can be a good idea to approach or write a letter to estranged spouses and partners if there are children involved. Though, to stress again, counsel should be sought before doing such a thing, since every situation is different. I have seen many people have good experiences with these amends. In some distressing cases where fathers had court orders placed on them forbidding access to the children, miracles happened, and they were allowed back into their children's lives. It may require patience, since former or estranged spouses often need time to be convinced that we are sincere.

I saw David deal with several fathers in this situation. He always suggested that first he make amends to the mother of his children, by letter if she will not see him. In doing so the father also makes it clear that he would like to make amends to the children and re-establish contact with them. However, he states clearly that the final decision as to whether or not he is allowed to see them is in the hands of the mother. He should tell her that he will not fight for custody in the courts because he believes that this will cause more distress for the children. Then the father assures her that he will not make any further effort to contact them unless he hears from the mother giving him permission first. This approach is suggested on the assumption that the children are in no immediate personal danger when in the care of their mother.

The outcome of this sort of approach was often remarkable. Most commonly, in cases where the relationship between them is poisoned there is no immediate response, but then with patience it comes, maybe after several months or even years. In this way contact is resumed gradually and on a better footing. This is the most common result that I have seen. The change in atmosphere that this seems to bring about can be so great that one would call it miraculous.

When I asked people who had experienced these very distressing situations, I was told that even if the worst happens and there is no contact with the children, then the children do seek the absent father or mother when they grow up. It is rare, however, that there is not some sort of contact before this.

Pray for the willingness to approach those whom we must approach

Once we decide that we must approach someone, we may nevertheless feel some sense of trepidation at the prospect. If this is the case, pray to God for the willingness to do what is right, until you are able to take the course of action you have decided is appropriate.

What form does the approach take?

Beforehand, I was told, we pray for guidance and for the strength to do the right thing. Sometimes a direct approach is preferable, sometimes a letter. If we think it will be distressing for the other party if we suddenly barge into their lives again, a letter might be best. We are always considering what is best for the other person.

For those whom we have harmed emotionally the general approach is as follows:

1. **We explain the harm we did and express regret for any former ill feeling**

    As we do so, we contrast the harms we have done with a positive account of their behavior and indicate that they did not deserve the treatment they received. Our aim here is to build them up and praise them. If they have harmed us, we do not touch on this aspect at all. This is important — we are dealing only with our own conduct. Very often, once approached in this way they will admit to harms they have done to us, but if they do not, we must not try in any way to steer them toward this.

2. **We ask for forgiveness for all these harms** It is important that we go beyond simply saying sorry for what we did, so we actually say: "Please forgive me." Note, we *ask* for forgiveness. We do not demand it. If they are unable to forgive us or simply do not wish to do so, then that is their right.

    Sometimes we have done things unknowingly that have hurt others, so we must give people a chance to tell us this. This is very often the case for people with whom we have long and close relationships. Much has gone on between us and each party can remember different things. So we say also, "if there are any harms that you are aware of that I have not mentioned then please let me know."

3. **Give them time to respond**

   Give them a few moments to think about this and to say anything else that they wish to add. Don't let this extend into so long a silence that it pushes them into saying things just to fill the silence and stop the embarrassment. The idea is simply to make sure that each person has an opportunity to say everything that is on his or her mind.

Where they bring up harms, ask for forgiveness for those too.

We conclude by wishing them well in the future and saying that if there is any way we can be of help, then they should not hesitate to ask us.

What if I have lost contact with someone and can't trace them?

If we were unable to trace someone after making a reasonable attempt then we said a prayer and did nothing further. However, if subsequently we happen to bump into them, we must grab the opportunity. This means that we must think about what we would say if we were able to see them, just in case. It is surprising how often such coincidental meetings do occur.

Debts

We should be willing, at the very least, to pay off all debts. In regard to dealing with creditors it is usually possible to make an arrangement. On the whole, they don't want to send us to prison – they want us to pay off the money and will cut a deal provided they feel that we are sincere in our desire to set matters straight. Most people will do so reckoning that if they can't get everything, then a guarantee of some money is better than none.

Criminal activity

Some people have committed crimes. Even in these cases we must be prepared to own up, make reparation, and ask for forgiveness. Depending on the seriousness of what has been done, it might be best to make such an approach through the justice system, rather than direct.

If others are to be implicated or are going to be affected by this, which is usually the case, we should seek advice as to how best to go about it. This is one case in particular where there are so many different possible situations that it is difficult to give specific advice, beyond the general principles already articulated, as to how to go about this.

Restoring faith in human nature

I had a variety of reactions to my approaches. The close friends and family whom I approached were all generous and forgave me.

Some did think I had not done very much harm and that I was probably building it up into something that much more serious than it really was, but nevertheless they let me say my part and forgave me afterwards. Some, particularly the guys, were a little embarrassed and wanted to close the conversation quickly. However, even then I noticed that it changed the nature of the relationship for the better. Usually, from that point on we were trying to get along with each other rather than trying to antagonize each other.

I was struck by how forgiving people were once they realized that I was sincere. It was the frank admission of harms done without excuse, I think, that started everything off on the right foot.

One or two to whom I sent letters did not respond and I don't know why. Perhaps they couldn't forgive me. David told just to let these go. I had done what I could, I should do no more and move forward with my life.

An Examination of Feelings, Thoughts and Actions

Part Five – Common Objections and Questions

Some people who are introduced to this self-examination question the premise that we are responsible for our own resentments and fears. When they do so, I do my best to answer all the objections that are raised (if I believe they are genuinely interested in the answers) and I have listed many of the common ones below.

'I don't have resentments or fears'

This is possible if you are a redeemed saint, otherwise you are almost certainly mistaken. Reacting to the events around us with at least some resentment and fear is an inevitable part of our fallen human condition. You may not be harboring resentments at the intensity of blazing anger, but if you have ever been irritated, fed up, or annoyed about something – even slightly, and even against those whom you love the most – then that is resentment. If you have ever been worried or anxious about anything, even slightly, then you have had self-centered fears. We should not be surprised or ashamed that this is the case. We should simply recognize the fact and take the sin that causes it to God and ask for his mercy.

This is true, by the way, even once we have been through the process. On a day-to-day basis we will react resentfully and fearfully to events around us. The healthiest thing is to recognize this and then to write them down and ask for forgiveness as part of our daily routine.

Denying our true feelings stores up greater unhappiness in the future.

'Can't I just express my feelings as a way of dealing with them? Do I really have to do all this writing?'

There are those who stress the importance of 'expressing' our emotions (i.e., telling people how we feel) as a way of dealing with bad feelings. Although bottling up emotion is not a good idea, the best way of dealing with the anger we feel is not to express that anger. A better approach is to acknowledge our true feelings and maintain self-control as best we can until we are in a position to release them through the analysis that this book has described.

Some people go as far as to say that if we feel resentful or angry at someone we should confront him with it and tell him we are angry. In my opinion, this is likely to lead to greater problems and won't help either party very much anyway. It is more likely to escalate the situation and generate more angry exchanges than to cause it to dissipate. The exercises described in this book allow for the dissipation of such feelings without causing more suffering for others.

'Isn't it right to be angry sometimes?'

This is a common reaction. They ask – aren't there situations when it is right for us to feel angry? Isn't this what causes people to campaign for justice? Would slavery ever have been repealed if people hadn't been angry about it?

Our model here is Christ. I turn to St. Alphonsus Liguori, a Doctor of the Church, who wrote about the anger of God and contrasted it with human anger:

> It is well to remark that when Holy Scripture speaks of God's anger, we must understand that God never does anything in anger, as men do, who act through passion and trouble of mind: since the Lord disposes and does everything with perfect calm: "Thou judgest with tranquility" (Wisd.12:18). When, then, God is said to be angry, we are to understand that He is chastising sinners, not now with a view to their eternal salvation, as He often does with those whom He chastises in order to bring them to repentance, but that He is punishing them solely to punish them, and to give free course to justice.[1]

Although, as I have said, I have never found the expression of anger toward the object of my ire useful at all. But this is not to say that we should not take firm action to resist wrongs and to right injustice. It

---

[1] St. Alphonsus Liguori, Commentary on Psalm 2

is right to resist evil and sometimes we must and this requires decisive action. For the saint, the desire to correct injustice can be passionate and felt viscerally, but when it is motivated by love it is a good feeling and not one that disturbs his inner peace.

Taking God's anger as the ideal, we should always strive for a peaceful disposition as we act. Inner peace and decisive action are not mutually exclusive. In fact, if we act when we are angry and resentful then it is likely to impede reason and cause us to act in way that we would later regret.

Hatred of injustice does not cause internal unrest, but hatred of evil *doers* does. Thus, the ideal we aim for is one of taking decisive action against evil while loving those whom we act against. To the degree that we do so, we feel at peace as we act. However, those toward whom our action is directed might still assume that we are feeling angry, because they would naturally associate such action with that feeling (just as the psalmists who are receiving just punishment describe the anger of God in very human terms). Righteous anger is a zeal or passion for what is right and it is expressed in actions that resist evil. It is never driven by hatred of a person— only a by love. Righteous anger, therefore is associated with an inner peace.

So St. Paul tells us to be rid of anger and to strive for forgiveness of those who wrong us:

> You must be rid of all these things: anger, passion and hateful feelings… You must put on compassion, kindness, humility, gentleness and patience. Be helpful to one another, and forgive one another, whenever any of you has a complaint against someone else. You must forgive one another in the same way that the Lord has forgiven you. (parts of Colossians 3:5, 12-13)

Similarly, the psalmist tells us:

> Take your rest in the Lord and hope in him: do not envy the one who thrives in his own way, the man who weaves plots. Abstain from wrath, abandon anger: do not envy him who turns to evil, for

those who do evil will be destroyed, but those on the side of the Lord will inherit the earth.' [Ps. 36(37)]

Sinful anger loves to masquerade as righteous anger. When I am angry, my natural desire is to justify what I feel. I should be on the lookout for this tendency, which is trying to hide a bad motive behind a good. If I don't, I will self-righteously justify all sorts of selfish behavior.

Does this mean that until I am sure that my anger is pure and righteous or has dissipated that I shouldn't be taking any action? Usually, the answer is no, simply because we don't have the time to deal with the resentment in many situations, since we have to decide quickly. Even the best of us, in taking right and decisive action are likely to have some resentment against those to whom we are acting. If I was expecting to be free of resentment before acting, in many situations I may never act at all.

Here's the approach I take: while acknowledging that it is almost impossible for me to be free of some level of resentment when resisting injustice or acting to change what is wrong, once I have done my best to assess what I ought to do, if reason demands that I act, then I must. If I am resentful I try to put my personal feelings aside and do what is right. In other words, I try to do what is right *regardless* of how I feel. However, to the degree that I am able to deal with such resentment, my actions are likely to be more reasonable and I will feel greater peace in my life. Once the action is finished and I have time to reflect, then I also have time to make an examination of my feelings and then be free of all resentment in the way described in this chapter.

Here is a meditation on anger – two verses from St. Ephraim the Syrian's *Hymns of Paradise*. He is describing the redeemed heavenly state to which we can aspire:

> *Bind up your thoughts, Old Age, in Paradise*
> *Whose fragrance makes you young; whose wafting scent rejuvenates you,*
> *And your stains are swallowed up in the beauty with which it clothes you.*
> *In Moses he depicted for you a parable: his cheeks, ashen with age became shining and fair,*
> *A symbol of old age that in Eden again becomes young.*

No blemish is in them, for they are without wickedness;
No anger is in them for they have no fiery temper;
No mocking scorn is in them for they are without guile.
They do not race to do harm – and so themselves be harmed;
They show no hatred there, for there they are without envy;
They pronounce no judgment there, for there no oppression exists. (Hymn VII, vv10,11)

'Grief is a bad feeling, but isn't it necessary as part of the process of overcoming the loss of loved ones?'

We are told that it is good to feel grief; that the grieving process is part of the process of dealing with the death of a loved one. Is this so? I would say the answer is that it depends. It depends on the nature of the grief. In order to understand this, we should divide grief up into two components: the self-centered and the compassionate. Each is a very different feeling but, as with anger, might result in apparently similar outward signs of emotion.

When someone I love dies, quite naturally part of me feels bad, but this is often driven by self-centeredness and self-pity. Although it is understandable that people feel this way, we can see also that this self-centered grief is not desirable or helpful to anyone. Self-centered grief says: 'How could this happen to me?' or 'How am I going to manage without this person?' It never feels good. It has never helped me to indulge in this form of grief. Neither have I ever found it necessary to the process of dealing with the loss. It is understandable that any of us might have this self-centered grief, but that doesn't make it good – it is not a sign of a genuine love for the person.

There is also a healthy grief based on compassion. When I lose someone I love it is a somber moment. The death of anyone is a reminder that we would not have death at all if it were not for the sins of our first parents. However, we can be sure that all people will, at the moment of death, have the chance to accept or reject God's love, and this will be true for the one we love, too. Rather than focusing on my own loss, I can reflect with gratitude on the time that I have had, through God's grace, with this person. Certainly, I am not pleased that this has happened, but with the eyes of faith I can be certain that this too has happened so that a greater good can emerge. Compassionate grief is a bright sadness, like the emotion that we see in the faces of the saints in holy icons. It is one of those occasions when we acknowledge our sense of powerlessness before what happens, but we are comforted by God's grace. To acknowledge our helplessness and need for God and then feel God's support when we need Him is a wonderful thing; as Jesus says: 'Blessed are those who mourn for they shall be comforted.' (Matt 5:4) 'Blessed' means 'happy.'

'Compassion for those who are suffering'

This relates not to the death of a loved one, but their suffering in life. One of the most difficult things to deal with in life is the sorrow we feel when someone whom we love is suffering and we are powerless to do anything about it.

My experience tells me that like anger and grief, compassion can have two components: one born of self-centeredness, which is a bad feeling; and one born of love, which is opens the door to intense joy.

When I am driven by self-centeredness, I look at the person who is suffering and I feel sorry for myself. This self-pity can be intense and almost unbearable as long as I see the other person's suffering as the cause of my anguish rather than my own self-centeredness as the true cause. It is easy to deceive myself and think that this is an expression of love, but if such empathy is rooted in self-centeredness it can be profoundly destructive to my life, while doing nothing to help the other person. I might imagine so vividly that I am suffering with this person, that I feel sorry for *myself*. At a mild level this is why I feel embarrassed for someone if he makes a fool of himself in front of many people. I am not so much concerned for him, but rather imagining myself in his position so that I feel the self-pity that I would feel if I were in his shoes. Hence the discomfort.

At a deeper level, when someone we love is the author of his own suffering – perhaps an alcoholic or a drug addict – then our own suffering can be driven not so much by the loving reaction of 'how can you do this to yourself?' but rather the self-centered one of, 'how can you do this to me?'

A cold, uncaring detachment is heartless and shuts out all joy in our lives too.

But there is a different sort of detachment in which we do not empathize but *sympathize* with the suffering one and act with love. We act lovingly toward the other, but do not share in the emotions that they are experiencing as we do it. I have heard this described by some as 'detaching with love.' Certainly this is greatly preferable to the self-centered anguish that causes us to feel sorry for ourselves when others are suffering. For many of us this may be the best approach for us to aim for.

The Church Fathers seem to suggest that there is an even higher form of Christian grief born of love, of which Our Lady is the model. The highest response to the suffering of others is a compassionate grief in which we do suffer with the other – compassion means literally 'to suffer with' – but that suffering is then transcended by Christian joy. This is the grief felt by Our Lady at the foot of the cross as she gazed at her suffering Son. It is an anguish born of love; as with all that arises from love, it opens our hearts so that we can have a fuller union with God and experience an even greater joy.

In order for me to try to understand this, I had first to consider the situation when I was the one suffering directly. I know that God always gives us grace to deal with any situation and that through cooperation with his grace, we can transcend any injustice and any suffering. When this occurs the suffering is not necessarily removed, but is likely to be overwhelmed by the sheer joy of experiencing God's consoling love. The writings of the saints indicate just how powerful this joy in suffering is.

If that consolation is there for us when we are experiencing suffering directly, one might argue, then it is there too when we experience pain or injustice indirectly, arising from an empathetic sharing in the suffering of others.

However, this is true only to the degree that our anguish arises from love. It if arises from a self-centered desire to right the suffering of others then we shun God's grace. We must first free ourselves of that resentful attitude. To do this, one might have to go back a step and adopt the 'detach with love' approach. When our anguish is a sharing in the suffering of others born of love for them, then it is a sharing also in Christ's suffering on the cross. It is a genuinely holy suffering that opens the door to a greater joy.

The Church's liturgy on the Feast of Our Lady of Sorrows is very instructive on this. In the Office of Readings there is a long passage from a sermon of St. Bernard of Clairvaux. He describes Our Lady's anguish at the foot of the cross as real, but arising from a genuine compassion that is born of charity, i.e., love. He calls it a 'martyrdom of the soul':

> We rightly speak of you as more than a martyr, for the anguish of mind you suffered exceeded all bodily pain. 'Mother behold your son!' These words were more painful than a sword thrust for they pierced your soul and touched the quick where the soul is divided from the spirit. Do not marvel brethren, that Mary is said to have endured a martyrdom in her soul. Only he will marvel who forgets what St. Paul said of the Gentiles that among their worst vices was that they were without compassion. Not so with Mary! May it never be so with those who venerate her. Someone may say: 'Did she not know in advance that he Son would die?' Without a doubt. 'Did she not have sure hope in his immediate resurrection?' Full confidence indeed. 'Did she then grieve when he was crucified?' Intensely. Who are you brother, and what sort of judgment is yours that you marvel at the grief of Mary any more than that the Son of Mary should suffer? Could he die bodily and she not share his death in her heart? Charity it was that moved him to suffer death, charity greater than that of any man before or since: charity too moved Mary, the like of which no mother has ever known. (From the Office of Readings, Feast of Our Lady of Sorrows)

Following this is a quote from St. Paul in his Letter to the Colossians in which he says directly that this sharing in Christ's sufferings through love is a source of happiness:

> It is now my happiness to suffer for you. This is my way of helping to complete, in my poor human flesh, the full tale of Christ's afflictions still to be endured, for the sake of his body which is the Church. (Col. 1:24)

The antiphon for the Benedictus on Lauds for that day echoes this and takes it even further: 'Rejoice grief stricken Mother, for now you share in the triumph of your Son. Enthroned in heavenly splendor, you reign as queen of all creation.'

This is a wonderful how the Church, through her liturgy, tries to lead me upwards to a full, joyful, spiritual maturity by which I engage fully with life, but disengage from sin.

If the loving grief in the death of a loved one is a 'bright sadness,' then the loving grief in the suffering of a loved one is a 'fiery anguish' – an anguish burning with the fire of love that overwhelms and transcends all before it and gives us an intense joy.

'What about loved ones who are going to hell?'

Someone once asked me this question directly. "Surely, if we love someone and they have rejected Christ," she said, "then we will be unhappy too, for we know that they will suffer in hell."

My response to this is that this is indeed a difficult situation to face, but I don't believe that we need be consigned to unhappiness. First, I find it difficult to believe that there have been any Christians who did not know someone who has rejected Christ. If this really is a barrier to happiness then no one can be happy. There would be no one who could demonstrate 'the art of living joyfully,' to use the phrase of Benedict XVI in his paper on the New Evangelization.

Second I look at my own response to my own family and friends who are not Catholic or Christian. I am aware that I don't know for certain that anyone is going to hell. Furthermore, I shouldn't try to judge the sinfulness of others before God. I am being arrogant in making such a judgment for it is not for me to do so. I often do make such a judgment of course, but it only makes me unhappy when I do. There is always, right up to the last moment, the possibility of repentance. I always think of my own case – I was in an apparently hopeless situation yet through God's grace I found happiness. I believe that at every moment, everyone is free to make such a choice should they want it.

Having said all this, it must be admitted that some people are likely to go to hell, and some of those may be people I care for. Although I am not happy about this fact, to say the least, it does not affect my general state of happiness because I know that everyone has free will and is given the chance to choose heaven or hell at the end of their life. If God respects their free will, then probably I should too and console myself that they are choosing their destination freely, whatever it might be. Again, I have to detach from thinking about this; it is beyond my control. When I am agonizing over such a thing it is because I am trying to control people against their will and I am hurt that they won't do what I want. I flatter myself when I think it is my concern that they do God's will. If it were the latter, then it would be, as in other cases, an emotion of love and so would be a bright sadness.

'Isn't fear necessary for survival sometimes?'

Some will argue that in certain situations fear is necessary – perhaps for our survival, so that we flee from danger. Once again, I would split this emotion into two forms.

First is an anxiety to save oneself which is rooted in self-centeredness; second is a 'reasonable fear' which is driven by the desire to save oneself also, but in order to carry out God's will. Reasonable fear is not a destructive emotion, it is a grasp of the truth of the situation to be avoided. This latter form of fear is most certainly necessary for survival. Fear rooted in a self-centeredness (which might be best described as a state of *unnecessary* anxiety) does not leave us in peace.

Very often in the heat of the moment we are likely to experience both. This is natural. If someone runs at me with a knife, I am likely to be afraid. However, even in these situations, it is the reasonable fear that is going to save me. The reasonable fear leads me to take the right evasive action. The self-centered aspect of fear, if too great, is likely to hinder us. It can be so great that it paralyzes. Therefore, even in this situation, it would be better for me to have only the reasonable fear if possible, which would subside once the danger was over.

Furthermore, we can know that a situation should be avoided without actually feeling fearful. This is reasonable fear. This reasonable fear is for the good – especially when there is impending peril. These occasions also remind us of our own powerlessness and direct us to God, on whose constant support we rely. It is the *reasonable* fear that will induce us to take all appropriate and necessary action to avoid danger. Part of any reasonable action is to seek help from God. We are more likely to be calm in difficult situations if we go to God and cooperate with his grace.

This dynamic of reasonable fear, a cry for help, and God coming to our comfort is – as with the comfort that comes with grief – a wonderful thing. It is there whenever we face danger or risk. When we cooperate with it, it reinforces our sense of his love for us. This is expressed in Jesus' prayer in the garden when faced with the most unjust and cruelest of deaths. It is a model of prayer for us in times of fear:

> Father, everything is possible for you.
> Take this cup from me;
> Yet not what I will,
> But what you will. (Mark 14:36)

St. Augustine explains how the pain and anguish that Christ felt in his passion is due to His bearing our sins and agony. The blood that streamed over his body when experiencing the agony in the garden was not due to anxiety for himself but, as Augustine says, 'Surely this bleeding of all his body is the death agony of all the martyrs of his Church.'

Consider the accounts of the martyrs and how they bore the pains of death. Perpetua and Felicity, for example, bore their grievous mutilations that eventually killed them cheerfully and willingly. I wonder at their purity and cooperation with grace and I wonder also at the fact that this pain is only part of what Christ is choosing to experience on their behalf.

Most day-to-day experiences of fear are not reasonable fear, but unnecessary anxiety. Unnecessary anxiety is more than just superfluous to our needs; it can be crippling. Many of the things we anticipate never materialize anyway, and the anxiety based upon self-centeredness reduces our capacity to think rationally so that even if the worst happens, we not are prepared to take the best action. Reasonable fear on the other hand leads us to act appropriately and with greater freedom.

Consider the following example. When I drive my car, I am aware of how terrible motor accidents can be, so I take a reasonable course of action and drive on the same side of the road as all other drivers, doing my best to conform to the rules of the road for safety. Even then, there is still some risk of death. It is a reasonable fear of an accident that leads me to act in this way. Even though there is still some risk of death, I do not feel anxiety when I drive. I barely give it a second thought. I have responded to a reasonable fear and behaved in a reasonable way. I do what I can to avoid danger and then trust in God that he will protect me in accordance with his will. I know that there is still a small chance that I will die on the road, but when I do occasionally think about it, I know that he will give me sufficient grace to deal with it. If I am at fault here, it is my lack of gratitude. I barely give a second thought to the fact that God is with me on the road and that it is through his grace that I am not anxious, even about the small risk that exists.

In contrast, when flying I am inclined to feel a pang of anxiety. This, thankfully, is not so great that I ever hesitate to fly anywhere. This is an emotion of fear that is not reasonable. The chances of being killed in a plane crash are far less than when I drive my car. It takes some effort on my part, but when I fly I am able to look at the self-centered irrational fear and see it for what it is. I choose to follow reason and take the flight while, of course, following the safety recommendations for air travel given by the airline.

We should expect to be fearful in the face of sudden danger, but we should try to act reasonably in response to it. Usually we don't have time to sit down and analyze the situation. We have to act. It would be foolish in the face of clear and present danger, to sit down with pen and paper and analyze our feelings first. However, once the moment is past, we do have time to analyze our feelings, using the technique of the examination of feelings to remove any residual anxiety.

What about fear of God?

To be 'God-fearing' is a virtue. Fear of God in this sense is not an emotion, but a rational response to faith in God in which we take acts to avoid his judgment against us by, for example, avoiding sin. A healthy fear gives us peace, never anxiety. There is no need for anxiety over God's judgment against us. God himself gives us the means by which we can avoid a harsh judgment by offering every one of us the chance to go to heaven.

Nevertheless, some people do have an anxious, distorted fear of God. Those that I meet often tell me that it is due to their education about the Faith as young children. Whatever the reason for this anxiety, it is a terrible shame; certainly, it is wrong to try to induce others to follow God's teaching by generating the emotion of anxiety about his judgment. In the end it is usually counterproductive. All the people I met who were educated in this way at Catholic schools when they were young are no longer practicing Catholics.

As a convert, I never experienced this myself. I converted to the Faith in adulthood. I chose to become a Catholic for positive reasons, like the life of joy that I believed was available to me by making that choice (and it has surpassed my expectations).

That is not to say that we shouldn't be aware of the perils of wrong action. Certainly, we all need to be aware of the existence of hell so that we can choose not to go there. We do need to make steady efforts to do what is right, but the point is that there is nothing to be anxious about. We are aware of the existence of heaven and we know that with God's loving and certain help, we can get there. In truth, the Church is not the source of anxiety. Rather, it is the solution to it. It is sad that the misrepresentations of its teachings by some of its members is such that it gives the opposite picture.

'Do I have to do all of that? Can't I just live in the moment, forget the past and ignore the future?'

On the face of it, this would seem to be a reasonable suggestion. Living in the moment would shut out all the resentments of the past and the fears of the future. However, even if it is possible, it is not proper to human nature and cannot result in happiness. It would reduce us to living the life of an animal, unable to respond rationally to what happens around us and relying on instinct alone to make decisions. We would have no sense of our purpose in life because that requires us to have a picture of the future ideal to which we are directing our actions. Finally, we could not learn from our experience of the past.

The Catechism tells us:

> There are many passions. The most fundamental passion is love, aroused by the attraction of the good. Love causes a desire for the absent good and the hope of obtaining it; this movement finds completion in the pleasure and joy of the good possessed.[2]

Love, then, by its very nature looks to the future in hope. Accordingly, the human person, who is made for love, must look forward to the 'possession of the absent good' in heaven to be true to his nature.

To go to any destination, we need two things. First, we need to know where we are going. This requires us to have an idea relating to the future and it is why St. Paul implores, 'set your mind on things above, not on earthly things' (Col 3:2). Second, we must know practically what to do to get there. Love is the principle that guides our actions on the heavenly path. Put simply, we get to heaven through acts of love (in cooperation with God's grace). To know how to act lovingly today we must apply reason to historical information picked up through experience via the senses and stored in the memory. Here is the point: in order to get to heaven, the human person must both recall the past and anticipate the future.

---

[2] CCC 1765

Happiness *does* require us to live in the moment, but in order to do that fully we must have also a true picture of the past and properly ordered hopes for the future. This is not about forgetting the past and ignoring the future, but rather in striving to see the events of the past, present, and future as they really are, in the eyes of faith and hope driven by love of God.

THE VISION FOR YOU

An Examination of Feelings, Thoughts, and Actions

Part Six – More detail of my personal experiences of this part of the process, and how my life improved as a result

Once I was shown the technique of a moral examination of past feelings, I was ready to start writing down all my resentments and fears in earnest. I took a week off work (easier to do in Europe than the U.S.) and set to it. First, in order to be systematic in the dredging of my memory, I wrote a list of people, places, and institutions from my past as an *aide-memoire*. I worked in clusters of people: I listed family members; I listed all school friends I could remember, class by class; university friends; all ex-girlfriends, and all ex-friends including girls but not girlfriends; I listed the places I had lived; I listed the places I had been on holiday, the places I had worked and so on.

Then I started at the top of the list with the first name and wrote down the first resentment. Usually, what I found was that this resentment would spark a whole string of memories of other resentments. For some the connection with the first resentment seemed obvious, for others there seemed to be no connection that I could discern at all – the second resentment was against a different and unconnected person and about an event that occurred at a different time from the first. Nevertheless, I wrote both down and all the others they sparked to create whole string of resentments recorded in the order that I remembered them. After I had mined that particular seam of my memory fully and had written them down, I then went back to the list of names again and wrote down the next resentment against the person at the top of the list. Again, I wrote all the secondary resentments that the memory of that first one seemed to trigger. I repeated the process until I had exhausted all the resentments against the first name, and then looked at the second name and so on until I had gone through the whole list.

This meant that although the process of actively dredging my memory was systematic, the order in which they were written down was closer to random because I always made sure that I recorded and analyzed these secondary resentments too.

I was told that this was absolutely fine. The order in which the resentments actually appeared in writing was not important because we were not looking for patterns to psychoanalyze (beyond the analysis of putting the self-centered impulses into that third column). We were just interested in thoroughness – getting all the resentments I could remember down on paper.

At the start of the process, the size of the task ahead seemed daunting. I had a good memory; especially, it seemed, for bad things. I thought I probably had weeks of work ahead of me. In fact, in the end I found that by steadily chipping away at it, I dealt with the bulk of it in about three days. My memory suddenly dried up, and right up until the point that it did so I had assumed that there was lot more to come. It was a pleasant surprise, therefore, to reach the end much sooner than I expected.

In my experience of helping others through the same process, I have found that the time it takes to complete the process varies, depending on how naturally resentful the person is, how good their memory is, and how quickly they are able to write. I would say that in comparison to others I am naturally given to taking resentments very easily and am unfortunate that I have a good memory for bad memories. Therefore, I had a lot to write down. I am lucky, however, in that converting the memories to the written word happened quite easily for me. So the writing part of it was less of a difficulty. Some are not so fortunate and struggle with the discipline of writing.

Sometimes I found this part of the process uncomfortable because I was reliving the situations that had caused anger and resentment. I was told that the best way to deal with this was to write it down and move on to the next item on the list once I had written down the components of self-centeredness connected with it. I was digging up some very painful thoughts, but I found that I was okay as long as I didn't dwell on any one resentment and stayed close to God by following my daily routine of prayer, meditation and good works.

After I had finished the writing, the process of reading all of these out loud was in itself an anticlimactic and surprisingly tedious process. Sin is, after all, rather dull.

Once I had read everything to David, I expected to feel a sudden and dramatic change for the better, like a swimmer coming up for air after holding his breath under water. But in fact, I don't remember feeling anything at this point except the relief that I no longer had to put the time aside to read out the list.

However, a few days later, I noticed that I felt connected to everyone in a way that I could not remember ever feeling before. It was as though I was part of the human race for the first time. The loneliness that had been with me for as long as I could remember had evaporated. This was an astounding change, one that I had never believed possible.

The wonderful thing about this is that I can have that feeling every single day for the rest of my life if I want it. Whenever I am not feeling great, I can sit down and ask myself what is troubling me. It's always resentment or fear that is causing the problem. Then I can apply the moral examination to whatever it is and as a result, peace and contentment return once more.

Another blessing that arose from this process was a clear identification of the direct link between sin and unhappiness. This modified my behavior in a couple of ways. First, I was more motivated to be virtuous and to avoid doing bad things, because I knew that failure to do so would increase my unhappiness. Also, I was less inclined now to be envious of those who were behaving badly and seemed to be getting away with it. I began to feel compassionate toward such people for the suffering I assumed that they must be going through, regardless of how happy or unhappy they appeared to be.

The conviction that there was a loving God present in my life now intensified and has continued to do so ever since by following the daily program. Since this time, as difficulties inevitably arise from time to time, I feel carried through them and protected. This is a way of life that works even when times are hard. Sometimes the tough times are caused by my own selfishness or foolishness. I can still make very bad decisions from time to time. But as soon as I recognize this I can move forward from wherever I am and toward the Light. Immediately I have that joy of living.

When I practice the principles I have been given, my life feels ordered and structured and good even when all around me is chaos. I am able to feel genuine gratitude for the gifts I am given on a daily basis.

By continuing the work of doing my best to be free of resentment and fear, God continually reveals more and more to me. I have maintained a sense of a spiritual journey ever since.

None of this is due to my own wisdom, skill, or natural ability. I can take no credit. It is simply that I was blessed to meet people who offered me this simple process, and my pride was battered enough that I was prepared to listen.

About four years after going through this process I converted to Catholicism. One reason was the realization that it was due to the presence of the Church, the mystical body of Christ, in this world that the process had worked so spectacularly well for me and given me this new joy even before my conversion. In my experience, God is very generous to those who seek him. He meets you where you are and leads you to him on a path that is never too difficult to follow. He is not contained by or restricted to the sacraments of the Church, but reaches out beyond them to draw us in.

Once I was received into the Church, it deepened and intensified the joy of the spiritual journey further. The Church is a never-ending well of grace that continues to give my life purpose and direction and increasing joy to this day. I am participating in the creative love of God, which had always been the answer to my problems. I am now part of the Church that offers joy to so many others in the world, who perhaps do not know Christ yet as I did not when he first reached me.

Maintain this on a daily basis: add the process of self-examination to your daily prayer and meditation

After dealing with my backlog of resentment I wanted to preserve this newfound peace. I was encouraged to incorporate this method of self-examination into my daily examination of conscience. Generally, I do not need to write down every small resentment I feel – just noticing a resentment and then mentally acknowledging its origin in self-centeredness will cause most daily resentments to evaporate. However some will persist beyond this mental exercise; then I do have to reach for pen and paper.

Each evening as part of my review of conscience I check to see that all seems right with the world before my head hits the pillow. If there are any bad feelings I deal with them, asking God for forgiveness on my knees after writing them down. If I have caused harm to someone, then I must make full restitution as soon as I can.

Now that we have cleared away resentment and fear we are open to God's inspiration in a new way. The next stage is to try to discern his calling – our personal vocation.

Now pray:

Bend my heart to your will, Oh God.
I ask this in the name of my Lord Jesus Christ.

12 The Deepening of the Mysteries

Contemplative Prayer

Once we have been through the spiritual exercises of the process as described in Part 2, we begin to have a greater sense of God at work in our lives. This sense of progress continues if we keep doing the daily program that has been suggested, including a daily examination of conscience.

Many of us feel at this point that we have experienced a spiritual awakening – a change in outlook and deepening of our faith that is having a profound and good effect on our lives. By practice of daily (ideally) reflection/meditation and contemplative prayer, we exercise our own spirit, so that we continue to develop our capacity to cooperate with the Holy Spirit. As a result, the gifts of the Spirit come to fruition more completely. For example, the application of our common sense and judgment in ordinary matters of life will become wiser, our intuition will become stronger and more accurate, and each of these improved faculties will better direct our thinking and be more in accord with reason.

If you can do the following daily, even for just a few minutes, the practice will serve you well. Of course, many will not find the time for daily practice, so as with all else, do your best.

Meditation and contemplation

These two words often go together in people's minds and are often used interchangeably, although they do have distinct meanings in the traditional Christian understanding. There are many forms of both and I do not suggest that the methods described in this book are the only appropriate methods to choose. If you know someone, especially an experienced contemplative layperson, religious or clergy, then it might be a good idea to approach them and ask for some help.

We have already been introduced to one spiritual exercise that involves reflection, which in the terminology of the Western tradition, could also be called a meditation. As mentioned, meditation in the Western tradition is a process of the *conscious* mind. It is *directed thinking*; that is, we direct our thoughts to heavenly things and ultimately to God. Put simply, we put aside time to think about subjects that are good to think about. The higher the things we think about, the better it is for us.

Contemplative prayer, in contrast, is a passive form of mental prayer by which we quiet the mind so that we are in a 'listening' (receptive) mode of thought, waiting and watching; rather than an active mode of thought where we expend energy generating ideas.

In practice meditation often precedes contemplation. Not all meditation needs to be directed toward contemplation – the writing of the gratitude list usually isn't, for example – but meditation *can* be practiced in such a way that it leads the mind into that contemplative state. God can make himself known to us at any moment of his choosing, not just when we schedule 'contemplation' into our calendars, and he does not need us to meditate in order to do so. All we can do is develop our faculty for the reception of God; in the event that he should choose to grace us in that fashion, our ability to respond is enhanced.

What does contemplative prayer feel like and does it matter?

We know what the 17th century sculptor Bernini thought it was like. One look at Bernini's sculptures of the mystic St. Teresa of Avila in ecstasy and his Blessed Ludovica will give you a sense of the ecstasy that they experienced. I cannot confirm how accurate a depiction Bernini's art is (but regardless they are wonderful sculptures).

While we can prepare to listen and accept the gift of contemplation if God chooses to give it to us, we cannot compel God to speak to us and so it is not in our power to see contemplative prayer through to its final end. It is God's choice whether or not he makes himself present to us in this way. God's reasons are a mystery to us and so we should not interpret the receiving of such an experience as reward for holiness, or skill at contemplative prayer; nor should we interpret the failure to experience it as a punishment.

We can be in this passive state and benefiting from the presence of God, without having any obvious or dramatic feeling that God is there. He doesn't always make himself known to us, and when he does it might not be in ways that we expect. The passages of God speaking to the prophets Elijah and Samuel come to mind here. In 1 Kings 19, Elijah is searching for the voice of God. He searches in a great wind, in an earthquake, in consuming fire, but eventually God reveals himself as a "still small voice" (verse 12). In 1 Samuel 3 the Lord calls Samuel, who is at this point a boy in the household of a very elderly Eli. Samuel hears a voice calling and three times he goes to ask Eli what he wants, mistakenly thinking that it is Eli who is calling him. He was not yet able to recognize the voice of the Lord. Finally, Eli realized what was happening and explained to Samuel how he should respond (verse 9).

When I pray contemplatively, I seek out a quiet place with a comfortable chair. Then I begin. During the meditation stage I tend to experience a gradual quieting of the mind and a restful state of peace and calm. I do get distracted from time to time and when I notice this I return to the meditation as directed, and the process of quieting the mind continues. Quite often at a certain point I feel very still and at ease and it seems to me that I am observing the thoughts that come into my mind rather than initiating them. This is pleasurable. Sometimes, very occasionally, I even get to the stage where I am in a state of what I can only describe as happy and restful expectation – I am ready for the thoughts that cross my mind, but very little happens.

In my experience, these periods of deep rest do not necessarily last long. Typically what happens is that I experience it, then I notice that I'm feeling like this, and this thought then sparks other thoughts (not all good). The passive state is immediately broken and I go down a train of distracted thought. Then I notice that I am distracted, and I consciously direct my thought back to the meditation whereby my thoughts are refocused so that they might lead me closer to the desired passive state. Most of this mental to and fro is happening at a low level of quiet thought. After the period of contemplative prayer, I usually feel rested and relaxed, but not always.

It's not about how we feel during the prayer

Although it is usually pleasurable (depending on the thoughts that occur), I do not remember ever being moved in the way that St. Teresa appears in Bernini's sculpture. I have never, to my knowledge, seen the Light of God through this method and would guess that even the great Bernini would struggle to make a sculpture of *David Clayton in Contemplative Prayer* worth looking at. However, I don't think the fact that I haven't been transported into such ecstasy matters very much.

Why? First, because, as I have said, it is up to God to bestow upon me useful "feelings" during this stage. Second, I think of contemplative prayer as an exercise that develops a faculty of the soul that will benefit me later, when praying in the sacred liturgy, and when trying to serve God as I go about my daily business.

It's like tuning the radio – the old-fashioned sort where you actually turn a dial and see a needle moving through all the wavelengths – and hearing it play whatever is received. The tuning process might be noisy or it might be quiet, depending on where you start on the dial. It doesn't really matter how quiet or noisy the tuning process is; what counts is where the needle ends up so that I can stop tuning and actually listen to the program.

The period of contemplative prayer is as much about the tuning, in this sense, as it is the receiving. I think of it as a routine that is training the soul to be more cooperative with God's grace and with the workings of the Spirit, which generally are going to be given to me outside the period of meditation. The fruits of this practice, to the degree that they are noticeable, are more likely to be seen in the course of my day; these are the fruits of the Holy Spirit. This doesn't rule out direct contact during contemplative prayer, but I try to remember that the purpose of prayer is to make me better able to serve in the whole of my life, not to achieve some sort of spiritual high with little useful connection to real life. There is little difference between this and looking for a drug-induced hallucination.

More about my practice of contemplative prayer

As already mentioned, there are many good books on this and many good priests and spiritual directors who can help you. If you know of any, these should be consulted. I am just going to describe two methods that I have used. The first is *lectio divina*[1] and the second I call *conspectio divina*, a form of contemplative prayer that involves sacred art.

Lectio divina

This is a process whereby the point of engagement of the mind is scripture. The phrase *lectio divina* means literally 'divine reading.'

In his apostolic exhortation, *Verbum Domini EN 87*, Pope Benedict XVI wrote about *lectio divina* in the following way:

> The documents produced before and during the Synod mentioned a number of methods for a faith-filled and fruitful approach to sacred Scripture. Yet the greatest attention was paid to *lectio divina*, which is truly "capable of opening up to the faithful the treasures of God's word, but also of bringing about an encounter with Christ, the living word of God".

I would like here to review the basic steps of this procedure. It opens with the reading (*lectio*) of a text, which leads to a desire to understand

---

[1] The first, *lectio divina*, will be mentioned in less detail here because I have already written about it in *The Little Oratory* and also because there is much information available elsewhere.

its true content: *what does the biblical text say in itself?* Without this, there is always a risk that the text will become a pretext for never moving beyond our own ideas. Next comes meditation (*meditatio*), which asks: *what does the biblical text say to us?* Here, each person, individually but also as a member of the community, must let himself or herself be moved and challenged. Following this comes prayer (*oratio*), which asks the question: *what do we say to the Lord in response to his word?* Prayer, as petition, intercession, thanksgiving and praise, is the primary way by which the word transforms us. Finally, *lectio divina* concludes with contemplation (*contemplatio*), during which we take up, as a gift from God, his own way of seeing and judging reality, and ask ourselves *what conversion of mind, heart and life is the Lord asking of us?*

In the *Letter to the Romans*, Saint Paul tells us:

> Do not be conformed to this world, but be transformed by the renewal of your mind, that you may prove what is the will of God, what is good and acceptable and perfect (12:2).

Contemplation aims at creating within us a truly wise and discerning vision of reality, as God sees it, and at forming within us "the mind of Christ" (1 Cor. 2:16). The word of God appears here as a criterion for discernment: it is "living and active, sharper than any two-edged sword, piercing to the division of soul and spirit, of joints and marrow, and discerning the thoughts and intentions of the heart" (Heb. 4:12). We do well also to remember that the process of *lectio divina* is not concluded until it arrives at action (*actio*), which moves the believer to make his or her life a gift for others in charity.

> We find the supreme synthesis and fulfilment of this process in the Mother of God. For every member of the faithful Mary is the model of docile acceptance of God's word, for she "kept all these things, pondering them in her heart" (Lk 2:19; cf. 2:51); she discovered the profound bond which unites, in God's great plan, apparently disparate events, actions and things. (Verbum Domini EN 87)

Some simple directions on how to do Lectio Divina based upon Benedict XVI's directions[2]

We begin by calling on the Holy Spirit, asking for his assistance. Then we proceed to read and to meditate the Sacred Text in Five Movements, using each time a different human quality. It is helpful to remember the words of Our Lord here: 'Seek and you shall find, knock and it shall be opened to you.' (Lk. 11:9)

The First Movement is called **Lectio**, which is to read the sacred text: using the Intellect we seek for the objective meaning of the text. In words of Pope Benedict XVI: "It opens with the reading (*Lectio*) of a text, which leads to a desire to understand its true content: what does the biblical text say in itself? Without this, there is always a risk that the text will become a pretext for never moving beyond our own ideas" (VD 87).

As you do so consider the following questions and write down answers to them: Who are the characters in the reading? What are the circumstances for the events described – when, how, where, and why? – and finally, what is it teaching us, what does the reading actually say?

The Second Movement is called **Meditatio**, which is to meditate on the sacred text: using the heart we find what the text is saying to me. In the words of Pope Benedict XVI:

> Next comes meditation (*Meditatio*), which asks: what does the biblical text say to us? Here, each person, individually but also as a member of the community, must let himself or herself be moved and challenged (VD 87).

Now we write down the answers to the following questions: What is the text telling me? How does it affect my life? What does it remind me off?

The Third Movement is called **Oratio**, which is to pray with the sacred text: using our whole being we knock by engaging in conversation with God through prayer. In the words of Pope Benedict XVI:

---

[2] I am grateful to Fr Marcel Navarro, a priest of the Institute of the Incarnate Word (IVE), for this presentation.

Following this, comes prayer (*Oratio*), which asks the question: what do we say to the Lord in response to his word? Prayer, as petition, intercession, thanksgiving and praise, is the primary way by which the word transforms us (VD 87).

Petition arises from an awareness of our relationship with God and so we consider what the text is asking me to do or to change. Then comes intercession: That God may give me the grace to do it; then thanksgiving: To the Lord beforehand for the gift; and finally praise: In God's providence to achieve the goal.

We note here that these are movements in prayer that are present in the sacred liturgy.

The Fourth Movement is called **Contemplatio**, which is a passive act of contemplation: using nothing, we let the Lord open to us and reveal to us whatsoever, however and whenever. In words of Pope Benedict XVI:

> Next comes contemplation (*Contemplatio*), during which we take up, as a gift from God, his own way of seeing and judging reality, and ask ourselves what conversion of mind, heart, and life is the Lord asking of us? [...] Contemplation aims at creating within us a truly wise and discerning vision of reality, as God sees it, and at forming within us "the mind of Christ" (1 Cor. 2:16) (VD 87).

Contemplate: God's love through the message He has given me; Comprehend: that I am a part of his plan & that despite my faults he loves me; Taste: I Enjoy the beauty of his gifts and the healing power of his mercy.

The Fifth Movement is called **Actio**, which is an active resolution to make the text come to life: using the power of the Will, we resolve to cooperate with God's grace to act upon the Word (following the example of Our Lady). In the words of Pope Benedict XVI:

> The process of *Lectio Divina* is not concluded until it arrives at action (*Actio*), which moves the believer to make his or her life a gift

for others in charity. We find the supreme synthesis and fulfillment of this process in the Mother of God. For every member of the faithful, Mary is the model of docile acceptance of God's word, for she "kept all these things, pondering them in her heart" (Lk 2:19; cf. 2:51)" (VD 87).

Recognize: What is it that I am supposed to do? Plan: How I am to do it? Evaluate: How am I progressing?

We conclude our Lectio by offering a prayer of thanksgiving to God for all gifts received.

Conspectio divina – divine watching – contemplative prayer with visual images

I adopted the practice of *conspectio divina* to help me stay focused during the period of quiet contemplation that follows *lectio divina*. I found that my mind wandered too much, and I wanted to find a way into that quiet, receptive state. However, *conspectio divina* can be practiced as a form of contemplative prayer in itself – it does not need to be done in conjunction with scripture reading.

There is also a longer version in which 30 minutes is put aside. The shortened version can be adapted to fill any few minutes in the day. Since it is about looking at the image of the invisible God, who is Christ, I call this practice *divine seeing – conspectio divina*.

When you first attempt this sort of contemplative prayer you might like to find copies of the same images and look at them as you pray. They are standard images for the core of an icon corner, as explained in *The Little Oratory* book in more depth.

You may begin by looking at the image itself as you pray. Part way through the prayer time, close your eyes and continue to pray with the image in your memory. Eventually you will not need the actual image at all, in order to begin. It will be ingrained in your memory sufficiently strongly for you to just close your eyes and see it.

Visual beauty conveys aspects of the truth that cannot be articulated in words

As you pray and gaze at each image, either directly or in the imagination, try to avoid conscious analysis of the painting such as might form a written commentary. Rather, let its form speak to you directly and silently as you look upon it and repeat the prayers. Holy images speak to us of things in ways that words cannot, through their style and beauty. If you spend the whole time creating in your mind a description of the image that could be used in a book about religious art, you are shutting out those aspects that are *beyond* words. The other side of this, of course, is that there are also some truths which cannot be said in art that <u>can</u> be said in words, so it is important to practice *lectio divina* meditating upon words and texts as well.

Conspectio divina, long version:

First, I find somewhere quiet to sit.

1. **Preparation:**
   a. **If you have not done so yet today, complete a written examination of conscience** looking at all resentments and fears using the method of analysis described in this book. Ask God for forgiveness for your sins, to remove your resentments and fear and to redirect your thoughts so that you may serve him better. Pray briefly for all those for whom you experience resentment.

   b. **If you have not done so yet today, write a gratitude list for the day.**

When you have done this, set a timer to 30 minutes or so and begin.

2. Pray to the Holy Spirit to lead you to Christ

Pray silently to yourself eight times: *Come Holy Creator Spirit Blest, lead me to Christ* or similar words that express this sentiment.

Focus now upon an image of the Holy Spirit. The Spirit has appeared as a dove or as fire in scripture and so you might like to have a picture of the baptism of Christ in the Jordan or of the fire at Pentecost. I prefer to think of the Spirit in relation to the Father and the Son – the personalization of the *agape-eros* dynamic that exists between them – so I choose an image of the hospitality of Abraham in which the three strangers whom he welcomed to his tent were in fact angels. The Fathers of the Church interpreted these three angels as a symbolic representation of the Trinity. In what is perhaps the most famous representation of this scene (which has become a common prototype), the Russian iconographer Andrei Rublev paints the figure on the left with ethereal clothing and the other two are looking at him. The central figure is identified as Christ, and commentators differ as to which of the other two is the Father and which symbolizes the Holy Spirit. I identify this angelic figure on the left with the Father.

3. Approaching Christ on the cross with the saints showing you the way

Next imagine Christ as a Lamb on the altar with all the saints and angels adoring him. If you can, find a picture online of the Van Eyck Ghent altarpiece in which the multitude from various distances are adoring a lamb 'standing as slain' on the altar. You might like to study that and commit it to memory. Alternatively, look at Zurbaran's famous painting of the Lamb of God and imagine all the saints and angels looking at that Lamb along with you. If you search for these images on the internet you can find them and print or order reproductions.

Pray with John the Baptist who is quoted in scripture saying: *Behold the Lamb of God.* Pray this quietly, or even silently, eight times. If you bring to mind any saints to whom you are devoted, you might say the same prayer and imagine you are saying it with each one in turn: *Behold the Lamb of God.*

4. Our Lady, Queen of Heaven, shows you her son

Now move to a picture of Our Lady showing us her son. I shall not suggest a particular one as there are so very many from which to choose.

Pray eight times silently: *Hail, Mary, full of Grace, the Lord is with you.* Note that this is not the whole Hail Mary prayer, just the first line.

5. See her son, Jesus, on the cross and imagine him taking upon himself all your sins

Now study a picture of Christ on the cross.

Pray eight times: *Lord Jesus Christ Son of God, have mercy on me a sinner.*

With the picture still before your eyes, recall the resentments and fears that you wrote down in your examination of conscience before starting to pray. Imagine that all the self-pity, anger, and fear that you felt in connection with these is lifted from you, and Christ is now feeling them for you instead, willingly taking them on himself. Then remember that he is feeling all the resentments and fears that you have ever given him and that he has freely chosen to take them all upon himself. Reflect further, that he is feeling all the resentment and fear ever experienced in the past, or to be experienced in the future by all as a consequence of every single sin whether or not ever acknowledged and forgiven. Imagine the torture he is experiencing, and the love for us that he must have in order to choose to bear all of that spiritual suffering for us. Then thank him for this and for all the blessings that have come into your life that you wrote on your gratitude list.

In his Confessions (VIII, 7), St. Augustine tells us that as a young man he prayed, "Grant me chastity and continence… but not yet." Try to think especially about those sins for which we have least sorrow and so repent least. Think about how they are contributing all the more to the pain and suffering that Our Lord experiences on the cross and how callous I am not to regret this more. Because I am conscious that true contrition for sin is lacking in me, I now always ask for forgiveness for my lack of sorrow for sins and my tendency to harbor a wish that I could get away with repeating some of them. I ask for the grace to help me become more fully contrite.

Compunction of the Heart

Rather than offering only those current sins that are on our mind some might prefer at this point to do an exercise referred to in the Rule of St. Benedict as "Compunction of the Heart." St. Benedict suggests that this is especially helpful during the penitential season of Lent, but I want to suggest that it is a good practice at any time of the year and especially in this context. Compunction of the heart is a process whereby we remember past sins that we have already confessed. We remember first the unhappiness and discomfort we felt as a result of this, we remember the sorrow we felt for our sins, and then we remember how this lifted when we confessed them. This leads us to wonder at the power of the mercy of God and his love, for he bore our pain, along with that of all other sins that have ever been confessed and ever will be. He took this vicarious spiritual suffering on himself freely and in addition to the great physical pain that he experienced during the Passion. When we ponder on this we can only say another prayer of gratitude to Jesus for bearing the pain of our sins willingly.

6. See the face of Christ in glory

Now, whether in fact or in imagination, move to an image of the face of Christ in glory – perhaps from a blessing Christ, a Sacred Heart image or a mandylion like we saw earlier in this book. If you have a picture of the Ghent altarpiece then the face of the enthroned figure is the image of God, that of the Son (and the invisible God, the Father). Just gaze upon the face and nothing else

Pray eight times quietly or silently: *Lord Jesus Christ Son of God, have mercy on me a sinner.*

7. Pray to the Holy Spirit to lead you to the Father

Now in the Spirit and through Christ we can approach the Father.

Pray eight times: *Come Holy Spirit, lead me to the Father through Christ.*

Focus on the image of the Holy Spirit. Once again, I choose the Rublev Trinity and imagine now the Spirit leading me to the Father.

8. Address the Father

Now we come to the Father who is the ultimate object of our praise and worship.

Pray eight times: *Our Father who art in heaven.*

Then, as Jesus told us we could, ask the Father whatever you want, in prayer, in the name of Jesus. I do ask for things for myself at this point, asking that they be granted if they will help me to serve God and man. I also make a point to pray for others. I start with those toward whom I have felt resentment and those I think might be resentful of me. I pray also for those that I love and anyone who comes to mind who might need help. I make a point of asking for these things 'in the name of Jesus Christ our Lord.'

When praying to the Father, keep in mind the image of the face of Christ, the Son in glory that we prayed to before. We are told by St. Paul that Christ is the image of the invisible God (Col 1: 15).

9. Repeat the Jesus Prayer until your time is finished.

After this more active opening phase of the meditation I return to the Jesus Prayer – 'Lord Jesus Christ Son of God, have mercy on me a sinner' – and repeat it until the end of the allotted time. It is during these repetitions with the image of the face of the Christ in my mind that I might become deeply relaxed and quiet.

10. Conclusion: returning to our daily lives in peace to serve God and to love God through love of man

When you finish, imagine hearing the final words of the Mass, the dismissal, in your imagination. If you want precise wordings, there are four variations, so take your pick.

I imagine the voice of Christ telling me: *Go in peace, glorifying the Lord by your life.*

Then I pray: *Thanks be to God.*

Then imagine yourself going out into the world. I might just let my mind gradually awaken, so to speak, regaining a more active conscious state of mind for a couple of minutes.

Why contemplative prayer is structured in this way

The structure of meditation in *conspectio divina* is designed to lead us from this world into the mystery of the Trinity in our imaginations and then take us back out into the world from which we came, ready to serve God. This is done in order to prepare us for what happens in reality and by degrees when we worship God in the sacred liturgy.

The Christian life is one in which, prompted by the Holy Spirit and with the help of the prayers and example of Our Lady and the saints, we have an encounter with Christ. We can be fit to do so only because Christ takes our sins upon himself on the cross and then gives himself to us so that we have a personal connection. Through our relationship with Christ as man we are intimately connected with Christ as God and are raised up to partake of the divine nature. Now the Holy Spirit leads us to the Father and we worship the Father, through the Son in the Spirit. In this life, this is not the end of the story. We encounter God in the liturgy and are partially transformed, but we must return to the temporal, albeit better able to participate in the Christian life.

The method of repeated prayer is intended to take us to a point of regarding the image silently, so that our prayer is developing in us that faculty for receptivity of the truth that is contained visually.

Note that neither this nor *lectio divina* are 'don't think anything' methods in the manner of some forms of Eastern meditation; rather they are methods of developing different faculties of thought, active and passive. This passivity is not inactivity because we are giving the mind something to accept whether words, images, or music. We are receptive but alert: watching, reading, or listening.

The hope is that we will be prepared through our daily practices of prayer to engage in the full dynamic of communication that takes place in the liturgy: through words, vision, music, ritual, posture and so on. By this, our loving desire for God, *eros* can be consummated in the reception of his love.

Numbers – how important are they?

At this point it might be worth mentioning the numbers. As anyone who has read my two earlier books will know, seven is the number of the old covenant going right back to creation in seven days. Eight, seven plus one, is the number of the new covenant ushered in by the incarnation, the life, death and resurrection of Christ. Christ is the eighth day and his day is the eighth day of the week, Sunday, which is simultaneously the first day of the next week.

In this context, the number seven points to its resolution in the eighth repetition. It is as if we were to hear someone singing a musical scale who then stopped abruptly at the seventh note. We could not help but be aware of the lack and wait expectantly for the eighth to complete it. Without the eighth it is unresolved.

This seven plus one pattern is contained within the pattern of the liturgy in the weekly cycle, as described, and the daily cycle in the traditional number of hours in the Liturgy of the Hours in a 24-hour period – seven offices in the day and one at night. The number 150 is the number of the psalms in the Book of Psalms. The Psalms are songs composed for worship and are sung in the liturgy. This book is said to be unique in the Bible because, according to St. Thomas Aquinas, it contains 'all of theology.' The number 150 is also created by adding 80 to 70. In his commentary on the psalms St. Thomas Aquinas tells us that this ratio of 7:8 speaks of the relationship of old covenant to the new covenant. That is why in the traditional rosary (Joyful, Sorrowful, Glorious mysteries) there are 150 repetitions of the Hail Mary in the decades.

The number of repetitions speaks to us of the liturgy both through our comprehension of the number symbolism, and through the pattern of prayer that we conform to, and so when we conform to this in the liturgy our souls are impressed with this mark of worship.

We can see that this *conspectio divina* is, when prayed, forming us for worship even through its numerical structure.

Loud thinking and quiet thinking

Multiple repetitions of brief and simple phrases can help lead us into quieter and quieter internal prayer. Imagine first you are saying the suggested words of each prayer, then imagine you are hearing them, then just know that they are being said – and finally think of the whole as a truth that exists as a single utterance that occupies both the tiniest fraction of a second and all time continuously and simultaneously. At this final stage sit with that truth and look continuously at the image within your mind, silent but ever alert.

When distractions occur, and you notice that you have strayed from the prayer, you can do two things. If it is a good thought – perhaps about God or the saints or the Church or your personal vocation of service to God – then see it through to its resolution and at that point return to the repeated prayer. You might have pen and paper handy so that you can record anything you wish to return to after the contemplative prayer is over. That way you don't need to worry about forgetting it and don't need to hang on to the memory. Once recorded you can happily let it go and return to the repeated prayer.

If the distraction is a bad thought then return to the prayer at a mental volume, so to speak, that is louder than the distraction. If the distraction is strong, you might even have to say the Jesus prayer out loud to bring you back to the right place. Once the prayer has displaced the unwelcome distraction, allow your 'thought volume' to be attenuated moving towards an ever-quieter repetition as before.

Beware! This prayer is not in itself a shortcut to the presence of God

This method should not be seen as a shortcut. Its purpose is to help us on the true path by deepening our participation in the sacramental life of the Church. It is through the Church, with the sacred liturgy at its heart, that we achieve our ultimate end in the next life, which is full and eternal union with God. Contemplative prayer is not higher than the sacred liturgy. Having said that, God is not limited by or restricted to his sacraments and can make his presence known to us in either situation. This prayer is very powerful in helping us to make the whole of our lives liturgical, a living expression of the love of God that extends even beyond the formal worship of the Church.

Be careful, too, about attaching too much significance to the thoughts that occur to you during the meditation. Your memory may throw up many angry, resentful and somewhat uncomfortable thoughts and emotions. When this happens, don't indulge in them. When you notice that you have strayed from the prayer you are supposed to be repeating and the image you ought to have in mind, just observe that they are still there and gently return to the prayer. Resist the temptation to make any psychological analysis of yourself based upon what memories your subconscious throws up. Just move back to the prayer.

My experience of combining contemplation with the spiritual exercises from the preceding chapter is that this has been an extremely powerful and beneficial purification process which deals not only with all long-held resentment and fear, but also the ups and downs of each day. I can't prove to you that this is so; it is based upon an inner conviction that is reinforced as time goes on, that this is helping my day. It just seems to me that the days seem to go better and happier when I do it.

A shorter version

It is quite legitimate to reduce this to a much simpler meditation by, for example, reducing the number of repetitions or perhaps simplifying the approach to the Father through Christ in Glory in the Spirit. You might simply move from the face of Christ as the Son, to the face of Christ as the image of the Father, for example. A simple repetition of the Jesus Prayer with the face of Christ in mind is powerful too.

Even longer versions – it can be part of a Holy Hour

To do a longer version, you can extend any part of the meditations as a special focus – for example, gratitude, the acceptance by Christ of your sins and suffering and so on. You can also extend the periods of repeated prayer and especially the Jesus Prayer. Also, this can be done as part of time spent silently in the presence of the Blessed Sacrament, such as in a Holy Hour.

Divine listening

A similar argument to that made in regard to the beauty of art could be made, I suggest, about the beauty of music. I leave it to the musicologists among you to devise a properly worked out aural equivalent – a divine listening – in which sacred music speaks to us through its form as much as through the sense of the words that are connected to it. Speaking speculatively, there may be a place for this in the Sacred Liturgy itself. This might be the value, for example, of having the Gregorian Latin propers sung at Mass after the congregation (which mostly does not understand Latin) has heard it chanted clearly and beautifully in English.[3] Then when they hear the Gregorian chant in the Latin, they know the meaning of the text in advance, and this frees them to be receptive to the form of the music which is linked intrinsically to the meaning of the text, and which speaks through its beauty of things that words cannot. It is preferable for the congregation to be *singing* or *listening* to text in English or Latin rather than to be simply reading it from a book before hearing the Latin sung (as I might do if I was just reading the translation in the Missal at the Latin Mass). That additional participation through a comprehending engagement with music and text leads us more powerfully and completely into that receptive state of mind. Then we can grasp more fully those aspects of the truth that words cannot express and are communicated through the form of the music.

What I have just described assumes, of course, that the style of music is one such as chant, in which the form is intrinsically linked to the meaning of the words. It is desirable to hear the Latin chanted, even if English is used as well, because the Gregorian tradition is the one in which form and content are most perfectly integrated. In the ideal we would know the Latin too, and in time this might encourage some to learn it. Unless the words of the Latin are known by the listener to the degree that hearing them immediately communicates the sense, then the singing of the vernacular is desirable, too. This does not mean that we need to be

---

[3] Using, for example, Adam Bartlett's Propers in English from the *Lumen Christi Missal*.

fluent Latin speakers – we simply need a sufficient level of familiarity with the Latin texts that we are aware of what the words are pointing us to in the liturgy. Those parts of the Mass – for example, the Ordinaries – that are repeated every week will quickly become familiar enough that we do not need to have them in the vernacular first.

Also, any form of chant which is sung antiphonally – that is, alternating with call and response, for example in the singing of the Office – naturally engages the person in both the active and the passive faculties of prayer. The opportunity for meditation and contemplation is built into the singing of the Divine Office and those parts of the Mass in which there is call and response.

All of this trains us to participate more deeply in the liturgy and especially the Eucharist, where we encounter Truth Himself and accept *h*im in love – our *eros* to his *agape* – and then return it – our *agape* to his *eros*.

Whatever form of contemplative prayer you choose, do it regularly

All the spiritual literature that I have read on contemplative prayer emphasizes regular practice. Circumstances vary, and what is possible for one person may not be possible for another. Whatever form you choose (or your spiritual director guides you to use) do something that you can do regularly and for a period of time that you know you can repeat. Aim for an ideal, at least, of once a day and resolve to persist even during those periods when the novelty wears off and it starts to seem dry and boring. Remember the reward is not the pleasure of the prayer itself, but the effect it has on the rest of our lives. I heard a talk recently about the Jesus prayer and the speaker quoted a Church Father who said, "The greatest reward in prayer comes not through the pleasure it gives us, but in the toil we take."

Now pray…

Bend my heart to your will, Oh God.
I ask this in the name of my Lord Jesus Christ.

Part 3

13 The Vision for You

Discerning Your Personal Vocation and How to Make It Happen

'It was not you that chose me, I chose you. The task I have appointed you is to go out and bear fruit, fruit which will endure; so that every request you make of the Father in my name may be granted you.'

John 15:16 (Knox translation):

At this point you will ideally have done what this book and the *Little Oratory* have suggested and incorporated the daily practices into your life as habits. You do your best to practice a liturgically-centered piety and go to Mass, pray the Liturgy of the Hours, have a prayer life that is a balance of liturgical, para-liturgical, and personal prayer, along with a life that incorporates a pattern of good works. Clearly the degree to which you are able to participate in this depends on whether or not you are Catholic and in a state of grace. If you are doing these things in a harmonious pattern, then all of this prayer and meditation will lighten the load of your daily life. It will not be an additional burden. You have done all you can to clear away the resentment and fear from the past that has been separating you from God, and you continue daily to examine your feelings and your conscience to maintain a clear connection with God.

Now that you have maximized your receptivity to God's call you are in a position to try to start listening to that call and to discern exactly what it is telling you. You are ready to discern your personal vocation.

This is a lot simpler and quicker than many people think. The assumption behind the method I am about to explain is that God speaks to us clearly and simply in various ways, including our imaginations. The imagination is a means by which we picture what does not exist, but which might exist in the future. It is also the means by which remember things seen in the past.

We do need to be discerning. We must be aware that we are as capable of imagining something bad as well as something good and so be able to distinguish between the two. As long as we keep this in mind, you will see that this is a simple process.

Here is the question that David asked me to consider to start:

If you inherited so much money that you never needed to work again, what activity would you choose to do, 9am - 5pm, five days a week?

Ask yourself this question and try to answer it. When you do so, allow yourself to dream wildly. Provided that what you do want to do is not contrary to moral law, then there is every reason to believe that your dream comes from God and is his calling.

Our personal vocation is not necessarily the dream itself so much as the life we have when we strive for the realization of that dream. God's will for us is what results each day as we do so. The result may or may not correspond to what we are striving for – that is in God's hands (although in my experience it often does). But this call, or 'homing signal,' is meant to be heeded and it will take us to where we are meant to be.

Anything is possible with God

Remember that we are answering a call from God, who has all power. If we are seeking to conform to his will, anything is possible for us. If you are meant to be President, he can make that happen more easily than a snap of the fingers and regardless of what expert political pundits might think of your chances. Recall St. Scholastica, who was so completely conformed to God's will that she could pray to God and the weather followed her desire. If we aim for holiness first, then to the degree that we become holy then this can be true for us to. Everything contained in this book and in *The Little Oratory* has been written to direct you to this holiness – a supernatural transformation in Christ that sets you apart from the person you used to be. Such holiness is within the grasp of all of us if we believe it is possible and have sufficient humility.

Therefore, allow yourself to dream wildly. You can dream for any occupation or situation that you want – painting, performing music, or composing – as long as carrying out that occupation isn't inherently immoral.[1]

Don't restrict yourself to jobs that other people do

There is no need to restrict yourself to an activity that other people already get paid for. You can dream of doing things that people don't normally get paid for – remember the initial question, we are thinking about what we would do if we didn't need the money. If this dream is realized, then you might find that you have the money you need to live, but by another source, or you might become unique in being paid for it. Who knows – you might very well become the first professional Abyssinian nose flute player in your hometown.

This is about what we want to *do*, not what we want to be

It is important when answering this question that you consider the *activity* that you will do each day. This means that 'pop star' is not an answer to this question, but 'sing' or 'write songs,' or both, is. Having said that, once you have established that singing is what you would like to do, there is nothing wrong in seeking to be a chart-topping and successful singer.

What sort of dream is right for me? Don't be scared to say what is on your mind

---

[1] One would imagine, for example, that it is unlikely that God would view the desire to be a successful drug dealer or pimp with any great favor.

Sometimes when presented with this question, people know instantly what it is and will say it. Sometimes they know instantly but are afraid to say it and it has to be coaxed out of them. I knew immediately what that activity was for me – painting. Yours might not be so obvious, or it might be something that you have always wanted to do, but never had the nerve to admit to anyone else before, let alone try to achieve.

Don't ignore or reject immediately anything that your imagination presents to you. Don't be discouraged by worries about whether or not you will ever be able to do it, about your lack of natural ability or talent (provided you enjoy it). It is very likely that what you are naturally good at and what you enjoy doing is the same thing (even if you are not aware of this talent at this point). Even then, the talented need work and training in order to do what they want to do well. It might be that you tried it and because you weren't as good as you thought you ought to be, you interpreted what was still raw talent as an absence of talent altogether. Forget the worries about how good you are, just think about what you think you would enjoy.

Don't let worries about how you will manage to support a family or meet other financial obligations stop you from articulating your dream. The method that we use to make it happen will not put these necessities at risk.

Talk about this, but only with those who encourage you

Don't get too caught up thinking about what others will say about what you want to do. Some people will try to discourage you for various reasons: perhaps they are envious that you are trying to follow your dreams when they are afraid to do so themselves. Perhaps they are afraid, or simply do not understand your approach to following your dreams because they lack faith and are not accustomed to leading a life in which decisions are based upon reliance of a loving God. To such people what you are aiming to do will seem an unrealistic fantasy.

In fact, as you will see, the approach to achieving your goals that we are suggesting is perfectly rational, once we accept the initial premise that we have a loving God who wants us to be happy. But anyone who does not accept this premise will inevitably struggle to understand what we are doing. Therefore, as a guiding principle, confide only in those who you think will understand and encourage you in your broad mission. If someone tries to discourage you from the very idea of following your dreams, don't waste time persuading him to agree with you, just drop the subject and stop confiding in him.

Those who do understand this approach to leading a joyful life are rare, but when you do find them, hang on to them. Aim to create circle of confidants, people who are close to what you are doing, are supportive, and are prepared to help and give advice. Before you take each large step, you may seek advice from one or more just to hear an objective viewpoint. If subsequently, one of these people, whom you know and trust raises a note of caution about a particular aspect of what you are doing, then it *is* worth listening to. They are probably not trying to put a dampener on the whole project, but are just questioning one aspect of the way you are going about it. This might be good advice.

If I have several ideal activities, which one do I choose?

If this is the case, write them all down and do your best to prioritize them. Again, don't agonize over this. Remember, this is not a pledge that is going to be used as a rod to beat you with afterwards if you change your mind and do something else. If two or three possibilities occur, then put them all down on paper and sort them out, as best you can, into an order or preference. Then follow the procedure I am about to describe, below, on the first item until either you achieve your dream, or you decide that your initial choice is not for you. If it is the latter, draw up another dream-activity list, pick the item that is now on the top and follow the same procedure.

The way in which we go for our goals allows for a pragmatic, see-what-works approach in which we can change direction on a dime if necessary. As long as you make a start, taking just one small step toward what you think most likely to be the right thing for you, and then continue to take each little step that you see in front of you, you will get to where God wants you to be in the end. Even if your choices aren't the wisest, God will make sure that somehow you stumble across what you are meant to be doing. You will know when you are at your final destination because you will love doing it and you will be good at it.

Be sure of this – happiness and a personal vocation are not denied to anybody. You will discover what you are meant to do despite your doubt and uncertainty. Until that moment when you find it, just patiently make progress, one little step at a time, and focus on enjoying the great gifts that God gives you each day on your journey.

Fears that might stop you from writing down your wildest dream

Here are some other reasons that I have seen keeping people from articulating their wildest dream:

Some people find that what they want to do is so far removed from where they are now that they simply don't believe that it is possible for it to be realized. This is a limitation in faith. As they see it, they would rather not face the situation at all and drop out of the process rather than test God and find him lacking if it isn't realized.

The most effective way to overcome this is to try to coax people into saying what their dream is and reassure them that no harm can come of simply telling someone else what it is. Then we can examine it together and make a judgment – is it selfish, or too wild or silly to happen?

Once people articulate their goal and hear about how they are to go about achieving it, they very often heave a big sigh of relief, for they discover that it is in fact a low-risk strategy, as you'll see.

We will never eliminate all doubt

We are all human and only the fully realized saints among us will have a perfect faith. Each of us is likely to feel some doubt. We should keep on fighting the good fight and trust God despite all our inadequacies. In regard to the search for our dream therefore, we do not wait until we feel a pure and unadulterated conviction that it will happen before acting. Even if you harbor some doubts or some fears, provided you have sufficient faith to take the small steps, it can happen.

Here is another reason why people won't say what they want to do. They think that their dreams are childish because it is the dream that they had as children and it hasn't changed much since then. They are embarrassed to admit it. There are more people in this situation than you might think. Some people have wanted to be nothing but a train driver or a gardener or a nurse since they were seven. They never followed this dream and when they made career choices, did something more 'sensible' and 'grown up.'

Sometimes these inclinations of our childhood are worth listening to. It might be that you end up doing exactly what you wanted when you were seven years old, but sometimes we can look at it and use it to unearth what is right for you now given that you have more knowledge of the world. You can think about what it is that a train driver or a gardener does that you think would delight you. When this is considered it is quite common to find these activities in many other different roles and so the field is opened up. Also, it is common that this simple dream of childhood will be included in the goal we set, but it is not the full story. It might be complemented by other activities that you didn't know about when you were seven.

It was a bit like this for me. My stated dream was to be an artist. I had always loved drawing and painting when I was seven and I might well have said that I wanted to be an artist too. In fact, by being prepared to reach for this simple vision, my life has opened up and the path I have followed has led me to things that I couldn't have imagined myself doing when I was seven…or even 27 – teaching, giving invited talks, writing, blogging, presenting TV shows, being interviewed on the radio. All this came to me by following my simple homing thought and taking the first basic step toward being an artist nearly 25 years ago – that step was signing on for evening classes at the local art school.

What will I lose if I do this?

Another common fear is that people are afraid of what they will lose. This is especially true for those whose lives are in many ways comfortable. In this respect, I was lucky. I had very little to lose and, frankly, things could only get better from the point where I was at the time I first started to consider this.

However, that is not true for all. There are plenty of people for whom life is quite good, but they would like it to get even better. Even though they are not fulfilled in their current situation, it might be stable and comfortable and relatively risk-free. Again, the fear here is that if they start to follow their dreams they will have to risk all of what they now have. The person who wishes to thatch roofs assumes that he is going to have to resign from his position as partner in a law firm, pack his bags and head for the nearest wetlands, sickle in hand, to start harvesting the reed beds, with nothing but the clothes he is wearing and a smile of spiritual joy.

Once again, I have to reassure these people that at no point will chasing this dream require recklessness or having to choose to make any sacrifices that they are not happy with. It might mean giving things up gradually, but it will be at a pace that you can manage, and because you are enjoying the journey you will want to do whatever God asks you to do. God makes it easy for us to do his will, and there are no exceptions – people with or without families… and even lawyers.

It doesn't have to be 'spiritual' it just has to be good

Many people think that because we are talking about doing God's will we have to do something that looks 'spiritual' or holy, such as charity work or working for a church. These sorts of activities will be part of the personal vocation of some people, but not everybody. Anything that is not intrinsically evil or immoral is good and can be directed to good ends, so the field is much more open than you might think.

Write it down

Once you have that dream, write it down. David was adamant about this. As with the gratitude list, he said that actually putting pen to paper has a special value. It forces us to crystallize in our minds exactly what it is we want in life. Write down the full vision of your nine-to-five activity and then add all other aspects of your ideal life that fit around it. If you have no other details, or you feel that your situation in other regards is fine and you don't want to change anything, then don't worry, you don't need to write anything else down. You can remind yourself of what is on this list from time to time. As you go on your journey, it is very likely that your idea of what you want will develop or change because you will be experiencing new things. When this happens, go to the statement and modify it or add to it.

Test your vision against a standard of what is good

Once you have written down your dream, ask yourself is there anything contrary to moral law in what you want to do? If there is, then it does not mean you reject it out of hand necessarily – it might just mean modifying your vision. As long as there is nothing that requires you do something contrary to Church teaching – the standard of what is good – then you can assume that it is legitimate to aim for. Then the big question is, will I enjoy it? If you think you will then you can be sure that not only is what you are aiming for good, but also that it is especially good for *you*.

It's not just the nine-to-five – extend your dream to your whole life situation

The focus of directing your dreams so far has been on our main occupation, but you can extend this to the whole picture of your ideal life. Where would you like to work? What other things would you like to be able to do as well as your main preoccupation? What state would you like to be in life, married or single? What sort of house would you like to live in? If you don't really have any great preference then don't worry about it; but if you have a dream connected to any aspect of your life situation, write it down.

Relax! You don't have to chase all aspects of your dream. Chase the big things and the let the little things chase you

Some might worry that broadening the vision in this way, commits you to a gargantuan task of managing every fine detail of your life. This is not so. When you start to follow your dream in the way that I am about to describe, you do not actively follow every little thing. Many of these things are like the list of six dreams we wrote down at the start of the process. We find that somehow by declaring them they happen to us or are given to us without even trying to chase them directly.

The rule of thumb here is that we chase the big things, but let the little things chase us. In other words, react to those opportunities that present themselves to you. If you do this many of the smaller things on your dream list will come into your life.

You may also find that this is how some of the big things are realized too. I have found on a number of occasions that while I was struggling to work out the next step to take because my choices weren't working, a door just opened in front of me in a totally unexpected way and all I had to do was walk through it. Therefore, be alert for these open doors. It seems to me that the act of actually writing down what I want seems to print them indelibly on my memory and so this means that I am more likely to spot such opportunities when they occur.

Sometimes, something previously unimagined can just happen

Be flexible. If you get offers or opportunities that weren't on your plan and they appeal to you then take them seriously. This has happened a number of times and I ended up doing some things that seemed unrelated to my dream. However, now that I look back at these I still get a sense of being guided to my goal because so many of them gave me skills or experience that, although I didn't realize it at the time, were to become very useful later.

For example, I had never considered myself a writer. I was not good at it at school. My essays never got top marks, and I studied sciences from age 16 through university. As I became more and more interested in art and culture I started to develop my own insights and wanted to talk to others about them, so I started to approach people I thought might know about this subject to ask them for help in forming and developing my ideas. I was lucky enough to meet someone who ran a journal called *Second Spring*. His name was Stratford Caldecott. He encouraged me in what I was doing and asked me to write an article about Catholic art and art schools for his journal. I told him that I couldn't – I wasn't a writer. He said he would help me. He invited me to Oxford for a week's guided reading and we discussed what I had read each day. Then, as promised (even though I knew it would be useless), I wrote a piece encapsulating my ideas which I called the *Way of Beauty*. This was the first time I used this phrase. The article was published in *Second Spring* and was the first of this type that I had ever published. It was in 2003.

At that time, the writing of this was a long slow process and I am amazed at the patience of Stratford in dealing with me. He corrected my poor grammar and spelling, he rephrased things in such a way that it still felt as though it was my voice, but the style was greatly improved. Because I was so slow in getting words onto paper I would hold the process up at every stage.

Eventually I wrote another two or three articles for "Strat," and each time I learned from the way he edited my work and was a little more fluent in getting my thoughts down.

Sometime later, I was approached and asked to write for a prominent blog, the New Liturgical Movement, by the founder and then-editor, Shawn Tribe, who had read these three articles. I told him that I didn't think I was good enough. I had needed so much help for those articles that I couldn't possibly write for a blog, which required the ability to write thoughts down quickly. Nevertheless, Shawn persisted and asked me again over the next few weeks several times. In the end he suggested that I write a piece as a one-off at whatever pace I could manage. I did this. Then he suggested that I do it again, so I did. Then he suggested that I do it monthly. After the first four or five, I found that I had sped up and with a little push from him I started to write weekly articles.

Then on the strength of these blog articles it was suggested to me by someone else that in addition I create my own blog on themes of culture and beauty. I thought I would give it a go and this became the website www.TheWayofBeauty.org. At the time of writing, I have been writing for both of these for over seven years and I typically write two articles a week.

Writing opened up many other doors. I was asked to write and present a TV series called the *Way of Beauty*; I have published books and created online courses. On the strength of these I am invited around the country to make speaking engagements. I still don't think of myself as a natural writer, but I can see now that I had to learn to be a competent enough writer, at least, for people to be aware of what my ideas were and to respond to them. While I don't describe the act of writing as my great joy, I enjoy it enough at least to do it regularly. What motivates me is the need to articulate and communicate my ideas. That I do find fulfilling.

Here is the point – I had never planned to be a writer and never actively pursued it as a career. Yet somehow, I ended up doing it and this created the opportunities for me to fulfill many things that were on my wildest dreams list, many of which I had never actively pursued. They just landed on my doorstep. One of these was the TV show. In one of the revisions of my dream list, after seeing someone on television talking about art and being convinced I could do a better job, I wrote down that I wanted to be on TV (…now that's something I haven't admitted to anyone before!). Out of the blue I was offered the chance to create a *Way of Beauty* TV show by Catholic TV, which aired in 2011.

What about those six wildest dreams I listed when I first started reading this book, what do I do with those?

Keep the list but as I initially suggested, don't look at it until a year is up. At that point when you do look at it, it will be a measure of how far you have come.

As I described earlier, all, bar one, came true for me. Equally interesting to me was that by the time I came to review my list, I took these blessings for granted. I had become used to the them. My sense of what was possible for me and what I could hope for in life had moved forward so much that what had seemed just a dream initially seemed almost to be a part of normal life now. Therefore, I took the opportunity to thank God on my knees for giving them to me. Second was that although I had these things, I could see that my values had changed since this time, and my horizons had widened. The things I had asked for were not bad things in themselves, but they now seemed less critical to my happiness than they had when I started.

Remember that I started from a pretty low point in faith and in the spiritual life. Many of you will already be much further along the path than I was, and so for you the change might not be so apparent.

Taking the first step

Back to discerning our personal vocation: now that you have written your dreams you can take the first step. Remember, you don't need to worry about the second step until you have taken the first and any motion in the right direction, no matter how small, will get the ball rolling. Even though it seems to be a small part of the enormous gulf between you and your final destination, take it. We build the bridge one brick at a time.

What sort of steps are these? David told me that in principle there are two different approaches. The first is to start doing the activity that you enjoy on a regular basis. Even if only a small amount of time each week is all you have to spare. This might seem like an obvious bit of advice, but even though I always wanted to be an artist, before I went through the process I wasn't actually painting very much. This was because I felt that it was so unlikely to happen that I had almost given up before I had even started.

Only a faith in God could change this for me. Before I had this, I lacked confidence in my ability and didn't know how to teach myself. When I looked at my work, although I knew that I was good in comparison to most people, I knew also that I wasn't as good as the great artists I admired, and I couldn't see how that would ever change.

But now, with David guiding me, my first step was simple – sign up for an evening class at the local art school. Even if such a class hadn't been available, I would have put time aside to paint on a regular basis. Even though my natural reaction was to think the class was a waste of time, I did it anyway. I felt I needed so much training that it would take lifetime of evening classes to accumulate the hours of a degree. How would I ever make progress? David reassured me that as long as I started the work somehow, God would help me, and the way would appear before me.

Another way of making the first step – mix with people who are doing what you want to do

The other approach to this first step is to put yourself in an environment where people are doing what you want to do. At this stage it doesn't matter what you are doing in this favorable environment, as long as you are in contact with others who are doing what you want to do. David said that in my case if I couldn't get into an art class I might try to get a job as a janitor in an art school or art studio. Then, he said, once I am there, if God intends for me to do this I will be given opportunities to move laterally and start doing what those around me are doing.

There are many ways that you can do this lateral jump approach – you don't always have to be the janitor. This is where any transferable skills that you might possess come in handy. For example, almost any workplace of any size needs people with IT skills, bookkeepers, or handymen.

What if I don't know what my first step is?

If you still don't know what that first step is, then the first step is to work out what your first step is.

This is how you can do that research:

Go and find people who are experts in the field you want to get into

Talk to experts in your chosen field. Ask them how they got to where they are now. Ask them to suggest ways that you can begin to follow their example. If any are discouraging, drop them. If they are encouraging and happy to see you again, go back to them for as long as they are helpful. You will be surprised at how readily experts who see a genuine enthusiasm in someone else for what they love to do will take people under their wings. Great friendships can develop from these initial contacts.

Until you know someone well, it is usually not always a good idea to ask directly for a job from the person you are talking to when you have these exploratory conversations. Most people approached in this way know that you are looking for employment and if they are able to give you work and want to do so they will offer. You don't need to ask. On the whole people don't like saying 'no,' so if they think you are going to ask directly, they will try to avoid the meeting because they don't want to feel awkward turning you down. However, nearly everyone likes to be asked for advice and if in your initial approach you are clear that it is just advice that you want, many will agree to see you.

Draw up a list of 10 people and try to see each.

Pray for rain and dig for water

Talking to experts can have spectacular results. I had one friend, who I will call Mike, who was a tradesman – an electrician if I remember. He was employed with a large firm and felt stifled and was not earning enough to support his family. His desire was simple: he wanted to have the freedom of being his own boss and to build up his own electrician's business so that he could earn more to support his family. However, he couldn't see how to break away and make a start. He asked me for advice. I had no knowledge of this field, so I suggested to him that he list 10 people who were self-employed electricians or had electrician's businesses, then phone them and ask to go and see them. Then I suggested, when he was in front of them, ask how they got to where they are now, explaining that this is what you were hoping to do yourself.

He was reluctant to do this because, as he put it, "In my business people don't go around doing that sort of thing, especially if it increases the competition." Regardless of the field, it takes a certain sort of person who naturally enjoys cold-calling, and Mike was not one of these. He sat on the list and did nothing. I had no other ideas so I couldn't offer anything else.

Eventually he got so fed up with his situation that he thought he would give even my strange advice a try. He chose an electrician that he knew about but had never met and building up his nerve, telephoned him. The first thing that surprised him was how open this man was to Mike's telephone call, "Sure, thanks for phoning," he said. They arranged a meeting in the next couple of days. Mike went to see him and they had a friendly conversation. However, afterwards Mike was somewhat frustrated. When he had asked the suggested closing question "Can you suggest anyone else that I should speak to who might be able to help me?" He had been told "No, I can't but give me your number and I'll call you if I think of anyone." Assuming that this was a polite brush-off, he was discouraged. Furthermore, this man had started from a position that was very different from where Mike was now, and he couldn't see how the experience could be applied to his personal situation.

He then looked at the second name on the list and ruminated over that for several days while he tried to work up the nerve to call him, too. While in this renewed state of inertia, he got a surprise phone call from the first guy, the self-employed electrician. He had a big job on, he told Mike, and it was too much for him and not in his exact specialization. He wanted to know if Mike could take this work as independent contractor, starting in two weeks. Mike jumped at the chance. He recognized that he was being given his next step, took the time off work, and took the contract. As it turned out, he never went back to his employment. This first job immediately led onto others and Mike found himself doing exactly what he had wanted to do.

There are couple of points to draw from Mike's story. First is just how quickly this can work if it is meant to be. And second, that even though Mike was not a natural networker or schmoozer, he did what he could and God did the rest. There is a motto that fits this description: 'Give it your best shot and God will do the rest,' or as I have heard it said, 'Pray for rain, and dig for water.'

If no one person does all that you want to do, go to people who are doing *part* of what you want to do

My experience has always been that if people love what they do, they like to talk about it and the like to help others do it too. As my vision of what I wanted to do evolved it became an eclectic mix of painting, lecturing, prayer, and research. There was no single person doing the exact combination of things that I wanted to do anywhere in the world. I started to seek out those who had achieved things in one aspect and ask for advice, starting with the most important. I was as hesitant about doing this at first as Mike had been, but once I realized how open most people are to helping others when approached in this way, then I started to enjoy it. As a result, I have never stopped doing this. I always try to be ready to listen to and learn from those who are good at something that I want to do. It becomes one of the great pleasures of the journey.

Remembering my earlier efforts, I try to be open now to giving time and thought to people asking me for advice, which does happen occasionally.

Sometimes introductions can happen in ways that you couldn't contrive. Here's how I found out what to do in order to take my first step. By chance, right at the start of this process I heard someone talk about how he had given up his job to become an art student at the age of 50. I immediately went to talk to him and asked for help. He listened to me and said, "Do you see that guy over there?" I looked around. He was pointing to someone I didn't recognize. "Go and talk to him and say I sent you over. He is a very well-established artist and a member of the Royal Academy."

I went to him and introduced myself expecting great things. This was exciting! Perhaps he would take me on and I could apprentice myself to him. In fact, it went differently. He listened to me intently and asked to see drawings of mine. This was great, I thought. By chance I had some photos with me. He looked at them and said, "Your first step is to learn to draw. You should take an evening class in life drawing." He then told me to get a directory of art schools so that he could recommend one.

I was dismayed. I had been full of expectation that I would be launched to stardom and now here he was pretty much telling me I couldn't draw, so he was pushing me on to someone else. I went and told David. David's reaction was to tell me that this was exactly what I was looking for. This famous artist wasn't bound to do anything and, David said, there was no reason to think that the advice he was giving wasn't the best available. Rather than being so negative, I should be more grateful for the time I had been given.

Reluctantly I accepted David's advice and putting aside my fear and resentment, I went back to the working artist and asked him to recommend schools. Then I took my next step, I signed up for a weekly life drawing class at Chelsea College of Art.

Get knowledge or skills appropriate to the field you want to enter

This is something else that you can do. Read books, take classes, watch and study experts in the field, if they exist, and observe how they do what they are good at. In regard to classes and courses, the information or skills you learn is much more important than the qualification received. Don't get caught in this trap of thinking you must always have a qualification in order to be able to do something professionally. In most professions there are different ways to get there. And even if the qualification is vital, as in medicine for example, and this really is what God wants you to do, then you will end up with the qualification one way or another. Very often we discover that we do something different from what we imagined, but that still fulfills our basic criteria in a different way. For example, there may be many other roles in which I help people in a very similar way to that of a doctor, and for which the barrier to entry is not so great – where I do not necessarily need six years' of very expensive education, for example. If I do end up in this slightly different place from the ideal I imagined, it will be because it is even better for me and others.

If you enjoy study, have the time and money, and if the qualification you get at the end of all that time and expense is useful then, of course, go for it. However, if this isn't open to you, there are always other ways. When I look at my current situation, I have no formal qualification for any of the things I am paid to do. I am paid because people value the quality of the work that I do for them. They are uninterested in how I got to be able to do it.

Change your goal if you no longer think it would make you happy

As a rule of thumb, the more you do something that you are meant to do, the more you enjoy it. For example, once I had completed the first art class I signed up for, I immediately wanted to sign up for another. The next year, I was getting impatient to do more and persuaded the company that I worked for to give me one day off per week for less pay (making sure that I could meet my financial obligations first), so that I could do a weekly day class at the same art school. I always felt this sacrifice was worthwhile because I enjoyed the classes so much.

It might not have been like this. For example, I might have quickly reached saturation point and decided that although painting is great for a hobby I just didn't enjoy it enough to make it central to my life plan.

If you find yourself losing enthusiasm as time goes on, then the chances are that you have the wrong goal for a personal vocation. Sit down and re-write your dream. This doesn't mean that the time already spent is wasted. At least you know enough to cross something off the list and not be plagued by the doubt that you should have followed it. There is every chance that along the way you saw or learned something new that will be useful later. Having said that, don't just give up at the first moment that you feel slightly disillusioned. None of us is perfectly patient, faithful, or hopeful and we are likely to suffer occasionally from inertia caused by acedia. If we don't get precisely the results we want and when we want it, we feel some self-pity. As a safeguard, before you change your goal make sure you are, as far as possible, free from fear and resentment.

If there are setbacks, change the path, but persist in following your dream

It is likely that along the way there will occasionally be people or events that seem to be frustrating you in following your path. If you are in one of these situations keep on going. Do not give up on the goal. Sometimes you just have to ignore the negative influence and stick to the path you are on. Sometimes you might have to change the path. For example, if you feel you hit a dead end and doors aren't opening in front of you, change your path, but don't change your goal. This is not a failure because all the time you are learning about what works and what doesn't. Don't persist in making the same unsuccessful actions time after time.

It's a cinch by the inch, but hard by the yard

Trust that many little steps will add up to significant change. It is easy, especially at the beginning of this process to feel that the start you are making is such a small move in comparison with the huge distance that you think you have to travel, that it is hardly worth taking. Take heart – as long as you are moving and striving to take some sort of action then things will happen. Very often it seems that by beginning the process in this way, things can come to you as much as you can move to them. My experience has been that huge strides are sometimes made suddenly and in ways that I couldn't possible have anticipated. At these moments I would get a sense that the future was flying to me just as much as I was marching forward in time.

A foolish decision is better than no decision at all

One of the fruits of the Holy Spirit is wisdom. We can expect at times to know intuitively how to do things that previously we could not. However none of us is likely to be perfectly wise all the time. We are capable of making foolish and selfish decisions as we follow this path and we are likely to face setbacks as a result and stray from the path. It is almost inevitable that we will do so at different times. This need not hamper us, provided we resolve to keep heading toward our goal from wherever we find ourselves afterwards. If we do our best to follow the process, God can make something better come out of our mistakes too. The wonderful thing about this process is that no matter how far off track we are now, all is recoverable through God. This is great news for me, it works even for someone like me who can be an arrogant fool. And even in these dead-end situations, with the process we can learn to be joyful as we tread the path to our happy.

The journey is part of your personal vocation too

You are living your personal vocation from the moment you start the process of moving to it. The journey is as much part of our personal vocation as the destination: our joy starts now. Each of us who is doing our best to work the principles of the process, is precisely where we are meant to be today, and that is the place that we are going to be happiest today. If we cannot be happy in our present circumstances, no matter how objectionable, then we will never be happy even when our circumstances are more agreeable.

The daily routine which includes the gratitude list, including a daily examination of our thoughts and feelings, will open the way for us to have this happiness – it certainly has done so for me. This is something that works even in the face of great difficulty. Along the way we are almost certain to face setbacks which are the consequence of own foolishness, or trials such as the malice of others, or just 'bad luck.' It is important that we don't fall into self-pity and we deal with each situation so that it doesn't fester and stop us from moving forward, which would eventually lead to despair.

Furthermore we are told that when we are doing God's will, we will inevitably face trials and even persecutions (cf. Mk. 10:30). But we should not fear these tests. If we stick close to God then we need not be swayed from the path and whatever the outcome, we will have joy.

Nearly all at some time are likely to face mockery, derision, discouragement, and rudeness. It is important the we do not allow these to get us down. In fact, the contrary is true. If we suffer for doing God's will we can rejoice for we are sharing in Christ's suffering, and through grace even these unpleasant situations can be a source of joy because of our hope rests in God and we know that an even greater good will come out of them. This is the message of 1 Peter 4:12-15, in verse 13 he says: 'But if you partake of the sufferings of Christ, rejoice that when his glory shall be revealed you may also be glad with exceeding joy.' [Douay Rheims translation]

My experience is I sometimes have to work hard to cultivate joy using the methods that I was shown; nevertheless, so far these methods have worked in response to everything that life has thrown at me.

More of my own story – how I dealt with setbacks and experienced unexpected opportunities

Many times I have had to face a disappointment of some sort that forced me to look for a new way to move forward, which in the end turned out to be better than what I was doing before.

For example, for several years I had to stop painting because of the circumstances I faced, but what I did during this period was invaluable to me when I did go back to painting.

I had been taking classes at art school in London for two or three years and slowly learning and improving. I had taken a job teaching physics at a high school on a part-time basis so that I had free time to paint.

The difficulty was that although I was getting by, my finances were on a knife's edge. One day I was extremely ill. Knowing that my contract required me to work the hours to get paid, I struggled into work. I was living in London and took the 'tube' (as London's subway is called) to work. I was very weak and felt hot and nauseous in the enclosed space of the train. Although I had a seat, I started to feel worse and worse and my vision started to close in. I knew I was going to faint and tried desperately to focus on the posters in the carriage so that I wouldn't pass out. It didn't work. Next thing I knew I woke up with someone holding his hand in front of my face, asking me how many fingers I could see. Then I heard the intercom on the train – 'we apologize for the delay. It is because a passenger has collapsed on the train.' It took a few seconds for me to realize that I was the passenger. I must have been out for several minutes.

It was the rule of London Underground that when this happens they have to call an ambulance for the passenger who is ill. The whole train had to wait until the paramedics arrived. Even though I thought I could walk by this time, I was told that the regulations stipulated that I must be stretchered to the ambulance. I lay on this stretcher as the other passengers looked on, politely and patiently waiting until they could continue their journey to work.

The ambulance took me from Hammersmith Station to Charing Cross Hospital emergency ward. When the doctor examined me I can remember him saying. "You have gastric flu. You just need to rest for a couple of days and you'll be fine… but what on earth are you doing going to work when you are that ill?"

As I returned home (on the tube again) I reflected on my situation. I realized that I needed to find some new way of paying for my painting time. Although I was nearly staying afloat financially by teaching, I needed to accept more and more teaching hours in order to stay solvent. Once I took into account time spent grading papers, I had a lot less time than I had originally thought I was going to get. Furthermore, I was lacking a firm purpose in my painting. My skill level was going up gradually, but I was struggling because beyond wanting to paint and knowing that I wanted to produce something beautiful, I didn't know what to paint or why. I knew I was beginning to drift. Taking all of this into account I decided that a break from painting would help me.

I remembered the guy whom I had seen speaking about giving everything up and going to art school a few years earlier. He had been working as an executive in the City of London and had enough money put away to be able to retire at 50. Maybe I could do something similar, I thought. I decided to get a job in the city, earn a huge salary, and hope to retire early.

As a result of this decision I stopped painting almost completely for about five years. I tried to get a job at an investment bank but failed – it wasn't as easy as I thought it would be. I did manage to get a job working for a recruitment company whose clients were these banks. I did quite well at this – I certainly earned more money (at one point a lot of money) and did well enough that someone approached me and asked me if I wanted to be her partner in creating our own recruitment business. I thought this would be the way that I could become independently wealthy most quickly and so, flattered by the approach, I went for it.

This business didn't succeed, and after about 18 months it folded. This time, however, to my surprise, events pushed me back to painting sooner than I expected. The difference from when I had been teaching physics part-time was that I had learned great lessons that made me better able to succeed.

First, throughout this period of more conventional work, although I enjoyed the experience and did well financially, I never felt completely fulfilled. This increased my conviction that painting really was a key part of me and that I would go back to it at some point.

Second, I had developed a different attitude towards business, businessmen, and entrepreneurs, and above all, bankers.

Before I actually started meeting and working with these recruiters and bankers, I had a deeply ingrained prejudice against all of them. I took the attitude that doing business was something that was intrinsically bad and necessary involved one person taking advantage of another. Bankers in particular, I thought, were not only the most grasping and uncaring, they were dull and unimaginative – uncultured – which was even worse. They succeeded because they didn't care who they stamped on in pursuit of their goals while justifying their behavior by claiming that by spending their huge earnings self-indulgently, they were putting money back into the economy, so their wealth trickled down in tiny quantities to everyone else.

In fact I discovered a whole range of personalities. On the whole, those who succeeded and reached a high level in large organizations struck me as at least as good and honest as any other section of the population. Furthermore, most seemed as interested in the well-being of their fellow workers and the poor in general as anyone who you might meet in a Labour Party activists meeting (which I had attended in the past). I'm not going to claim they were all saints, but neither were they all the self-absorbed charlatans that I had believed them to be. They were like any other group of people from any other walk of life, including those professions that one would think would attract a higher proportion of good people such as nursing and medicine, charity work, and social activism.

Generally those bankers or consultants who rose to the top in management positions did so because they were good managers, which meant they were in part at least genuinely interested in the well-being of the people they worked with, and good at dealing with people. It was as much of a surprise to me to find a charity worker could be callous and self-centered as it was to find a banker who could be warm and well-intentioned. I now see that in each case I was surprised because I had been prejudiced, with too high an expectation of charity workers and too low an expectation of bankers.

I could see that entrepreneurship created jobs and opportunities for many people and I realized that the process of actually doing business might be intrinsically good. Some people genuinely thrived in this world. I met people who were fascinated and excited by bond trading. These were people for whom bond trading was their personal vocation. They were using their imaginations and abilities to contribute positively to society.

While I was pretty sure that I was not one of these people – doing business was not my personal vocation – spending time in a commercial environment did teach me some business skills: sales, networking, marketing, and some insights into business strategy, which later opened the door to different ways of funding what I did want to do. It gave me a new freedom.

The other benefits of this period away from art were spiritual and intellectual. With a demanding full-time job I couldn't find the large blocks of time I needed to paint. Besides this, I found myself drawn far more to reading and studying. Throughout this period I started to learn a lot more about traditions in art and theories of culture. I also delved deeper into my spiritual reading and started to connect the two together. The main fruit of this period was my conversion to Catholicism and the second – connected to it – was a whole new direction this gave to my art. I knew now that I wanted to serve the Faith.

Equipped with this new purpose, I started to contemplate painting again. I wasn't in a position to retire but when my business folded I did have enough to last for a few months and so decided to use this time to get back to into painting in some sort of financially viable way. The first thing I did was investigate whether or not there were art schools that taught religious painting. I think I even tried to look up 'Catholic art school' under C in the yellow pages. I couldn't find any! Having exhausted the British possibilities, I investigated the art schools at nominally Catholic universities in the U.S. This was disappointing, too. When I looked at the students' work it looked no different from what those at secular and aggressively anti-Christian art schools were producing, and which I disliked intensely. If there was a school that taught both the skills and the understanding of the Catholic traditions in art, then I couldn't find it. I started to develop ideas about what such an art school would look like. I directed my study and reading to this end as well as the continued development of my spiritual life (which was under the direction of an Oratorian priest in London at this time).

Through this process of study and reflection my goals became modified. I now wanted to establish an art school that promoted traditional skills and had an ethos in which Catholics could flourish. Then, I thought, I would enroll as its first student.

As I talked to people who were interested in traditional art forms, I realized that there was no single person who had all that I was looking for. I decided to learn the necessary art skills first from a number of different artists who had part of what I wanted. If I could at least get up to a level where I could teach, I thought, then I would be able to create this school around me.

I went to Florence for a year to study portrait painting and signed up for icon painting classes with the iconographer Aidan Hart. I discussed my ideas with anyone else I could find who would help develop my thinking as well as my skills, such as Stratford Caldecott, who coached me into writing my first article for his journal, *Second Spring*.

One day during this period, when I was visiting my brother in Berkeley, California on holiday, I decided to sit down and write out a fresh statement of my goals. I still had painting down on the list, but now I had also the goal of establishing a Catholic art school. I wanted to create a school that would train students who would paint so beautifully that their work would be in demand; thus, this school would become the model for all art schools.

Then I stopped for a moment. If God is behind this, I thought, and anything is possible with God, why not aim for the very highest goals I could think of. So I wrote down, "I want to transform Western culture and Catholic culture so that we have culture of beauty that draws people to God and his Church."

I remember feeling excited about this because I knew I had something that I was passionately interested in. Even though it seemed absurdly ambitious, I couldn't see any reason why I shouldn't aim for the highest ideals. If a culture is to change, *somebody* has to be involved in changing it – why not me?

Although I was certain that I still wanted to develop as an artist, from this point on painting became a secondary aim and not a primary one. I have had a steady stream of commissions since then, but I have never made marketing my art the main focus of what I do. I thought then, and still think now that at some point – perhaps at a later stage in my life – I might focus on painting alone, but now I had a different mission.

Nevertheless I wrote out a goal for my painting career. I decided that the ultimate achievement for me as a religious painter was to have a painting hanging in the Brompton Oratory. This is the church in London whose liturgy and priests had been so influential in my conversion. If I could do that, I would feel that I had achieved what I wanted to do, I thought.

So fired by this new goal, I resolved to write more for *Second Spring*, if Stratford would let me and then see where it took me. I flew home to London. When I got into my apartment in Wandsworth in South London I saw that there was a new message on my voicemail. It was from one of the Fathers of the London Oratory. I couldn't believe it – he was asking me to come see them, because the Oratory wanted to commission a painting from me. One of the Fathers there had seen some of the studies that I had done.

Here I was, an aspiring artist who had never sold a painting before, and who just a few days earlier had decided that having a painting in the Oratory would be one of his wildest dreams. Less than two weeks after first writing it down on my personal mission statement, I had a chance that what I had hoped might be the height of my career would now be the very first painting I would sell.

This made me nervous as I went in to see them. I didn't know what to charge them, assuming I got the commission. I wanted a reasonable price, but also didn't want to price myself out of the job. When I went to the Church the provost told me that they wanted a 6-foot portrait of a newly canonized Oratorian St. Luigi Scrosoppi. I explained to them what I would do.

The provost then asked me what price I would charge. I tentatively suggest a price. Without blinking he said, "I'm very sorry but I can't offer you more than…" and named a price three times higher than what I had asked for. I said, "That sounds good." "You drive a hard bargain," said the provost with the faintest hint of a wry smile. I had my first sale and the patron had negotiated me up!

I thought I had done pretty well out of this until I delivered the painting three months later. I went with the provost to the framers. He ordered an ornate gilded baroque frame which looked like something that would go around a Titian at the National Gallery. I was very excited at the thought of seeing my painting in this frame in the church.

Then they quoted the price for the frame. It was double what I was paid for the painting. I was momentarily dismayed, but still I didn't care that much. I had fulfilled my ambition as an artist with my very first commission.

As a result, I have never felt frustrated about lack of success as an artist. In fact, I've become even more focused on the wider mission of changing the culture. If you want to see the painting in the Oratory, by the way, you won't find it. It was taken down several years later. I was sorry, but in some ways was relieved because I think I am a much better painter now than I was then.

The other side of my vocation developed in the following way. I was starting to get articles published in *Second Spring* and other journals; as I did so, I could point to a commission in a church known throughout the world. As a result of this, people in the Catholic world took me seriously and listened to my ideas.

By another series of 'lucky breaks' I started to get national coverage in Britain as an artist. After my business venture failed I looked for work that would give me time to paint. I had been through this before and was trying to find something other than teaching this time – a part-time job that paid at a higher rate and fewer hours. It wasn't easy to know what to look for and I was beginning to wonder if I should just go back into full-time employment and put active pursuit of my mission on the back burner again.

One day, I was describing this to my regular tennis partner. He worked at *The Sunday Times* newspaper as a senior sub-editor and suggested that I try some shifts as a sub-editor. If it worked out I could do two or three days a week, and it paid more than teaching. It hadn't crossed my mind before that this was a possibility – I didn't even know what sub-editing was. I had no experience of working in production in publishing. I can only guess that he thought I had what it took based upon our conversations about nothing-in-particular between sets on the tennis court.

For those who don't know, sub-editing is a different role from editing. The 'sub's' duties consist mainly of proofreading, checking the accuracy of all factual information, writing the headlines and captions (for approval by the editor) and cutting the article subtly to fit the available space in the page.

I went and tried out at *The Sunday Times*. To this day I still don't really know why I was hired. It was not my friend, but his boss – the chief sub – who hired me. It can only be that they thought I had potential, because I was very raw and not particularly literary, to put it mildly. Once given the chance, I did work hard to learn and to contribute. By the time I left, a few years later, while I was not the best sub there, I was worth my place on the team. Sub-editing gave me the chance I was looking for. It gave me the means to support myself and continue painting and working towards my goals.

As with my first painting commission, this new opportunity just landed in my lap. I found myself starting in sub-editing at *The Sunday Times*, one of the premier newspapers in the UK. Once I had worked there, I was able to get shifts at other magazines and newspapers. One of these was *The Catholic Herald*, the national Catholic weekly paper, where I ended up writing a couple of articles about art and music, which I submitted speculatively to the editor.

I also did a handful of shifts for *The Times*, the daily sister paper to *The Sunday Times*. *The Times* did a regular feature on people who did strange jobs. From memory it was called something like "Someone's gotta do it." One Saturday we had just cleared the feature for the coming week – about (would you believe) a woman who made a living offering spiritual healing through colonic irrigation. The editor was stuck for a topic for the following week.

The chief sub, who was vaguely aware that I had painted religious art, asked me if I would like to be the subject of the article. Spiritual colonic irrigation was a hard act to follow, I thought, but I told him I was up for it. He suggested my name to the editor and the next day the journalist contacted me for a telephone interview and the article about my painting duly appeared the following week. I found myself featured in a national newspaper as 'the icon painter.'

The following week, another UK national daily, *The Guardian*, contacted me because they had seen *The Times* piece and asked me if they could use me for the front cover of their educational supplement. I can't remember why I was relevant for their education weekly, but they sent a photographer around, and the whole of the front page of this tabloid-sized paper was a photograph of me, brush in hand, painting an icon. I remember that the caption read, "There's lots of talk of icons in all walks of life these days, well here's someone who makes the real thing."

So now my credentials read: "Artist commissioned by the London Oratory, whose work has been featured in the national UK newspapers, *The Times* and *The Guardian*. Writer and commentator on art and culture with articles published in *Second Spring*, the international journal of faith and culture, and the national Catholic weekly paper, *The Catholic Herald*."

I began to attract attention abroad. I was invited to speak at a conference in Washington D.C. on religious art, and on that trip met the president of Thomas More College of Liberal Arts who offered me the position of Artist in Residence and Lecturer in Liberal Arts. I moved to the United States to work for Thomas More College in New Hampshire. This gave me the platform in the U.S. from which I started to write for blogs on liturgy and culture, to appear on Catholic TV and give numerous radio interviews. Then invitations for paid speaking engagements started to come in.

All this and I had no formal qualifications connected with any of the activities that I was doing on a day-to-day basis. All the opportunities opened up because people believed, based upon my past record, that I could do the job they wanted me to do. Since I had the spiritual tools of the process available to me, I was able to enjoy life all the way through this journey.

This is available to all

I recount this because I believe that every single one of us can have a joyful life regardless of our current situations and, with God's grace, have a life beyond our wildest dreams. There may be a few surprises in what that life turns out to be, but we will get the life God intends for us so that we can be happy.

We just have to do the best we can in following these directions. It is okay to make errors as long as we acknowledge them, pick ourselves up and start again. If we use the tools available to us, put one foot in front of the other, and keep a positive attitude, then God will do the rest.

Now, with faith in God's power and goodness, ask the Father for whatever you want in life – in the name of his Son, Jesus Christ.

Before you do so pray:

Bend my heart to your will, Oh God.
I ask this in the name of my Lord Jesus Christ.

Epilogue

Hope for the Best and Be Ready for the Worst

The Lesson of Job

Wickedness is therein, deceit and guile go not out of her streets. For it is not an open enemy that hath done this dishonor, for then I could have borne it; Neither was it mine adversary that did magnify himself against me; for then peradventure I would have hid myself from him; But it was even thou my companion, my guide and mine own familiar friend. We took sweet counsel together and walked in the house of God as friends. Let death come hastily upon them and let them go down alive into the pit. For wickedness is in their dwellings and among them.

As for me I will call upon God, and the Lord shall save me. In the evening and the morning and at noon-day will I pray and that instantly he shall hear my voice. It is he that hath delivered my soul in peace from the battle that was against me.

Psalm 55

'Forgive us our trespasses, as we forgive those who trespass against us.'

Matthew 6:12

This book is about the joy of living. The philosophy of life that underlies this is optimistic in that it is rooted in a faith in a loving God who is all powerful and wants us to be joyful and gives us the means to be so. This is the vision that David inspired me with when I first met him, and he showed me how to make a reality.

The danger in pushing this message, I know, is that some will get the impression that nothing bad ever happens to those who are on the *Way of Beauty*. Those who think this are probably in for a shock. Inspired by this picture of a rosy future, you set your sights on all that you want in life, confident that, provided it is good and it is God's will, it will happen. This all sounds great and you are on your way, full of optimism... but if this is the picture you have, then when something goes wrong, which it very likely will at some point, you will not be ready for it and might become disillusioned.

When I talk about things going wrong, I don't mean superficially wrong – the sort of thing where it is easy to see that I am being childish about minor things not going my way (like having to wait longer than I want in the supermarket line). I *am* talking about real and bad things – things that we cannot pass off as illusory: great illness or injury, or real hardship. I am not saying that these things are guaranteed, but most experience something of this nature if we live to a significant age.

Scripture confirms this, as mentioned at various points in this book already. It tells us that in addition to all the good things that God gives us, those who are following God's will can expect trials and persecutions as well.

Certainly, I can say that I have had difficulties in my journey. This is not magic – we cannot control events perfectly to our liking ever. I have found that unless I accept this fact, I am always wishing things were different. Once I accept it, the problem – which is in me – is removed.

Nevertheless, with the process, we can look at even these reversals in the Light of faith in a loving God and be optimistic. When we do so we are confident that God will give us the grace to deal with anything that life can throw at us. We need not have fear.

In other words, the journey along the *Way of Beauty* will always be beautiful but will at times be shrouded in mist. Adverse weather conditions can distract us from our enjoyment of the path. Provided that we keep our attention on the guiding light that is a beacon, showing us the direction to travel, we need not fear. In fact, more than that, because we know we are assured of our safety, we can enjoy the journey still, despite the buffeting. A storm can be exciting and beautiful when you know there is no danger from it. And mist can have the veiled beauty of mystery.

I used to think that this 'caveat,' if I can call it that, was a cop out. 'We promise you everything you want; except when you don't get everything you want, at least we can help you deal with the disappointment.' This is not that great of a promise, I thought. Why does God allow a system in which bad things occur in the first place? Wouldn't a more loving God create a world in which there was a way to avoid bad things altogether?

I have to believe that the answer is no. My experience is that my faith in God is stronger for having gone through bad things with God's help and come through them happy and secure, than if I had never had to face them at all.

For me it is analogous in some ways to dealing with a good customer complaints department of a company. It has been shown that it is better PR for that company if they solve problems and deal with complaints sympathetically and efficiently than if the problem had never occurred in the first place.

Many times I heard David tell people who were going through very difficult experiences that these are just the times when we must keep doing what makes us feel good. I saw the example in his life. He suffered from ill health, but always was cheerful and dignified. I have already mentioned how he put bad things on his gratitude list. I adopted this idea too after I heard him talk about it and I found that it really helped me to deal with adversity.

David was a good man, but he was not perfect. He had his moments like all of us – for example, I once I saw him snap at someone who pushed a shopping trolley into him at the supermarket. She wouldn't have known that because of his ill health she had hit a very tender spot on his leg. Then I saw him regain his composure and go off after her to apologize for being rude to her. At other times David was impatient and bad-tempered with poor service in restaurants and hotels, especially if he needed special attention because of his health. I think that because he didn't otherwise look ill or pitiful, people didn't think to give him special care. He never hesitated to complain and could be bitingly sarcastic at times.

Nobody is perfect, and David certainly wasn't, but *generally* he was calm, dignified, and joyful. And he wanted you to be joyful too. Since he was like this generally, the little slip-ups were all the more surprising. I know that some people put him on a pedestal only to have their idealized picture of him destroyed when he showed some indication of human weakness or selfishness. Then they would swing in the other direction and characterize him as generally bad-tempered or impatient and drop him.

I looked at it another way. Seeing an ordinary, flawed human being get so much from a reliance on God even in difficult situations encouraged me to believe that this was on offer to me too.

In my own life I have suffered great setbacks and difficulties – most of them since David died. Nevertheless, his advice to others in similar situations was still ringing in my ears when I experienced them, and I knew what to do.

When bad times come, we can cultivate joy by freeing ourselves of all resentment and fear as we have been taught, by meditating on the blessings that are present in the day – even those days when nothing goes the way we want it to – and by taking the action that is consistent with love of God and love of man.

It is good to have these habits already ingrained before tough times occur, so that we instinctively reach for what is good in order to remain happy, rather than succumbing to despair. I once heard someone describe his philosophy of life as one of 'hope for the best, and be ready for the worst.' This works for me too. If I had to pick out one thing as the most difficult for me to deal with, I would say that it is not any physical pain, or financial hardship, but calumny – cruel and unjust accusations.

This systematic 'character assassination' has happened twice, in two completely different situations with different sets of people. Because there are other people involved, I will not go into details. But to know that there are people who believe that you are doing bad things because they are being told malicious gossip. It is difficult to deal with, all the more when you are helpless to stop what might even amount to a destruction of your reputation.

It is one thing when indiscreet people are gossiping about bad things you have done. Although tough to cope with, there is at least some sense that you have brought it on yourself and deserve what you get. But when it is truly unjust, and you must accept that it is happening and let events take their course, I found it particularly difficult to bear.

Why are people so cruel as to make false accusations? There might be any number of reasons. It is possible that the person is not deliberately lying but has made a mistake, and for some reasons believes that they are telling the truth. Also, I might be mistaken in my perception of what has happened – it is easy to hear about gossip secondhand and overreact, assuming that much more is being said, and more often, than is actually the case. It might also be that that although what is being said is malicious and untrue, I had played a part in what happened because I have in some way antagonized this person.

However, sometimes it is none of these things. Even if I behave perfectly, there will be times when I will not escape the ire of others. This is because some people are antagonistic to the Word. To the degree that I am doing God's will and my life is a witness to what is right and good, it will draw attention to Christ. Some people are drawn to the Light of course, and this is the hope of evangelization, but some do not want to see the Light at all.

The Light of Christ will touch those who are living badly and cause their consciences to sting. At this point they could respond by recognizing their own flaws and correct them. Or they might feel this discomfort and do no more than seek to avoid whoever is shining with the Light of Christ. Others, however, hate the Light so much that they wish to extinguish it. These people will do all they can to discredit you so that it might drive away whoever bears that Light and distracts others from it.

This causes the persecutions referred by scripture. If we are doing what God asks of us, chances are we will have to face them. You should be ready for people to try to pull you down, or frustrate your efforts to follow your personal vocation. There might be mockery, derision, malicious gossip, and false accusations right up to a level of seriousness that could ruin you. I have had to face situations where I could potentially see my good name destroyed, my friends deserting me, and the loss of much of what I hold dear, all through unjust accusation.

So much of the anguish in such situations arises not from what actually happens, but through a fear of what people who hear such gossip might think about me, and what they might do.

Even when I have faced these bad situations, I have found that provided I stay close to God by taking the actions described, I feel protected. My prayers don't necessarily change the external situation immediately (although sometimes amazing things do happen), but with the process my peace is preserved.

Then it is possible for me to be in accord with St. Peter, who rejoiced in his suffering because he believed he was sharing in the suffering of Christ:

> Always behave honorably among pagans so that they can see your good works for themselves and, when the day of reckoning comes, give thanks to God for the things which now make them denounce you as criminals.[1]

I have had difficulties and setbacks in my live, but none have been at the level of suffering that many have to face, but nevertheless in the context of my life they seemed difficult to me. The fact that the process worked even during the worst I have had to face has reinforced my faith and increased my trust in God.

---

[1] 1 Peter 2:11, quoted in the Office of Readings, Wednesday of Easter week.

THE VISION FOR YOU

The bigger question, why does God do this to me?

Each time I experience any sort of injustice or bad luck, serious or minor, I have to deal with the resentments against the perpetrators. In fact, I find this relatively easy to deal with, because of the power of *The Vision for You* process. I can understand that fallen people do bad things.

What I find hard to deal with is the question, why did God permit such injustice?

I have a bad tendency to fall into the trap of thinking that God's favor automatically brings good fortune; the other side of this trap is thinking that the lack of good fortune indicates God's disfavor. This being so my reaction is to ask, "What can I do to make God give me what I want? How can I get back in his good grace so that he will follow my directions and change this terrible situation for me?"

This type of thinking is dangerous. When I do this, I have fallen into the same error of the law-of-attraction book authors I described earlier. I have inverted the hierarchy and tried to make God subservient to me.

How can we reconcile suffering with the true picture of God? This is my approach:

Why don't we always get what we want? Reconciling suffering with divine providence and an all-powerful, all-loving and personal God

When something happens that I don't like, I pray to God and ask for help. I have to admit, I would prefer that he changed the situation and reversed my fortunes, rather than forcing me (as it seems) to rely on his grace and bear misfortune joyfully.

Sometimes the situation does change, and the bad situation goes away. Other times, however, nothing seems to change when I pray. Then, perhaps reluctantly, I have to examine my attitude to God as well as to the situation I am facing.

Put another way, the question is, "Why do bad things happen to *good* people... i.e., me!"

I find the Book of Job in the Old Testament helpful to me. It is named after its protagonist (apparently not an Israelite[2]) and treats just this problem of the suffering experienced by those who are innocent.

Job is a holy and prosperous man who loves God. Satan questions Job's sincerity and so God permits Satan to bring down a series of catastrophes to afflict Job, confident that Job will not lose faith in him. Job loses material possessions and suffers horrible and painful illnesses. While he is going through this, three friends come to console him. A cycle of speeches begins. Job's friends insist that his plight can only be a punishment for personal wrongdoing and an invitation from God to repent. Job rejects their explanations insisting that he has not done wrong and asks God to respond. Another person, Elihu, who is close by delivers four speeches in support of the views of the three friends. In response, Job insists again that their judgment is wrong and pleads that he be allowed to see God and hear directly the reason for his suffering. God's explanation is not one of the nature of divine justice, but rather a catalog of the wonders of creation. Job is content with this, and in the end all of Job's fortune and health are restored to him.

The conference of U.S. Catholic bishops (from which I draw my summary) sums up the books as follows: "The Book of Job does not definitively answer the problem of the suffering of the innocent, but challenges readers to come to their own understanding."[3]

Here is my understanding: this story reinforces the point that, other things being equal, reversals and setbacks <u>do not</u> indicate that we are not on the road that God intends for us. Our personal vocation is just that, a calling – it is a guiding light that directs our activity in the present moment. Although there is a good chance that this wonderful picture of our ideal life will happen, at least in part, the only guarantee is that if we

---

[2]Cf. Ez. 14:14, 20

[3]http://www.usccb.org/ U.S. conf. cath. bishops

do our best to follow it then God will bestow what is best for us. That might conceivably be, for some of us, something very different from what we would like it to be. After all, we are not always the best judges of what is good for us.[4]

If we face trials and reversals, sometimes these are large enough that they dominate our sense of where we are on the journey at any point in time. In other words, we would characterize our whole life with the suffering of the moment. For some people this is a fair characterization. For martyrs, for example, their suffering is emblematic of the meaning of their whole lives. But even here, the happy conclusion of the martyrs' stories is that they are received by God in heaven.

But for most others it is different. This is a temporary phase. Job was not a martyr, the happy conclusion for Job was that his good fortune was returned to him and he was prosperous for the rest of his life.

The story of our lives might be close that of the martyr, or it might be closer to that of Job – characterized by temporary suffering in a largely prosperous life. We are very likely to face some injustice at some point in our lives and however it all unfurls, we can be sure God's intention is that we be joyful throughout; he gives us the grace to allow that to be at all times. The story of the Christian life is one in which the ending is not only guaranteed to be happy, but the journey is also guaranteed to be happy, too, regardless of what we face.

Job was patient. He never lost faith in God even though he could not understand why he should be suffering. For rhetorical reasons we hear Job, thinking aloud, about the doubts he has but then he works through them and his conclusions are always the right ones. This is similar to what we read in Psalm 22 which begins, "My God, my God look upon me, why hast thou forsaken me?" and which goes on to describe unjust treatment at the hands of other men. While it begins with this cry of anguish, it works through the despair, bringing us along with the psalmist

---

[4]Alternatively, readers may wish to read the commentary on this book by Fr. William Most, which is at http://www.catholicculture.org/culture/library/most/getwork.cfm?worknum=97

and his emotions. Then in the final section he praises God: "My praise is of thee in the great congregation; my vows will I perform in the sight of them that fear him." (v32). The opening words of this psalm were quoted by Christ on the cross and quoted in the gospels on the assumption that the reader knew the rest of the psalm.

If we succumb to temptation and adopt a false 'new-agey,' law-of-attraction approach we will conclude wrongly that it is because we are not doing the process well enough that we suffer. The common explanation in the law-of-attraction books when things go wrong is that we are not being optimistic enough and so are not exerting our will power on the situation powerfully enough. However, the example of Job tells us otherwise. No one was more in favor with God, yet he permitted him to suffer for a greater good that Job could not know of. Job even got to the point of believing that he would never see the return of good fortune in this life, but nevertheless he still had hope in eternal life that consoled him during the sufferings of his earthly life.

For my part, I am reminded through reading this story that I cannot know God's plan in advance. Although we can be assured of God's love for us, we cannot direct God in the provision of his love. God does as he chooses, not as we choose. His acts are always in accord with what is good and always loving. His love is beyond our comprehension and certainly beyond our powers of foresight. However we *should* be optimistic. We are assured of his love and God will not give us anything we aren't capable of embracing joyfully. He is not trying to set traps for us in order to teach us a lesson for the sake of it or to demonstrate our inferiority. He does all he can to help us so that we might make decisions that will give us a happy life, while preserving – again, because of his love – our free will. He understands that we are flawed human beings and is not looking for loopholes in a contract that enable him to avoid fulfilling his promise to give good things to us. When we treat him as though he is like this then it says more about us than it does about God. It will also very likely reflect how we view others and how we behave in our human relationships.

In the Christian interpretation, suffering is given to the good and the holy for another reason. Benedict XVI said that one of the reasons to become a Christian is so that we participate in the creative love of God. We can be creative and loving in many ways, but one way in which we can participate in the love of God is to participate in the sacrifice he made for mankind, that all of us might have happiness. When we suffer unjustly, we can joyfully take on ourselves some of the suffering that Christ endured in the Passion for the love of him and for the love of mankind, for whom Christ suffered. This might be a silent, secretly borne suffering; or it might be one that is obvious, and by our visible bearing of it with dignity, brings greater glory to God and greater understanding in others of the sacrifice God made for us.

In the Office of Readings in the period after Pentecost, the first long reading is from the Job. On Thursday of Week 8 in Ordinary time, the Responsory (which is sung after reading the scripture passage) gives a very fitting interpretation of Job's suffering:

> We are in difficulties on all sides, but never cornered; we see no answer to our problems, but never despair; we have been persecuted, but never deserted.
>
> Always we carry with us in our body the death of Jesus, so that the life of Jesus, too, may always be seen our body. We have been persecuted, never deserted.

I have heard it said at times that Christianity does not guarantee happiness, rather it offers the truth. This statement is profoundly false. In fact, Christianity guarantees happiness to those who accept its teachings, *because* it offers the truth… and goodness and beauty.

Truth, goodness, and beauty are never in opposition with each other. Beauty draws us to what is good and true. If we accept the truth in our heart of hearts, then through God's grace we inevitably take those actions that are good. This is true, even in bad times. The times may be bad, but life can be good.

And the good life is a happy life.

I close with a passage from the first letter of St. Peter. I hope it will be an inspiration for you as you walk the joyful path – the Way of Beauty – towards God's vision for you.

> Through your faith, God's power will guard you until the salvation which has been prepared is revealed at the end of time. This is a cause of great joy for you, even though you may for a short time have to bear being plagued by all sorts of trials; so that, when Jesus Christ is revealed, your faith will have been tested and proved like gold – only it is more precious than gold, which is corruptible even though it bears testing by fire – and then you will have praise and glory and honor. You did not see him, yet you love him; and still without seeing him, <u>you are already filled with a joy so glorious</u> that it cannot be described, because you believe; and you are sure of the end to which your faith looks forward, that is, the salvation of your souls.
>
> 1 Peter 1:5-8

Appendix 1

Eight Principles for Progress

A summary of the step-by-step process described in this book

The following is a summary produced by a number of people who have been through the process, which has been developed in order to help others.

The Three Acknowledgments

1) We acknowledged that we are the cause of our own unhappiness through our self-centered behaviors, thoughts, and feelings (otherwise known as *sins*); the cause is not other people or circumstances, no matter how unfortunate.

2) We acknowledged that we are unable to control our thoughts and actions perfectly or to rid ourselves of unhappiness, which is in the form of resentment and fear.

3) We acknowledged that our sole hope for happiness is in God. We set ourselves this ideal for living: with God's grace we can do his will, be free of resentment and fear and have a good, beautiful and joyful life. Once we have accepted this truth, then we *do* have a choice and we can say that misery is optional.

The Five Spiritual Exercises:

1) We adopted a daily routine of prayer, reflection, and good works.

2) When the daily routine had become habitual, we undertook a detailed written self-examination, looking at our past thoughts, feelings, and behaviors in order to root out the resentments and fears arising from our self-centeredness. We admitted our shortcomings to God and to another trusted person.

3) We made amends for any harms done (provided that to do so would not cause more harm).

4) We discerned our personal vocation by consideration of what we would like to do *in our wildest dreams*, and then worked towards that goal.

5) We continued to deepen our spiritual lives through the practice of a daily routine of prayer, reflection, and good works.

Appendix 2

The Daily Routine

A Summary of the Habits that Lead us to a Happy Life

Commit to doing all of these things daily until they become habits of life:

Prayer:
- In the morning, on your knees in an action of humility say something like: – *'Please God, take care of me today so that I can be of service to you and my fellows.'*

- In the evening before retiring, again on your knees, say: – *'Thank you, God for looking after me'* – it's good manners to say thank you!

- Reactive prayers during the day:

    o If you are angry or annoyed at someone: Pray for the person; repeatedly until you feel better. E.g. *'Please give [name] everything that I would wish for myself.'*

    o If you are fearful or anxious: Say the Serenity Prayer repeatedly until you feel better – *'God grant me the serenity to accept the things I cannot change; the courage to change the things I can; and the wisdom to know the difference.'*

    o When you have been through the detailed **self-examination** as outlined in our spiritual exercises, apply this process to resentments and fears that crop up during the day as needed to remove them and have a happy life.

Personal Reflection:
- Write a gratitude list and thank God for each blessing that you find.

- Spiritual reading: read something each day that gives you an ideal to live by. For example, the *Just for Today* statement.

Good works:
- We adopt a general attitude of seeking to be of service to others. We ask what we can give to the world, rather than what we can take.

- We make a regular voluntary sacrifice of time devoted to the service of others in a way of your choosing. This might be by contributing to the establishment of meetings whose purpose is to pass *The Vision for You* process on to those who need it. Or by sponsorship – giving time to meet with others personally in order to take them through the process.

- We strove to 'do the right thing,' that is, to lead a good and virtuous life.

As we continue on our journey we keep in mind our eighth principle, which is the fifth spiritual exercise, and which allows us to add and modify this in according with its underlying principles as time goes on.

Appendix 3

The 17 component forms of self-centeredness used in this examination of conscience

The 17 'sins' I used are: *self-centeredness, self-pity, pride, acedia, dishonesty, hypocrisy, envy, jealousy, greed, selfishness, gluttony, lust, anger, arrogance, intolerance, impatience, and sloth.*

Self-centeredness: thinking of myself excessively and not giving due regard to others. This is a form of pride and is the umbrella defect so to speak – all the other 16 impulses listed below can be considered self-centeredness manifested in one form or another.

Self-pity: feeling down about my own situation. This is a defect that we feel directly. Because we feel it, it's one that lets us know that we have a resentment — 'poor me!' is how I feel. Self-pity is the manifestation of melancholy or despair associated with a sin called 'acedia' (see later).

Pride: the rejection of the love of God and his authority. An unreasonable and inordinate self-esteem: worrying about what people think of us — what would they think of me if they knew? How could he do that to the great me? This includes occasions where we are boastful of our achievements (which used to be known as vainglory).

Acedia: is the neglect to take care of something that one should do. It can be an inertia or spiritual sloth whereby because of a lack of faith and hope we do not reach for what is good and feel down. It is translated to listlessness; depression, and feelings of self-pity. If we sit with our self-pity it can become intense and in today's language would be described as depression. The true antidote to feelings of self-pity are virtuous actions and the cultivation of joy, such as those described in this process.

However, it can be a temptation to seek solace instead in lesser goods in order to distract us or to escape from our self-pity. These may not be bad in themselves, but they can only be a temporary fix for self-pity and so if misused in this way can lead to our seeking happiness through them fruitlessly, and neglecting our obligations. This is a root of addictions, workaholism, hedonistic lifestyles, giving in to the temptation to look at pornography and so on. Acedia describes the inertia towards doing what is right, while self-pity describes the emotional aspect that is felt.

Dishonesty: not being honest (lying, cheating, stealing). Dishonesty has a specific use in this analysis. If I am blaming someone else or an institution for making me feel bad, which is always the case when I resent someone or something other than me, then I am being dishonest.

Hypocrisy: in simple terms this is accusing others of faults that we have done ourselves. We can extend that further, so even if I have never done what I had resented him for, then in almost every case I can say, "There but for the grace of God go I." In other words, if the positions were reversed and I had been through everything that person had been through in life, then I have to acknowledge that I might have done as this person did, and there is potential hypocrisy. This reflects the idea that is commonly expressed as, don't make judgments about others unless you have walked a mile in their shoes.

There are certain situations where this would not apply: we cannot ever put ourselves in God's position. Other things being equal, if we resented God we would not include dishonesty.

Envy: wanting what rightfully belongs to others, their possessions, their abilities — For example, I might be envious of Fred's Mercedes and his good looks. (But in this case I am still jealous of him as well because Mary fancies him and not me.)

Jealousy: resenting affection that is given to others in preference to me — I am jealous of Fred because Mary fancies him and she doesn't fancy me.

***Greed*:** when I have what I need yet I want more. Refers to material possessions.

Selfishness: not being prepared to let others have some of what is mine (material goods, time). [*NB: although in common parlance selfishness and self-centeredness are interchangeable, in this context we use them slightly differently.*] If we are just thinking of ourselves, that is self-centeredness and not selfishness. Selfishness is about not being free with goods we possess or are in control of for the benefit of others and is similar to greed.

Gluttony: greed for food and drink (including alcohol).

Lust: an inordinate (i.e., disordered) desire for carnal pleasure. Usually used in association with sexual pleasure.

Anger: is an inordinate and uncontrolled feeling of hatred of the person who perpetrates injustice and is characterized by a desire for vengeance. It is something that is felt, viscerally and is, like self-pity, a fault that lets us know that we have a resentment. If self-pity makes us feel down, anger fires us up. It is particularly grave if a lack of self-control leads us to indulge in our anger to the degree that there are external expressions of it and others are on the receiving end of actions or words driven by it. It is to be distinguished from righteous anger which is a desire to right wrongs and is a hatred of vice, rather than a hatred of the person who is causing the injustice. Righteous anger is compatible with the love of God and reinforces rather than undermines our inner peace.

Arrogance: knowing better than my equals (not minding my own business, telling people who have not asked my opinion and over whom I have no authority, what to do); or thinking I am the equal of my betters (not accepting the authority of those I should — parents, bosses at work, teachers when I am at school). Also making judgments on the morality of people's behavior is arrogance, because ultimately only God is entitled to do that. This is a form of pride. St. Peter characterized a right approach to injustice from natural authority figures as follows:

> Slaves must be respectful and obedient to their masters, not only when they are kind and gentle but also when they are unfair. You see, there is some merit in putting up with the pains of unearned punishment if it is done for the sake of God but there is nothing meritorious in taking a beating patiently if you have done something wrong to deserve it. The merit, in the sight of God, is in bearing it patiently when you are punished after doing your duty.
>
> (1 Peter 2:18-20)

Note, this is not an endorsement of slavery, neither is it saying we shouldn't do something to stop it if we can (or any other injustice which might exist). It is telling us a general principle of how to be free of resentment against authority figures, regardless of whether that authority is exercised justly or unjustly.

This is a high ideal – taking an unjust beating patiently – but with God's grace we can move toward it. In the Lord's prayer, we ask God to 'forgive us our *trespasses as we forgive those who trespass against us.*' I found that acknowledgment of arrogance helped me to move toward this ideal of forgiving those who have perpetrated an injustice against me. This is the whole point about forgiveness, if that act against us is not unjust, then there is nothing to forgive. Its very essence is all about freeing ourselves from the resentment we bear in the face of unjust persecution.

Intolerance: not putting up with qualities in others that they cannot help — he is ugly; I don't like her accent; I don't like the English; I don't like the working/middle/upper class; I don't like his or her skin color/race/nationality. Intolerance is not used for when we don't like someone's behavior (see 'arrogance').

Impatience: I am fed up with waiting (bus queues, she hasn't returned my telephone call yet.)

Sloth: I am being lazy or procrastinating about taking action for ordinary activities. Although in many commentaries sloth and acedia are used interchangeably in this context, I was directed to use acedia for a spiritual sloth, not doing something that arises from a lack of love; whereas sloth here is used for more conventional way – being lazy, and so on.

Common combinations

At the core of every resentment that I have written, there is one of the two following combinations:

- *Pride, self-pity and acedia, self-centeredness*
- *Pride, anger, self-centeredness*

When I have someone other than Self in the first column I will usually have the addition of dishonesty and hypocrisy to the cluster, giving such possibilities as:

- *Pride, self-pity and acedia, self-centeredness, dishonesty, hypocrisy Pride, self-pity, anger, self-centeredness, dishonesty, hypocrisy*

Appendix 4

A summary of the method of reflection called conspectio divina for easy reference

Find somewhere quiet to sit.

1. Do a written examination of conscience

Ask God for forgiveness for your sins and for him to redirect your fear so that you may serve him better. Pray briefly for all those whom you have borne any resentment.

When you have done, this set a timer to 20 minutes and begin.

2. Pray to the Holy Spirit that he may lead you to Christ

Pray silently to yourself eight times: *Please come Holy Spirit and lead me to Jesus Christ.* Suggested image is the Rublev Trinity.

3. Approaching Christ on the cross with the saints showing you the way

Imagine Christ in the distance, with a lamb on the altar with all the saints and angels adoring him. Pray silently, with John the Baptist: *Behold the Lamb of God.* Say this prayer eight times. Suggested image is the Ghent altarpiece with the lamb on the altar.

4. Our Lady, the Queen of Heaven shows you her Son

Pray eight times silently: *Hail, Mary full of Grace, the Lord is with you.*
Note: this is not the whole Hail Mary prayer, just the first line.
Suggested image is an icon or gothic image of Our Lady showing us her Son.

THE VISION FOR YOU

5. See her Son, Jesus, on the cross and imagine him taking on himself all your sins

Pray eight times: *Lord Jesus Christ Son of God, have mercy on me a sinner.* Study a picture of Christ on the cross.

With the picture still before your eyes, recall the resentments and fears that you wrote down in your examination of conscience before starting to pray. Imagine all the self-pity, anger and fear that you felt in connection with these lifted from you and Christ is now feeling them for you instead, willingly taking them on himself. If you prefer, practice 'compunction of the heart' and remember the unhappiness of your past sins and how confessing them and receiving God's mercy caused the unhappiness to go and consider how Christ on the cross bore that pain. Then thank him for this and for all the blessings that have come into your life especially those items that you wrote on your gratitude list.

7. Pray to the Holy Spirit to lead you to the Father

In the Spirit and through Christ we can approach the Father. Pray eight times: *Come Holy Spirit, lead me to the Father through Christ.* Suggested image is the Rublev Trinity.

8. Address the Father

We come to the Father who is the ultimate object of our praise and worship. Pray eight times: *Our Father who art in heaven.* Suggested image is the mandylion.

Ask him for all that you desire in the name of his Son, Jesus Christ. Pray for yourself, but as that it be granted only if it will help you to be of service. Pray also for other people and the good of the world. When you have prayed for each thing ask for it *'in the name of my Lord, Jesus Christ.'*

10. Pray the Jesus Prayer many times until your time is up.

After the intercessional prayers, pray the Jesus Prayer ever more quietly in your mind until is so quiet that you imagine you are saying it! Have in mind the face of Christ in glory.

11. When you finish, imagine yourself turning around and the dismissal is said, *Ite, missa est*. In your mind reply, *Thanks be to God* and see all those you resented with the Face of Christ. Resolve to love them.

APPENDIX 5

A summary of how to discern your personal vocation and to follow the call

Eight Steps to a Life Beyond Your Wildest Dreams

Discerning Your Personal Vocation

1. Ask yourself the question: If I inherited so much money that I never needed to work again for the money, what activity would I choose to do, 9am-5pm, five days a week? Write your dream down on paper.

2. Add your lifestyle dreams to this. It's not just about work, it's about your whole life.

3. Hold this up against what is good and true. If it's God's will it has to be moral.

4. Take action. Look for the first move to make, however small, and then make it! Don't think about the second move until you have taken the first. If you take this step by step approach, you will get there, little by little.

5. Don't do anything that is reckless or foolhardy – you must pay the bills and meet your obligations. This is not an excuse to evade the responsibilities of life.

6. If you can, surround yourself with a number of people who will encourage you in what you are aiming to do, use them for advice.

7. Be ready to modify your dreams as you go along. You may discover that God has something greater in store for you – something that you cannot even imagine at this point. Something *beyond* your wildest dreams!

8. Finally, enjoy the journey – embrace all that happens to you as part of a loving God's plan for you and remember that you are living your personal vocation right now! We have found that misery is optional and even in the face of setbacks and trials, we can enjoy every single day because it has been created for all of us by a loving God. God is both the means to happiness and the source of happiness itself – he is the Way and the Truth and the Life. Give yourselves to him and join us on the Way of Beauty.

Appendix 6

Tips for Sponsors

Here are some thoughts that might help those who guide others through the Vision for You process. We are assuming that at this point the prospect is interested in doing the process. There are no hard rules about this. We do whatever works, but we have found the following helpful over the years. We suggest that sponsors read this book, *The Vision for You,* in detail before sponsoring:

- Remember that as with all things spiritual, it is in the *trying* that you are successful. We do not get disheartened or take it personally if our prospects do not complete the work. We are always just grateful for the chance to be of service and we can be assured that if that is our attitude, it will help us on our spiritual journey. Having said that many of us do find that we learn with experience how to pass this on more effectively and that is likely to be true for you.

- As far as possible rely on your experience rather than your opinions when you guide others. If you tell others what you did, rather than what they should do, then no one can tell you that you are wrong and, especially in the early stages of the relationship, your advice is more likely to be followed.

- It is not your job to solve the problems of others. We simply show them a process, and God, if he wishes, will solve problems and difficulties.

- Explain to your sponsee that your desire is to be helpful and you will not spend time trying to persuade him to do anything he doesn't want to do. Should he not be willing to do any part of this, we suggest that you step back and move on to someone else who does. Let him know, however, that the door is always open should he wish to change his mind. As a sponsor, never takes it personally if the sponsee changes his mind and decides to stop the process or to move to another sponsor. We should wish him well and be grateful for the chance to have been helpful to the degree we have.

- Explain to your sponsee that there is a condition upon your doing this: that if it works, he will be open to passing it on to others as you have passed it on to him. In fact, if he is not willing to pass it on, the effect will be much less powerful.

- Assure your sponsee that you will be discreet and that anything of a personal nature will go no further than you. This is important.

- We used the following 'lesson plan.' Tell your sponsee that you will work on the following structure too:

    1. Ask him to begin with the daily routine, the first Spiritual Exercise, until it becomes a habit.

    2. Discuss the Three Acknowledgements together.

    3. When the sponsee is convinced by his experience of the daily routine and consideration of his predicament in the light of the three acknowledgements, ask him if he is committed to going on with the process.

    4. If he is convinced, then take him through the remaining Spiritual Exercises in order. You will need to explain to him your experience at every stage, but the detailed reading of the book, *The Vision for You*, will support this and help you and him together to deal with many questions that might arise.

- When helping him through Spiritual Exercises 2 and 3, he is likely to be reticent about revealing details of himself. Gain his confidence by entrusting him with highly personal and private examples of your own. He is more likely to open up and trust you, if you open up with him first. Explain the technique for the self-examination and then show him how to do it by writing out examples from his past in the three-column way, so that he can see how it is done. Then ask him to go away and try to write a few more of his own resentments and fears in this manner and then meet up with him. Look at what he has done and correct any mistakes. You may need to meet several times at this stage, correcting him each time. The self-examination technique is quick and precise when we get the hang of it, but it can take a few meetings before sponsees do grasp it. Be patient and expect a few weekly sessions before he fully understands it.

- If you have questions at any point, ask your own sponsor for help! Seek the permission of your sponsee before doing so.

Appendix 7

Some More Scriptural Quotations that Support the Principles Outlined in This Book

What does the Bible have to say about praying for what we want?

Here are the principles as far as I can discern from my reading of the Bible and the Church Fathers. I am no biblical scholar, so I encourage readers to make up their own minds based upon the quotations given and any others they may find themselves.

We can have what we pray for if:

1. We remember that these goods will not make us happy in themselves. We should seek first God and then all things will be given to us. What we want should be in accord with love of God and neighbor.

2. We ask in the name of Jesus.

3. We believe that we already have it.

4. We are grateful for what we have today. If we are not grateful, we should cultivate gratitude.

5. We should be generous in giving away what we have now and not be attached to anything more than God.

6. We aim for the ideal of conduct in accordance with moral law.

7. We partake in the sacramental life of the Church (the Eucharist, the liturgy, etc.).

8. We recognize that the power that provides all of this is God and God is Love. The power behind this is *not* me; it is <u>not</u> the universe.

If we fulfill these criteria then we should expect the following results:

1. We will receive in abundance because it will glorify God.

2. We will receive also persecutions in this life for fulfilling these criteria – but even these persecutions can be a source of joy.

3. We will have joy.

4. We will have eternal life, as well as getting material goods in this life.

5. We will partake of the divine nature.

Biblical References and some quotes from the Church Fathers

2 Cor 9:6-8: Who sows sparingly will also reap sparingly, and whosoever sows generously will also reap generously. Each man should give what he has decided in his heart to give, not reluctantly or under compulsion, for God loves a cheerful giver. And God is able to make all grace abound to you, so that in all things at all times, having all that you need, you will abound in every good work.

2 Cor 4:7 Yet we who have this spiritual treasure are like common clay pots, in order to show that the supreme power belongs to God, not to us.

James 1:4-6: Perseverance must finish its work so that you may be mature and complete, not lacking anything. If any of you lacks wisdom, he should ask God, who gives generously to all without finding fault, and it will be given him. But when he asks, he must believe and not doubt, because he who doubts is like a wave of the sea, blown and tossed by the wind.

Psalm 23:1   The Lord is my shepherd
             I shall lack nothing.

Mark 10:29: Jesus said, 'I tell you the truth, no one who has left home or brothers or sisters or mother or father or children or fields for me and the gospel who will not receive a hundredfold now in this time, houses and brothers and sisters and mothers and children and lands, with persecutions; and in the age to come eternal life.'

Matthew 7:7-12: 'Ask and it will be given you, seek and you will find, knock and it will be opened to you. For everyone who asks receives, he who seeks finds and to him who knocks it will be opened. Or what man of you, if his son asks him for bread, will give him a stone? Or if he asks for a fish, will give him a serpent? If you then, who are evil, know how to give good gifts to your children, how much more will your Father who is in heaven give good things to those who ask him! So whatever you wish that men would do to you, do so to them; for this the law and prophets.'

Matthew 21:22: 'And whatever you ask in prayer you will receive, if you have faith.'

Luke 11:9-13: 'And I say unto you, Ask, and it shall be given you; seek, and ye shall find; knock, and it shall be opened unto you. For every one that asketh receiveth; and he that seeketh findeth; and to him that knocketh it shall be opened. If a son shall ask bread of any of you that is a father, will he give him a stone? or if *he ask* a fish, will he for a fish give him a serpent? Or if he shall ask an egg, will he offer him a scorpion? If ye then, being evil, know how to give good gifts unto your children: how much more shall *your* heavenly Father give the Holy Spirit to them that ask him?'

John 14:12: 'Truly, truly, I say to you, he who believes in me will also do the works that I do; and greater works that those will he do, that the Father may be glorified in the Son; if you ask anything in my name, I will do it.'

John 15:7-11: 'If you abide in me, and my words abide in you, ask whatever you will and it shall be done for you. By this my Father is glorified, that you bear much fruit, and so prove to be my disciples. As the Father has loved me so I have loved you; continue in my love. If you keep my commandments you shall abide in my love. Even as I have kept the Father's commandments and abide in His love. These things I have spoken to you, that my joy may be in you, and that your joy may be full.'

John 15:16-19 (Knox translation): 'It was not you that chose me, I chose you. The task I have appointed you is to go out and bear fruit, fruit which will endure; so that every request you make of the Father in my name may be granted you. These are the directions that I give that you should go out and love one another. If the world hates you, be sure that it hated me before it learned to hate you. If you belonged to the world, the world would love you for its own and love you. It is because you do not belong to the world, because I have singled you out from the midst of the world, that the world hates you.'

John 16:24: 'Hitherto, you have asked nothing in my name; ask, and you will receive, that your joy may be full.'

2 Peter 1:3-4: His divine power has granted to us all things that pertain to life and godliness, through the knowledge of him who called to us his own glory and excellence, by which he has granted to us his precious and very great promises, that through these you may escape from the corruption that is in the world and be partakers of the divine nature.

Phil 4:12, 13: 'I have learnt in whatever state I am, to be content... I can do all things in Him who strengthens me.'

Matthew 17:20 (The disciples have just asked why they couldn't cast out devils.) He said to them, "Because of your little faith. For truly, I say to you, if you have faith as a grain of mustard seed, you will say to this mountain, 'Move from here to there,' and it will move; and nothing will be impossible to you.'"

ABOUT THE AUTHOR

David Clayton is an internationally known artist, writer, teacher, and broadcaster. He is Provost of the online Catholic university www.Pontifex.University for whom he designed a unique program – a formation in beauty and creativity for all – Master of Sacred Arts. He has published two other books: *The Way of Beauty*, which describes the principles of a traditional formation for artists and how it can be incorporated into general education, and *The Little Oratory: A Beginner's Guide to Praying in the Home* (co-written with Leila Lawler). An Englishman who moved to the United States 10 years ago, he now resides near Berkeley, CA. He was received into the Church in 1993. His blog is TheWayofBeauty.org.

Made in the USA
Columbia, SC
04 June 2018